POLARIZED

POLARIZED

MAKING SENSE OF A
DIVIDED AMERICA

WITH A NEW AFTERWORD
BY THE AUTHOR

JAMES E. CAMPBELL

PRINCETON UNIVERSITY PRESS
Princeton and Oxford

Copyright © 2016 by Princeton University Press
Afterword to the paperback edition,
copyright © 2018 by Princeton University Press
Published by Princeton University Press,
41 William Street, Princeton, New Jersey 08540
In the United Kingdom: Princeton University Press,
6 Oxford Street, Woodstock, Oxfordshire OX20 1TR

press.princeton.edu

Cover art: Dome of the US Capitol Building with Columbia Statue
(photo) / Buyenlarge Archive / UIG / Bridgeman Images.

Second printing and first paperback printing, 2018
Paper ISBN: 978-0-691-18086-1
Library of Congress Cataloging Number: 2015047924
Cloth ISBN 978-0-691-17216-3

British Library Cataloging-in-Publication Data is available

This book has been composed in DIN Pro & Sabon Next LTPro

Printed on acid-free paper. ∞

Printed in the United States of America

3 5 7 9 10 8 6 4 2

To those who are

kind to animals

CONTENTS

FIGURES AND TABLES

FIGURES

TABLES

ACKNOWLEDGMENTS

This book has been a long time in the works. I began writing more than three years ago, but the book was percolating long before that. I have been reading and thinking about the polarization of American politics since the late 1960s. Polarization was not a commonly used term back then, but we all read a good deal about political pluralism and that was really the same subject. Both polarization and pluralism are about the extent and organization of political conflict and that spans the waterfront of American politics.

My thinking about polarization and American politics has been influenced by many interactions with friends, colleagues, and fellow students of polarization, both directly and through their writings. I am grateful to every one of them. Unfortunately, space prevents me from thanking them individually, but I would like to express my gratitude to many of those who helped make this book possible and who helped shape my thinking about American politics and my approach to studying it.

Three people, in particular, were especially generous in advising me about how this book might be made substantively stronger and stylistically clearer. At the top of this list is Jamie Druckman. Jamie was instrumental in this book's publication and offered unerringly good advice along the way. Mike Lewis-Beck provided sage counsel, encouragement, and insightful comments on the manuscript. I expected no less. Ed Cuddihy, a former managing editor of *The Buffalo*

News, volunteered his prodigious editorial talents to wade into my prose to offer on-the-money, page-by-page advice about how I might more effectively and clearly communicate the substance of the book. The book would not be what it is without the help of these three wise men.

I have also been fortunate to have had the good advice and support of many others. Mo Fiorina, Ralph Halpern, Ben Page, Bob Grafstein, Tali Mendelberg, and Jay Dow read all or significant portions of the manuscript and each offered very useful advice that I have incorporated into the book. I also appreciate the comments and views of John Aldrich, Phil Arena, Jim Battista, Jon Bond, Chuck Bullock, Larry Dodd, John Hibbing, Gary Jacobson, Tom Mann, Bill Mayer, Samuel Merrill, Diana Mutz, Dick Niemi, Andy Rudalevige, Larry Sabato, Sean Trende, and the students in my undergraduate honors seminars on polarization and my graduate seminar on American Politics at the University at Buffalo. Of course, none of these friends, colleagues, and students bear responsibility for what follows.

A good deal of my thinking and analysis reported in this book has grown out of previous research on polarization. Although my conclusions often differ from what has gone before, I have a high regard for that research and for those who grappled with these tough issues. Their names appear throughout the book and in the references, but I would like to thank several in particular. More than anyone, Mo Fiorina is responsible for the burgeoning body of research on polarization over the last decade. Alan Abramowitz's research has been the principal counterpoint to Fiorina's, and together they have framed the debate. I should note, too, that I can always count on lively political disagreements with Alan to enlighten me on how the other side of the ideological spectrum sees things. Keith Poole and Howard Rosenthal have also made major contributions to the study of polarization through their groundbreaking analysis of elite ideologies using congressional roll-call votes. I am grateful to them and to everyone else who has worked on the many facets of polarization.

The list of those from whom I learned about American politics and polarization is quite lengthy. I acknowledged many of them in my first book, *The Presidential Pulse of Congressional Elections*, and this book benefited from them as well. I learned a great deal about American politics from my friends, colleagues, and students at the University of Georgia in the 1980s, Louisiana State University in the 1990s, the National Science Foundation for a couple of years in the early 1990s, and the University at Buffalo since 1998. My experience in the APSA's Congressional Fellowship Program in 1980 also provided an up-close education on congressional politics. A Brookings conference in 2006 on polarization also refreshed my interests in the subject. I want to thank again Tom Mann, David Brady, Mo Fiorina, and Pietro Nivola for inviting me to participate in that stimulating meeting.

One of the things that surprised me most in writing this book is how often I reached back to my undergraduate days at Bowdoin College and to my graduate school time at Syracuse University. At Bowdoin, I was introduced by Professor Daniel Levine to the writings of many mid-century social theorists, who appear in chapter 2, and by Professors John Donovan and Richard Morgan to Scammon and Wattenberg's *The Real Majority*, discussed in chapter 8. At Syracuse, I was immersed in the American politics literature by Professors Bob McClure, Tom Patterson, Bob deVoursney, Linda Fowler, and later, by Jeff Stonecash. In particular, a small and intense seminar on *The Federalist Papers* refereed by Professor Ralph Ketcham made a deep and lasting impression on me, as did an independent study on political ideology that my great friend Karen Beckwith and I took under the guidance of Professor Phil Beardsley. Sometimes I can't remember where I parked my car, yet all of this stuck.

I am also deeply indebted to Eric Crahan and his exceptionally talented colleagues at Princeton University Press for their professionalism and dedication to this project. It has been a pleasure to work with such an outstanding team. I would also like to thank Dianne Fazio and Dick Murphy (my cousin) at Walch Printing in Portland, Maine for their first-class work in preparing an earlier draft of the book for distribution and comment as the manuscript made its way through the publication process at Princeton.

I thank my friends and family for their support and patience while I obsessively worked on this book. Polarization creeps into almost everything political, and as a political junkie, I see it, stimulate it, and learn about it almost everywhere. My polarization laboratories reach from The Front Room on Munjoy Hill and The Great Lost Bear in

Portland, Maine to MacGregor's Pub and Dr. Michael Katz's dental office in Amherst, New York to Saturday lunches with Buffalo's luminaries at Boomerang's Restaurant and, of course, any family gathering. I thank all of the participants, especially those reluctantly sucked into the political arguments I find so enjoyable and invigorating.

Finally, I thank my family and friends for being there: my mom, Mary Campbell; my brothers John, Bob, Dick, and Stephen and their families and friends; and my brother-in-law Tom Porter. Since beginning this project in earnest, I have also enjoyed the devoted companionship of two delightful and strong-willed basset hounds Rufus and Juliet. My wife, Susan Porter, has been wonderfully encouraging and amazingly patient as I obsessed about getting more work done on the book and as we traveled back and forth from the underappreciated city of Buffalo, New York to our home on Peaks Island, Maine. They were all very supportive, except on those few (maybe not so few) occasions when they told me to shut up about politics. Polarization?

POLARIZED

INTRODUCTION

Voters are not fools.

—V. O. Key, Jr. *The Responsible Electorate*[1]

America is polarized. Our political parties are highly polarized and the American electorate is highly polarized. By highly polarized, I mean there are substantial differences in political perspectives across a single ideological dimension. Liberals versus conservatives. Fundamental political differences slice through broad segments of the American electorate and separate the political parties on a wide range of important issues. The polarization of the American electorate is real and widespread. It is not an artifact manufactured by polarized political parties, manipulative politicians, rabble-rousing talking heads, myopic interest groups, or mischievous gerrymanders. It is not limited to rarified groups of political leaders or zealous activists, or even the politically engaged. Nor is it constrained to only a few contentious, hot-button issues. It is *not* an illusion formed by forced choices in elections or geographic clusterings of the like-minded. Political divisions in American politics are now deep and real.

Despite this reality, the idea persists that America is a moderate nation and that most Americans are moderates. That is a myth. Most

Americans are not moderates. Not even a slim majority of Americans voting in recent elections are moderates. Some are to the left, some to the right, and together they outnumber those in the middle. America is a politically divided nation, it has been so for some time, and has become more so in recent decades.

While the American electorate and its political parties are quite polarized, the extent of polarization should not be exaggerated. Though a majority of voters are *not* moderates, moderates are still a large and important minority. And even among the majority of the electorate who are not moderates, few could properly be called extremists. We are substantially polarized, but we are not a bimodal nation with half of the electorate at the leftist outer edge of the political universe and the other half on the extreme right wing. We are highly polarized between liberals and conservatives, not between totalitarians and anarchists. The polarization of American politics pales in comparison to the polarization of other nations with more combative political cultures or even our own in more combustible times such as the decades leading up to the Civil War. As polarized as we are, we could be more so. Moreover, despite the attention now paid to polarization and the evidence of its increase, the ideological composition of the American electorate has not changed radically in recent decades.

As rough as our political debates can be, and they can get quite vicious, happily we are not on the precipice of another civil war. Americans and both major political parties share a great deal of common ground. There are still core American values.[2] We all want peace and prosperity, a secure nation, equal opportunities and justice, an efficient government with fair elections, a successful educational system, a clean environment and ample access to energy, a well-maintained and efficient transportation system, reliable and technologically advanced communication networks, a compassionate system of safety nets for those who cannot fend for themselves, safe streets and suitable housing, wholesome food, plenty of safe and rewarding jobs, and so on. More abstractly, there still seems to be a consensus about many basic principles, from individualism to majority rule and minority rights, what Austin Ranney and Willmoore Kendall long ago referred to as the "American Creed."[3]

However, though these fundamental goals are shared, we should not be deluded into thinking that all is peaceful politically and that our differences are only superficial or slight. They are not. There are sharp and deep differences between large segments of the electorate and between the political parties about what these common goals mean in practice, how they might best be achieved, and what role government should play in achieving them. There are also a number of hot issues on which goals are not held in common (the abortion issue, for example). These further divide large segments of the electorate and the political parties.

So how is it that the American electorate is now polarized, if there is a large contingent of moderates and if the ideological composition of the electorate has not changed dramatically in recent times? First, like most things, polarization is a matter of degree. It is not an all-or-nothing matter. American voters are highly polarized, but not completely polarized. The nation can be quite polarized while still having a large number of centrists. By the same token, politics can also be intensely divided while having a good deal of common ground. Red Sox and Yankees fans may both like hot dogs, beer, and infield seats for the ball game, but their rooting for opposite teams overshadows whatever many other preferences they might otherwise have in common. So too with liberals and conservatives. They are all Americans, but that does not mean they are not also at each others' throats on the most important political issues of the day.

Second, though there has not been an enormous shift in public opinion in recent decades, the electorate has become more ideological, and a modest shift of this sort can have major political repercussions. A five- or ten-percentage-point shift in ideological preferences may seem like "small potatoes," but a nation that is 40% moderate and 60% ideological (liberal or conservative) operates quite different politically from one that is a 50-50 split. In the 1930s, the normal vote in presidential elections changed by only about 10 or 11 percentage points and that ushered in the huge change of the New Deal that restructured public policy for generations. Changes in the balance of the relatively ideological versus the relatively non-ideological in the electorate have not been quite this large, but they have been significant.

Finally, the electorate is highly polarized without having changed a great deal in recent times because it has been quite polarized for a long time. The electorate was not very polarized in the 1950s and early 1960s, but became much more so in the late 1960s and 1970s. For historical reasons dating back to the period of the Reconstruction after the Civil War and even before that, differences in the electorate were not well reflected by the political parties. The heterogeneous compositions of the parties, with many liberals in the Republican Party and many conservatives in the Democratic Party, essentially obscured and muted the extent of political differences in the electorate. This began to change in the 1960s with a prolonged or staggered partisan realignment, a process that dragged on into the 1990s because of the historical absence of a viable Republican Party in the formerly solid Democratic South and the power of incumbency. As the realignment took shape, first in presidential voting in the late 1960s, then in party identification shifts in the 1980s, and in congressional voting in the 1990s, the realigned parties themselves became more polarized (or, in Morris Fiorina's terminology, better "sorted"). As a result, they better reflected the polarization of the electorate. Rather than masking and muting that polarization, the polarized parties now reveal and accentuate polarization in the electorate. Polarization in the electorate begot polarization of the parties and polarization of the parties begot more polarization in the electorate.

This, in a nutshell, is the state of polarization in the American politics and how we got there. The chapters that follow develop this narrative, provide the evidence and analysis regarding it, and assess the consequences of polarization for the political system. They also delve more deeply into why the party system is polarized at all when the logic of party competition would seem to propel parties toward the political center in pursuit of the crucial swing voter, the majority-making median voter.

A number of books have been written in recent years about the polarization of American politics. Why another? The short answer is, to get it right, or at least to take my best shot at getting it right, and to tie together the various aspects of polarization into its big picture. Though there have been a number of excellent studies on the subject, a good deal of what has been written about the polarization of the electorate is mistaken in its evaluation of the evidence and in its fundamental conclusions. A more complete answer to the question of why another polarization study is that there is still a great deal to learn about polarization (a subject of chapter 1) and there are a number of problems with the theories and studies that dominate the debate about the level and change in polarization (a subject of chapter 2). This real and more complete story of polarization, from its theory to its analysis, has not been told before now.

The study is organized into three parts and a concluding chapter (so, four parts if you want to get picky). "Preparing the Foundation" is the first part and consists of the first two chapters. Chapter 1 takes stock of what we know and what we do not know about political polarization. There are some fairly settled questions about polarization. Among these is the fact that the political parties, both in the electorate and at leadership levels, are now highly polarized. This is not disputed, but several other questions (see above) remain wide open. Two of the principal remaining questions concern the extent and change in the polarization of the electorate and another three questions concern party polarization—why the parties have become increasingly polarized, whether one party has grown more extreme than the other, and why the parties are polarized at all.

Chapter 1 also highlights six important analytical concerns to keep in mind in examining polarization. Clear answers are more likely to come from clear questions and these require clear distinctions. It is important to maintain the distinctions between the polarization of the electorate and the polarization of the parties (leaders or party identifiers) and between questions about *change* in polarization as opposed to the *extent or level* of polarization. The question of the existence or level of polarization in the public should be understood as being quite distinct from the question of whether polarization has increased a great deal. The public may be quite polarized without polarization having increased greatly. Finally, answers to questions about either the change or level of polarization require benchmarks, some way of determining whether polarization should be considered high or low.

Chapter 2 offers some historical and intellectual background to the current debate about polarization. Though it is often forgotten, the extent and nature of conflict in American politics is not a new subject. The chapter also presents the several theories of polarization as well as a number of problems that may have impeded the determination of the extent and reasons for polarization. These problems range from the questions posed about polarization to the data used to examine them. Determining the level of polarization in a nation and how well it matches up with the polarization of leaders and political parties over time is a difficult task. Since polarization is a matter of degree, not an all-or-nothing condition, how do you tell whether the glass is three-quarters full or only one-quarter full?

Chapter 2 also summarizes the six major points of this study. The first point concerns the direct evidence of polarization. Although concerns about various methodological problems with the direct evidence may raise some caution flags about placing absolute confidence in the findings, analysis of both the self-reported ideology data and the issue attitude data yield the same results. While various data problems may provide reasons to hold findings based on them in abeyance, the second major point of the study is that circumstantial evidence about polarization is also available and extremely valuable. While offering an indirect view of polarization, the circumstantial evidence has impeccable credentials. From turnout rates to party identification, the measurement of this evidence has been meticulously vetted. Moreover, in every respect, it corroborates the findings of the direct evidence and goes beyond that evidence to shed light on polarization in the years before the direct evidence (self-reported ideology and issue attitude data) was available. The final four major points concern the extent of polarization in the electorate, the reason why parties are polarized at all (despite the centrist pull of the median voter), the masking of polarization by the pre-realigned ideologically heterogeneous (largely unpolarized) parties, and the revelation of polarization by the post-realigned ideologically homogeneous (highly polarized) parties.

The second part of the book examines the evidence of polarization in the electorate. The empirical investigation into the extent and trends in the public's polarization is based on three different types of data: ideological orientations in chapter 3, issue preferences in chapter 4, and circumstantial behavioral evidence in chapter 5. This three-part examination begins in chapter 3 with an analysis of aggregate responses since the 1970s to survey questions about the ideological perspectives of citizens. The ideology measure is based on direct questions to respondents about their general outlooks on political matters. In many respects it parallels survey questioning about a person's partisanship. The analysis draws together these self-reported ideological data from five highly respected sources: the American National Election Studies, the General Social Survey, the CBS and the *New York Times* surveys, Gallup, and the National Exit Polls. There are, of course, many differences among these surveys in how they pose the question and conduct their interviews, but each provides respondents with an option to declare themselves a liberal, a moderate, or a conservative, and some offer more fine-tuned options (extremely conservative, etc.). The analysis of the self-reported ideological measures indicates the American public has become somewhat more ideological and less moderate since the 1970s, but that it was already fairly well polarized in the early 1970s.

With these findings in hand, chapter 3 then evaluates the quality of self-reported ideology data for measuring polarization. A number of questions have been raised about the validity of the measure. Do responses reveal common thrusts in general viewpoints about politics or are they lightly held responses to symbols that mean different things to different people? On the whole, like party identification, there is a great deal of merit in vesting substantial credibility in what respondents tell us about themselves. Without compelling evidence to the contrary, to do otherwise is at least imprudent. After investigating some possible problems with self-reported ideology, including the competing measure of what has been termed "operational ideology," the self-reported ideology measure looks quite reliable and valid. Though some reasons for skepticism may remain, the ideology evidence of polarization is fairly solid. It indicates that the electorate is, was, and has become more polarized.

Chapter 4 continues the examination of the direct evidence by investigating what the public's attitudes on policy issues reveal about its polarization. Most prior research on polarization has been based on issue attitudes. This makes a good deal of sense. Voting studies had concluded that most Americans lacked the political sophistication to respond to politics in sophisticated terms. *The American Voter* study had estimated that less than 12% of survey respondents answered questions about the presidential candidates in the 1950s revealing ideological or near-ideological levels of conceptualization.[4] *The American Voter Revisited* revised these numbers upward for the 2000 electorate, but still found slightly less than 20% with this level of conceptualization.[5] Considering these limitations, the evidence of polarization or its absence might be more clearly seen at the less abstract level of practical policy issues (though issue attitude data have many problems of their own). Much of this issue-based research concluded that polarization did not increase over the years, and some push the findings further to claim Americans were not then and are not now highly polarized.

This chapter takes a fresh look at the issue evidence of polarization. Interpreting the evidence is more complicated than it might first seem and requires answering a number of questions. What are we looking for in the issue evidence that would shed light on polarization? Is it enough that attitudes are dispersed on individual issues? Since there are multiple issues in American politics, how might polarization be expressed across a range of issues? How can we evaluate whether issue preferences are widely divided or not? What benchmarks might be established to provide some perspective on the extent of polarization? What is the quality of the issue evidence? There are many problems with issue attitude data, from the temporary nature of issues and the evolution of their meaning in different political contexts to the sensitivity of issue attitude question wordings and their sky-high levels of random measurement error. What can we expect from such flawed data?

At the end of the day, even considering their many problems and the caution that should engender, a careful examination of issue attitude data offers some leverage on the polarization questions. Two exemplar issues from American National Election Study (ANES) surveys are examined in detail: the government guaranteed jobs issue and the government healthcare insurance issue. Despite their many problems, issue attitude data point to the same findings as the self-reported ideology data. Like the ideology evidence, the issue evidence indicates that Americans were quite polarized in the 1970s and have grown more so since then. Moreover, Americans line up on the issues much as they line up ideologically. The polarization of American politics is not a myth. It is very real.

Chapter 5 tackles the public polarization questions from a different angle. As in a criminal investigation, there may not be a perfectly reliable eyewitness (self-reported ideology) or direct physical evidence (issue attitudes), but there may be circumstantial evidence and that is the case when it comes to solving the mystery of polarization. Chapter 5 follows the circumstantial evidence trail by taking advantage of the one major aspect of polarization that is not disputed: that the political parties are now much more polarized than they were. The claim that the public is relatively unpolarized is inconsistent with highly polarized parties in an overwhelmingly partisan electorate. It is also inconsistent with several other well-documented changes in the electorate's attitudes and behavior. We would expect a relatively centrist electorate to have reacted quite differently than a relatively polarized electorate to the increased polarization of the parties. The analysis indicates that across several different criteria (turnout, partisanship, and ticket-splitting) the reaction of the electorate has been what we would expect from a relatively polarized electorate and exactly the opposite of what would be expected from a moderate electorate. In short, together with the ideology evidence of chapter 3 and the issue preference evidence of chapter 4, the circumstantial evidence demonstrates conclusively that the electorate is now quite polarized and has been so for quite some time.

Part 3 turns to questions of the polarization of the political parties. As already noted, there is no doubt that the parties have become much more polarized in recent decades. Chapter 6 attempts to explain why this occurred. Two factors contributed to the increased polarization of the parties: the increased polarization of the public and a realignment of the parties. The partisan realignment was a staggered process that dragged on over several decades. It can be traced back to the 1950s and its roots extend even further back into history. The seeds of the realignment were planted in the aftermath of the Civil War. The party of Lincoln, the Republican Party, was not welcomed across the post–Reconstruction South. In the late nineteenth century and well into the latter half of the twentieth century, there was no viable local Republican Party in the South. The Democratic Party's shift to the left in the 1960s, especially in advocating civil rights legislation, opened up the South to the Republicans, but there were few southern Republicans positioned to take advantage of this. Building a southern Republican Party was a slow process and the parties could not become fully aligned along ideological lines until it was completed in the 1990s. Once the staggered realignment was complete, the parties were more ideologically unified, more polarized, with a clearly conservative Republican Party challenging a clearly liberal Democratic Party. With a clear orthodoxy within each party, party discipline and each party's base reinforced the already strong ideological inclinations of the parties.

Chapter 7 addresses a twist in the polarization debate. Some claim the polarization of the parties is not the simple result of both parties moving equally to their ideological homes. As they see it, party polarization has been asymmetrical. The Republican Party allegedly has been captured by right-wing zealots while the Democratic Party has remained a reasonable center-left party. The claim of asymmetrical party polarization is half-true and completely understandable. First, there should be no mystery to asymmetry. If the parties are very competitive, as they are, and the public is skewed to the conservative end of the ideological scale, the parties should be similarly skewed. In a center-right nation, the right-wing party should be further to the right than the left-wing party is to the left. If the two parties were equally ideological, the Democrats would be in a permanent minority. That said, the increased polarization of the parties cannot be entirely attributed to the Republican Party becoming more conservative. Before the Republicans began moving to the right, Democrats had moved further to the left. Party polarization followed the staggered nature of the realignment. In the 1970s, congressional Democrats moved significantly to the left, while there was little change in congressional Republicans. The Republican shift to the right came later and was augmented by the growth of conservatism in the public. The polarization of the parties was a two-step dance—maybe three steps: One big step to the left and two smaller steps to the right.

Chapter 8 turns to a very basic question of party polarization: why are the parties polarized at all? Perhaps no political theorem is as highly regarded as the median voter theorem first advanced by Harold Hotelling and developed in Anthony Downs's classic treatise on *An Economic Theory of Democracy*.[6] As popularly interpreted and applied to two-party competitive politics, the pivotal electoral position of the median voter should compel the parties and their candidates to converge on the decisive swing voter who stands at the median or center of the political spectrum. With full information, rational parties should be entirely unpolarized as the median voter theorem is commonly interpreted. Moving as close to the center as possible is the optimum strategy of parties or candidates seeking to win a two-way race. By this argument, parties should not be polarized at all, much less as greatly polarized as they have become. And while the extent of current party polarization is historically high, numerous empirical studies over the years suggest that substantial party differences have long been the rule.[7]

What draws the parties away from the political center? The answer is that the more ideological bases of the parties have a good deal of leverage over their parties—not only in the nomination of candidates, but in general elections as well. This reflects the fact that the median voter is not a fixed position, but one that moves with the support each party receives from its base. Every additional vote brought out to the polls from the base moves the critical median voter one vote closer to the party's side of the spectrum. Every non-centrist voter who stays home pushes the position of the median voter one vote further away from the party. The turnout of the base is critical and it depends on non-centrists seeing a substantial difference between the parties and seeing their own party as representing their views. A party that moves too far toward the center risks losing votes from its base as non-centrists see less consequential differences between the parties (indifference) and feel less well represented by their party (alienation). Since these non-centrists are a large, growing, and loyal source of votes for each party, neither party takes its base for granted. Polarized parties are, thus, the result of each party's efforts to assemble a majority, to capture the vote of the median voter.

The book concludes in chapter 9 with a consideration of three basic questions about polarization in the American democratic system. The first is the very basic *Causal Question*: Why is the American electorate polarized at all? What is the basis of our political differences in the electorate? Does democracy breed polarization? As far as we know, there have always been political differences in the electorate and many of these have tended to fall along a single dimension (some degree of polarization). Is there some common explanation of these differences across time and, if so, what is it? Economics, race, views of government, or something else? The second question is the *Consequences Question*: What are the consequences of polarization of the parties and the electorate? Are we better or more poorly represented as a result? Can a government run effectively in a polarized state? How does polarization affect the relationship of citizens to their government? Does polarization pose a threat to civil and effective democratic government? The final question is the prescriptive *Cure Question*: What, if anything, is to be done about the dysfunctional consequences of polarization? Are there reforms to the government or the democratic political process that would ameliorate the negative consequences of polarization? Is polarization itself a problem or is the real problem in how some people handle their political differences? Other than endlessly complaining about them, how should Americans, the parties, and other mediating institutions (notably the media and educational institutions) deal with polarized politics?

In the end, V. O. Key's sage observation about voters may guide the way to the answers to many of the polarization questions. Voters may be lazy. They may not be very wise. They do not always make the best decisions for themselves or for the nation. They may be less informed and less attentive to politics than we would like. Most are not deep thinkers about politics. That said, Americans have their views about what is right or wrong. As Key reminds us, they are not fools—and neither are their parties. American political parties are highly polarized because Americans are highly polarized.

PART ONE
PREPARING THE FOUNDATION

CHAPTER 1
KNOWNS AND UNKNOWNS

Let's start at the beginning. Gentlemen, this is a football.

—Vince Lombardi, legendary NFL coach[1]

Despite an avalanche of studies in recent years, many important questions about polarization in American politics remain unsettled. Before delving into them, as Coach Lombardi ever so gently suggests in the epigraph, it is a good idea to begin with the basics, to establish what we know (or think we know) and what we do not know about the subject. This taking stock and clarifying the concepts and the questions of polarization is the principal purpose of this chapter.

It might seem unnecessary to state the case for why the subject of polarization is important, but it should be stated nevertheless. It is our football. The level of polarization is important because it affects every aspect of political life, from discussions of political issues in informal settings, to the conduct of elections, to interactions at the highest levels of government over national public policies. As noted in the Introduction, polarization is the condition of substantial and intense conflict over political perspectives arrayed along a single dimension—generally along ideological lines. Rather than political differences being aligned differently on a variety of unconnected issues on which opinions are weakly held, highly polarized conflict is aligned across different issues with strongly held and divergent views. In highly polarized politics, there are distinct sides who see the political world in diametrically opposite ways. Whether in discussions over a few beers in a pub or on roll-call votes cast in the halls of Congress, polarized conflict is not easily resolved or accommodated.

Some degree of polarization is a fact of life in politics. Politics, especially free and democratic politics, involves conflict over differing views. But the extent of polarization can vary, and this is important. The level of polarization in the public and between its political parties establishes the "degree-of-difficulty" that the nation and its political system confronts in governing. A less polarized public and party system makes the political process less contentious and its results more broadly satisfactory. Greater polarization translates into more difficult and combative politics. Considering the gravity of the stakes involved, anyone who cares about or who might be affected by American politics should have an interest in understanding its polarization. If you are not in this group, you are excused.

THE KNOWNS

To move further down the road of understanding polarization in modern American politics, we need to know where we are starting from—what do we already know about polarization? While we know a good deal about it, five observations and findings are most important. The first two are observations about the character or nature of polarization. These are relevant to understanding the magnitude of both polarization in general (first-order polarization) as well as polarization between the political parties (second-order polarization). The three remaining "knowns" are basic empirical findings about party polarization on which there seems to be general agreement.[2]

A Matter of Degree

Polarization is not an all-or-nothing condition. It is a matter of degree. Polarization is about antagonistic political perspectives confronting one another (a single dimension of conflict). Political differences are always present to some degree, but they are never all-consuming. Although the complete absence of polarization and the complete dominance of polarization are hypothetical possibilities, they are not realistic possibilities.

The idea that polarization is a matter of degree may be best appreciated by reviewing what the extreme conditions of no polarization and complete polarization would require. There are only two conceivable ways in which the politics of a free society could be free of polarization. The first of these is unanimity. If everyone were of one mind on all important matters of public policy, politics would be entirely unpolarized. This is, of course, well beyond the realm of possibility. The only other way to avoid polarization entirely is if differences on important matters were distributed in such a random way that there were no stable alliances formed across different matters in dispute—in effect, perfect pluralism. Allies on one issue were as likely as not to be opponents on the next issue. This, too, is beyond the realm of possibility. Common strands of thinking on issues build relationships—friends and foes.

At the other hypothetical extreme, politics would be completely polarized when two sides of equal size were as far apart as possible in their perspectives. Between two homogeneous and diametrically opposed perspectives would be a vast and vacant chasm of the political center.[3] Even civil wars might not reach this extreme.

Real world politics are considerably more messy than these hypothetical extremes of no polarization and complete polarization. Public opinion is complex, motivated in part by common interests, often not well formed and articulated, and routinely measured with error. With these characteristics, simple pictures of universal agreement or random differences, on the one hand, or neatly concentrated bimodal divisions, on the other, are not remotely realistic possibilities.

As a consequence, whether with reference to the public or to the political parties, there is no bright line over which normal political differences become polarized political differences. In statistical parlance, polarization is an interval condition, not a dichotomy.[4] No one would seriously contend that adding one more contentious ideologue to an otherwise unpolarized society or legislature would "flip the switch" and convert it to a polarized body. The real question is not whether American politics are or are not polarized, but to what degree are American politics highly polarized or relatively unpolarized?

This observation may seem obvious, but debates about polarization are often conducted as if they were about the extremes. We are polarized or we are not. Those seeing politics as fairly moderate tend to downplay the extent of real conflict. Those seeing a polarized America tend to look past the fact that differences among ordinary citizens as well as differences between the political parties could be larger and even more intense.

The interval nature of polarization has many implications. It is an important reason why: (1) polarization research has been so frustratingly inconclusive; (2) data used to address questions about polarization are often inadequate or problematic; and (3) the question about the extent of polarization so often becomes conflated with the question about whether the level of polarization has changed. Because polarization is a matter of degree, one needs a benchmark or some way to determine what is a large amount of polarization and what is a small amount. We are or are not largely polarized *compared to what?* It is difficult to determine with much of the data whether the polarization glass is two-thirds full or only one-third full.

The benchmark difficulty can be illustrated by a hypothetical example of two polling questions. Suppose a poll reported that only 15% of Americans loved their country. Most would conclude that this was a dangerously *low* number. On the other hand, suppose a poll reported that 15% of Americans advocated the violent overthrow of the government. Still 15%, but most would probably conclude that this was a dangerously *high* number. In both cases, we would have some basis for expectations and the observed percentage would have been lower or higher than those expectations. It is not self-evident what our expectations should be for a normal level of polarization, and so some benchmark is needed to make sense of the data. If half of the nation is ideologically committed with one-quarter strongly opposing another quarter, is this a high or low level of polarization and why should we think so?

Because polarization is a matter of degree and there are no established benchmarks for determining whether various measurements indicate that polarization is great or small, assessments of the level of polarization often slide into examinations of the change in the level of polarization. The past is implicitly used as a benchmark and one not carefully validated or calibrated. If polarization increased (or decreased or stayed the same), was this a change from a condition when political conditions were highly polarized or substantially unpolarized?

There is an irony in all of this. The one thing that we know or should have known all along about polarization, that it is a matter of degree, is a major reason why we do not know more about polarization. Examinations of polarization's direct evidence in chapters 3 and 4 and its circumstantial evidence in chapter 5 offer several solutions to the benchmark problem.

Small Change, Big Difference

Attention to the degree of polarization cautions us to be careful in interpreting evidence of the *level* of polarization. The second point warns us to be equally careful in interpreting the significance of any *change* in polarization levels. Changes in aggregate political conditions (macropolitics) may appear to be small, but seemingly small changes may have huge consequences.

Some perspective on meaningful changes in polarization may be gained from other aspects of macropolitics, particularly other areas that involve more deeply held and durable political dispositions such as changes in the normal vote and in macropartisanship. The normal vote division is the vote that one would expect in the absence of conditions temporarily favoring one party or the other.[5] It is essentially the electorate's default vote division. A sizeable change in the normal vote is an indication of a partisan realignment, a change in the balance of electoral power between the parties. A closely related concept is macropartisanship. It is an aggregate measure of party identifications. It is computed as the percentage of party identifiers (Democrats and Republicans) who identify themselves as Democrats.[6] Like the change in the normal vote, a sizeable change in macropartisanship may be read as evidence of a party realignment.

Realignments are infrequent but important in reshaping American politics. They have huge political repercussions. The historic changes arising from realignments are based on changes in the normal vote and macropartisanship that might at first appear numerically small. The momentous realigning changes in the normal vote division between the parties and in macropartisanship historically have been around ten percentage points and often smaller. The realignment of 1896 changed the normal vote by about six percentage points. This shifted the political balance of power from being quite even between the parties to one of Republican dominance. The New Deal realignment in the 1930s was undoubtedly the greatest political change in the twentieth century, ushering in a Democratic majority that dominated American politics through the 1960s. The New Deal realignment was a shift of about ten or eleven points in the normal vote.

The current era of competitive party politics resulted from single-digit percentage changes in macropartisanship and the normal votes. The realignment establishing the current parity between the parties came about through a shift in the normal vote of only about five percentage points.[7] Macropartisanship in this realignment (between 1980 and 1984) shifted about seven percentage points from a decided Democratic Party advantage to near parity.[8] These realignments had enormous political repercussions, but the extent of change could easily be misread as minor. The point is that since polarization involves long-term political orientations akin to partisanship and voting habits, significant changes in polarization may easily be misread as minor or even inconsequential.

The idea that what looks like a small change can make a big difference is by no means unusual or in any way limited to politics. Examples exist everywhere. A few feet to the left or right in a last-second 47-yard field goal attempt may not sound like much, but they can be the difference between a Super Bowl win or loss. A long fly ball hit a few feet to the left or right of a foul pole in a World Series game can be the difference between a walk-off win and just another strike. Outside of sports and politics, the change of a few degrees in temperature may not sound like much, but it could make the difference between water and ice. The global warming or climate change issue is based on concerns raised by a change of less than two degrees Celsius in the earth's average surface temperature.

The most dramatic illustration of how seemingly small differences potentially can have big consequences is offered by the bonobo. In politically incorrect times, the bonobo was known as the pygmy chimpanzee. Geneticists studying the bonobo's genome have determined that the genetic blueprint of bonobos differs from that of humans by a mere 1.3% to as little as four-tenths of 1%.[9] This numerically tiny difference obviously makes a huge difference (though the reader may have some possible exceptions in mind). Monkey business aside, while small change may not necessarily have great consequences, it can be a big deal.

The McClosky Difference

The third point in analyzing polarization is drawn from the seminal study "Issue Conflict and Consensus Among Party Leaders and Followers" by Herbert McClosky, Paul J. Hoffman, and Rosemary O'Hara.[10] The McClosky group and those following in their footsteps found that ideological and issue differences are greater between the parties' leaders than between their followers.[11] That is, the Democratic Party's leaders generally disagreed *more* with the Republican Party's leaders than the Democratic Party's followers differed with their counterparts in the Republican Party. Party leaders in the study were national convention delegates, and party followers were drawn from two national surveys of voters. Along the same lines, Philip Converse found that elites, this time congressional candidates, held more consistently liberal or conservative positions on issues than did average citizens.[12]

The importance of the McClosky group's findings is that they mesh with other research on differences between elite and mass opinions in suggesting that opinion formation is more definite and polarization much greater among those who care more and think more about politics—in this case, the elites or leaders.[13] This should not be surprising. It is actually the business of a party's elected officials to know about political issues and to articulate their positions on those issues. They are the most conversant with political terms and ideas and most able to express them in a sophisticated way. More sharply defined opinions lead to greater differences of opinion.

Moving down the scale of political engagement, when a question asking for their opinion pops up in a survey, one is likely to run into opinions that are less well shaped and adhered to, and somewhat fuzzier views of politics and certainly less well formed for expression.[14] Although less refined and less clearly articulated than the views of those more deeply immersed in politics, those opinions are no less real. Differences among those at these middle rungs of the political engagement ladder are likely to be more muted and to appear even less sharply defined as expressed. At the very lowest rungs of political engagement, we should expect no real opinions at all and, therefore, the absence of polarization. If someone is clueless about politics, completely unconcerned about it, we should expect non-attitudes—responses with no real cognitive content behind them. Without opinion, there can be no real conflict and no polarization. Essentially, the politically unconnected produce nonpolarized noise.

This point has several implications. First, we should not expect average citizens or voters ever to appear as polarized as political leaders (even when they may actually be as polarized). The views of leaders are more refined and focused and even practiced in their expression. The views of everyday citizens and voters are not nearly as well-honed or crystallized. As V. O. Key observed long ago, much of public opinion is latent or hibernating opinion that should not be confused with non-attitudes (an absence of opinion) or, for that matter, with moderate opinions.[15] Latent views are not expressed with the same clarity, certainty, and confidence as the views of leaders, but they may find a better expression in the more sharply articulated views of leaders. This is essentially a broader application of U.S. Supreme Court Justice Potter Stewart's observation about recognizing obscenities. Justice Stewart admitted that he had trouble defining what an obscenity was, but wrote that "I know it when I see it."[16] Voters also may not be able to identify their policy preferences at a moment's notice in a survey, but they know what they like and what they don't like when they hear positions articulated by political leaders.

The unrefined nature of much of mass opinion, along with the difficulty in measuring it very accurately, may make mass opinions appear more centrist than they really are.[17] In short, the use of elite or leadership standards to evaluate the polarization of the electorate is a straw-man standard. Based on the McClosky study and those who in various ways have followed since, it should be understood that the leaders of the parties (e.g., elected officials, candidates, activists) have been, are, and always will appear to be more clearly polarized in absolute terms than the electorate.[18] This is not news and it still leaves open the very real question of whether the current electorate is relatively polarized or unpolarized, as electorates go.

A second implication of the McClosky Difference (as extended to the full range of political engagement) is that the breadth of the public examined for polarization is inversely related to the amount of polarization one is likely to encounter. As noted previously, greater political engagement (caring and knowing about politics) tends to be related to more definite opinions and this lends itself to greater polarization. Conversely, lower levels of political engagement tend to be associated with less well-defined opinions and this lends itself to lower levels of polarization, at least as measured. Thus, examining polarization in the entire American adult public (which includes a large percentage of the politically disengaged) must inevitably yield a less polarized picture. Restricting the examination to the more politically engaged (say, those participating in politics beyond voting or to activists) will most certainly produce findings of greater polarization.

This raises the question of how broadly should the net be cast in examining polarization in the American electorate. From both an analytic and a political standpoint, evaluating polarization among the politically inert or clueless is of little interest. They will definitely be unpolarized and, even if they somehow were polarized, it would make virtually no political difference. They have decided, implicitly in most cases, to remove themselves from political life. At the other end of the spectrum, highly engaged citizens are quite likely to be fairly well polarized. That is what gets them engaged. However, if the criteria for engagement are very strict, we might be simply approximating the McClosky group's finding of greater polarization among party leaders (or, in this case, those with involvements just shy of leadership status).

The implications of the McClosky group's findings pose a Goldilocks dilemma. One mix is too cold and one too hot. In evaluating public polarization, we should neither cast the net so broadly as to include those who are fundamentally apolitical, nor cast it so narrowly as to include only a rarified group of political obsessives. Not too cold and not too hot. Based on these considerations, the focus in examining polarization in the public would ideally be on those who vote or who might plausibly vote in presidential elections. However, there is no bright-line division of the public into tuned-in plausible voters and tuned-out apoliticals.[19] This being the case, the routine oversampling of people with characteristics associated with voting is helpful in getting us closer to the real electorate.[20]

Increased Party Polarization in Government

The political parties are much more polarized now than they had been, both at the elite or leadership level (the fourth "known") and at the mass or party identifier level (the fifth "known"). Differences between the parties are now far greater than they had been, and differences within the parties, though still in evidence (sometimes glaringly so), are not as great as they once were. The days of Rockefeller Republicans challenging Goldwater Republicans are over, as are the days of Dixiecrat Democrats doing battle with northern liberal Democrats. The Democrats are now quite clearly the liberal party and the Republicans are now quite clearly the conservative party, whether referring to leaders, activists, party identifiers, or voters. At all levels, there are far fewer conservative Democrats and liberal Republicans than there were in the 1960s and 1970s.

The evidence is overwhelming that the leadership of the political parties (elected officials, candidates, activists, etc.) have become more highly polarized over the last several decades. Using Keith Poole and Howard Rosenthal's NOMINATE scores of congressional roll-call voting, Sarah Binder in the mid-1990s observed that, "The political center in Congress has shrunk markedly over the past 15 years. Hovering around 30% of House and Senate members in the 1960s and 1970s, the percentage of centrists in each chamber began slipping in the 1980s, and it has fallen to about 10% today. Centrists now can claim 11.3% of the House, down from 20% or more during the 1980s. And after peaking at 32.3% of the Senate during 1969–70, the first term of the Nixon administration, centrists make up less than 10% of today's Senate."[21] Summing up the situation as it stood at the time, Binder concluded that "the shrinking political center has left Congress increasingly polarized.... Democrats are perched on the left, Republicans on the right, in both the House and the Senate, but strikingly for both chambers.... Since the 1980s the distance between the two parties has essentially doubled."[22] They have only grown further apart since then.[23]

Revisiting the issue nearly a decade later and using the same roll-call measure of ideological voting in Congress, Bond and Fleisher found the congressional parties to be quite polarized and to have become more polarized since the mid-1980s.[24] They classified House members and senators from the 1950s to the 1990s in six categories of ideology and partisanship (liberal, moderate, or conservative Democrats and the same on the Republican side). Based on their classifications, the percentage of "non-conformist" representatives (House members or senators who are moderates or liberal Republicans or conservative Democrats) declined a great deal since the 1950s. In the House, at least 40% of members were nonconformists in the 1950s (42%), 1960s (45%), and 1970s (42%). The percentage of nonconformists dropped to 28% in the 1980s and only 15% in the 1990s. The decline in the Senate was similar. There was little change until the 1980s, when the parties became more polarized. At least 40% of senators were nonconformists prior to the 1980s.[25] The middle began shrinking in earnest in the 1980s (30%) and centrists were an endangered species by the 1990s (11%).

Poole and Rosenthal and Keith Poole's website thoroughly evaluate the history of party polarization in Congress.[26] They find that "by the 1970s, polarization took off in both houses."[27] One indication of this was the degree of ideological overlap between the parties. Overlap is defined as the "percentage of a party's members closer to the centroid of the opposing party than to the centroid of their own party."[28] Less overlap indicates greater party polarization. From the 109th to the 112th U.S. Congress (following the 2004 to 2010 elections), Poole and Rosenthal found no overlap whatsoever between Democrats and Republicans in either chamber. The least liberal Democrat was more liberal than the most liberal Republican in every Congress.

Beyond the party separation evidence of polarization, the parties are a good deal more cohesive or unified ideologically than they had been and the ideological differences between them are greater than they had been since the early 1900s, according to Poole and Rosenthal.[29] In the 1950s and 1960s, the median distance between the parties on the DW-NOMINATE measure was about .5 in both the House and Senate. In the 2000s (through 2010), that distance had increased to about .8 in the Senate and nearly 1.0 in the House. Individual DW-NOMINATE scores generally range from –1.0 most liberal to +1.0 most conservative. Party polarization is not only greater than in the 1950s and 1960s, according to this measure, it is "now at the highest level since the end of Reconstruction."[30]

TABLE 1.1. INCREASED UNITY WITHIN CONGRESSIONAL PARTIES, 1961–2012

Period	*Mean Party Unity Rates*			
	House		Senate	
	Republicans	Democrats	Republicans	Democrats
1961–1980	77.3	75.6	73.7	74.9
1991–2012	90.7	89.1	87.9	88.8
Difference	+13.4	+13.5	+14.2	+13.9

Source: The data were obtained from Keith Poole's Voteview website: http://poole androsenthal.com/party_unity.htm (Last updated, February 8, 2013 and Accessed June 5, 2013). Much of the data were obtained through an NSF funded project with principal investigator Elaine Swift (Study No. 3371, Database of Congressional Historical Statistics, 1789–1989).

Note: A party unity vote is defined as one in which at least half of one party votes in the opposite direction from at least half of the other party. The party unity score is the percentage of these votes that a member votes with his or her party.

For skeptics of measurement by complex algorithms (and there is good reason to be skeptical even when the complex scaling is well done), some less methodologically sophisticated and less processed measurements corroborate the findings that party polarization in Congress has substantially increased. The first of these is a measure of internal party unity in roll-call voting. Table 1.1 displays mean party unity scores in the House and in the Senate by party for two periods, the 1960s and 1970s when parties were thought to be somewhat less polarized, and in the 1990s and 2000s (up to 2012) when they were considered highly polarized. Party unity scores for individual representatives or senators reflect the frequency with which they voted along party lines when a party line could be determined. That is defined as roll calls in which at least half of one party opposed at least half of the other party.

Both parties, according to the evidence in table 1.1, have become more unified in their opposition to each other in more recent years.[31] Greater party unity is evident both in the House and in the Senate. In the 1960s and 1970s, a party could typically count on about three-

TABLE 1.2. INCREASED PARTY POLARIZATION IN CONGRESS, 1961–2008

	Mean and Standard Deviations of ADA Scores			
	House		Senate	
Party	1961–1980	1991–2008	1961–1980	1991–2008
Republicans	17.2	11.6	26.0	14.0
	(19.8)	(13.4)	(25.9)	(16.1)
Democrats	56.0	81.6	54.5	85.5
	(31.4)	(19.2)	(29.4)	(14.8)
Difference	38.8	70.0	28.5	71.5

Source: The data were originally scored by the Americans for Democratic Action. The original data are available at www.adaction.org/pages/publications/voting-records .php. The data used here were collected from the ADA by Timothy Groseclose and posted on the website: www.sscnet.ucla.edu/polisci/faculty/groseclose/Adj.Int.Group .Scores/, accessed June 3, 2013. The data are the unadjusted ADA scores. The Ns are 5,243 and 3,868 for Democrats in the House. For House Republicans: 3,347 and 3,631. For Senate Democrats: 1,211 and 867 and Senate Republicans: 756 and 894. The initial number in each pairing is for the 1961–1980 period.

quarters of its members voting together on roll calls. The other quarter would vote with the other side. This allowed the more frequent formation of bipartisan coalitions, whether combining to pass or to block legislation. By the late 1980s, however, the parties were becoming much more unified and potential bipartisan coalitions had fewer potential members who might plausibly be recruited. In the 1990s and early 2000s, about 90% of members supported their parties on party roll calls. This heightened loyalty was evident in both parties and in both chambers. During President Obama's first term (2009 to 2012), party unity averaged over 88% among House Democrats and over 91% among Senate Democrats. Republican party unity averaged 89% in the House and over 84% in the Senate.[32] By the 112th Congress (2011 to 2012), the average party unity score in the House had reached 91% for Democrats and 93.5% for Republicans.[33]

Table 1.2 displays the average liberalism scores in congressional parties as computed by the Americans for Democratic Action (ADA). The ADA is one of the oldest and most revered liberal organizations in the nation.[34] It began tracking the roll-call votes of representatives in the 1940s. After each session of Congress, the ADA selects a set of roll-call votes (usually about 20) it considers important and scores representatives according to whether they voted in accord with or in opposition to the ADA's position. The ADA score for each member is the percentage of votes they cast in support of the liberal position. As with the party unity analysis, table 1.2 reports on the voting of the congressional parties in the 1960s and 1970s compared to the 1990s and 2000s (up to 2008) in both the House and the Senate.

As the ADA's ratings make crystal clear, the congressional parties are now much more polarized than they had been. In the 1960s and 1970s, the average congressional Democrat was typically about 30 or 40 percentage points more likely to have voted for the liberal position than the average Republican. The Republicans, in both the House and Senate, were moderately conservative in this period, but the average Democrat was just barely left of center (just over the 50% mark). This reflected the split between southern Democrats and more liberal non-southern Democrats.

Now this has greatly changed. The party differences in the House and Senate of 30 to 40 percentage points have now expanded to a 70-percentage-point-wide chasm. Both parties are more unified (note the decline in standard deviations) and ideologically much farther apart. The Republicans have moved a bit more to the right (by about 6 points in the House and 12 in the Senate), while Democrats have moved much farther to the left (26 points in the House and 31 in the Senate). This increased party polarization in Congress is also evident in ADA scores adjusted for "shifting and stretching" related to the use of different roll calls in different years.[35] The evidence is overwhelming: the elected leaders of the political parties have become much more polarized.[36]

The voters are well aware of the increased differences between the parties in office. In response to the question of whether there were "any important differences" in what the parties stood for, only half of ANES respondents in the five presidential election year surveys from 1960 to 1976 said they saw significant differences between the parties. Many more are aware of differences now. In the five presidential elections from 1992 to 2008, that percentage increased to 68%. It exceeded 75% in 2004 and 2008.

In the 1940s and 1950s, the parties were considered so internally divided that they failed to offer voters clear alternatives.[37] Critics called for more programmatically coherent and responsible parties. In the 1960s, internal party divisions were so great that they created a virtual four-party system.[38] Crossing party lines was so common that a Conservative Coalition of Republicans and southern conservative Democrats often ruled the day.[39] Those days are long gone. For better or worse, the parties in government have become much more ideologically homogenous, with few centrists available for cross-party coalitions of any sort.

And lest one think that the increased polarization of party elites is confined to Congress, there is good evidence that the U.S. Supreme Court is more polarized by party and ideology as well. By 2012, each of the four justices who had been nominated to the Court by Democratic presidents had more liberal voting records on cases than any of the five justices nominated by Republican presidents.[40] The Court's polarization may also be reflected in the less "friendly" language used by justices in their written opinions.[41]

Increased Party Polarization in the Electorate

As in the leadership ranks, the Democratic Party has become more clearly the liberal party and the Republican Party more clearly the conservative party among average Americans. In a study of the values of Americans, Pew reported that "their values and basic beliefs are more polarized along partisan lines than at any point in the past 25 years."[42] Similarly, an over-time analysis of an interesting array of social distance metrics (including feelings about interparty marriage) by Iyengar, Sood, and Lelkes concluded that "American partisans are highly polarized in their feelings about each other."[43] Whether the parties became more polarized because of an increase of liberals and conservatives in the electorate or because the parties did a better job of sorting liberals and conservatives into their more aligned parties, there is a broad consensus that the parties in the electorate have become much *more* polarized.[44] This increase has been great enough that partisans are generally regarded as being *highly* polarized.

The consensus over party polarization in the electorate is built on a mountain of evidence. Party identifications are now more positively correlated with ideological perspectives.[45] In the 1970s and 1980s, the correlation of party identifications and self-declared ideological perspectives was moderately strong (a correlation of around .4); but by 2004, it was a good deal stronger (a correlation over .6). As Abramowitz noted in an analysis of party identification in the 2006 Cooperative Congressional Election Study, "the liberal-conservative scale alone correctly predicted the party identification of 91.3 percent of voters in the CCES survey."[46]Along these same lines, partisanship and the various issue positions of survey respondents have also grown more closely correlated.[47]

Assessments of presidential job performance also reflect the increasing polarization of partisans.[48] The partisan approval gap, the median difference in quarterly presidential approval rates between Democratic and Republican party identifiers in Gallup's data, has widened considerably. From 1954 to 1969 (Eisenhower, Kennedy, and Johnson), the gap was about 38 percentage points.[49] Presidents typically received support from about 84% of their own party and 45% from the opposition party. Partisans have been far more divided in more recent times. From 1993 to 2013 (Clinton, G. W. Bush, and Obama), the gap increased to 61 percentage points. Presidents still get strong approval numbers from their own partisans (typically about 84%), but much lower levels of support from the opposition party (only about 20%). Since 2004, opposition party support has routinely been in the teens and even lower.

While there is a great deal of prior evidence indicating the greater polarization of parties in the electorate, this development may be seen most directly in the increased alignment of the voters' partisanship and ideological perspectives. Table 1.3 reports the percentages of ANES reported voters in presidential elections since 1972 whose ideological and partisan orientations were aligned, unaligned, or misaligned. This reflects changes in the numbers in partisan and ideological categories as well as the increased correlation of ideology and partisanship. Reported voters are considered to have *aligned* party identifications and ideological perspectives if they were liberal Democrats or conservative Republicans. The *misaligned* were conservative Democrats or liberal Republicans. Those who said that they were moderates or did not know how to classify their ideological views or who were independents in their party identifications (not leaning toward either party) were grouped as *unaligned* voters.

TABLE 1.3. PARTY POLARIZATION AMONG REPORTED VOTERS, 1972–2012

Presidential Election	Party Identification and Self-Reported Ideology Alignment (%)		
	Ideologically Aligned Partisans	Moderates, Don't Knows, and Independents	Ideologically Misaligned Partisans
1972	33.0	53.4	13.7
1976	34.4	55.0	10.7
1980	35.8	52.4	11.8
1984	39.1	49.5	11.5
1988	41.0	47.7	11.3
1992	41.5	47.5	11.0
1996	46.3	42.9	10.8
2000	43.1	46.3	10.6
2004	48.7	44.2	7.1
2008	50.0	43.0	6.9
2012	54.8	38.0	7.1
Difference 1972 to 2012	+21.8	−15.4	−6.6

Note: The data are from the ANES cumulative file and the preliminary release of the ANES 2012 Time Series Study.

The electorate's partisanship and ideological perspectives are much more aligned than they had been. In 1972, one-third of the electorate held ideological views in accord with their party identifications. By 2012, more than half had ideological perspectives consistent with those that prevailed in their parties. On the other side of the ledger, the percentage of ideologically misaligned partisan voters dropped from about 14% to about 7%. This decline suggests the sorting effect contributed to the greater polarization of the parties among voters— liberals were more likely to be Democrats and conservatives to be Republicans. This was not the only decline to offset the rise in aligned voters. Self-declared moderates, those unable to identify their ideo- logical outlooks, and independents—the unaligned—made up a much smaller portion of the electorate in 2012 than they had in 1972. More than half of the 1972 electorate was unaligned. By 2012, fewer than four in ten voters were unaligned, a drop of more than 15 percentage points. These declines, at least in moderates and in the ideological "don't knows," suggest that an increase in the general ideological polarization of the electorate contributed to the polarization between the parties in the electorate.

So this is where we stand. Polarization is a matter of degree, and changes in it, like changes in other aggregate characteristics of politics, may have large consequences despite appearing to be of modest proportions. Polarization in the ranks of political leadership will always appear greater than among the less politically engaged. And finally, whether considering differences between the parties' leaders or between their followers, the political parties have become substantially more polarized in recent decades. The increase in party polarization has created a wide chasm between Democrats and Republicans in the electorate as well as in government. This is what we know or at least what seems to be settled matters. What important questions remain?

THE UNKNOWNS

Eight important questions about polarization in American politics remain unsettled. The first two concern polarization in the electorate. These are explored in the three chapters (3–5) of part 2. The next three questions concern party polarization at the elite or leadership level. They are the subject of the three chapters (6–8) of part 3. Chapter 9 offers some thoughts about the remaining three questions. These concern the ultimate causes and consequences of polarization as well as possible responses to it.

The Level Question

The first of the great unknowns is the question of whether the American electorate is largely polarized or substantially moderate. Are Americans substantially divided into two opposing camps of ideological perspectives or mostly pragmatic and commonsense centrists who have been forced to deal with the extremism of highly ideological political parties?

There is no question that many, perhaps most, Americans believe this is a settled matter, that the electorate is highly polarized. Public opinion scholars, however, disagree about whether a highly polarized public is a reality or a myth. In recapping the results of the 2012 presidential election, Feldman and Zaino writing for the CBS News website observed that "Americans are exceedingly polarized in their political beliefs. The U.S. electorate in 2012 was deeply divided ideologically—and it was reflected in their votes for president."[50] On the other hand, in his review of the research on polarization as of 2009, Hetherington observed that "despite all the talk about red states versus blue states, it is not clear that ordinary citizens are polarized today."[51] Certainly, as the McClosky Difference suggests, the public does not appear to be as polarized as its leaders are and never will be. But apart from this comparison, is the public nevertheless now highly polarized?

Some claim that what many see as the general polarization of the public—widespread ideological differences and a relatively small political center—may actually be the polarization of the better sorted or realigned parties, the exaggeration of relatively small ideological-geographic differences by winner-take-all electoral rules (as in the red state, blue state differences), or the polarization of the nation's party activists and leaders rather than the public. As Morris Fiorina forcefully argues, the sorting of a preexisting pool of ideologues into their respective left-wing and right-wing parties may create the illusion of a more generally polarized electorate even when a large majority of citizens remain comfortably in the political center.[52] The ideological choices that voters are forced to make between the parties' candidates create a false impression of the voters' true preferences. The centrist electorate, so the argument goes, would opt for a more centrist choice if one were offered, but that choice is not offered by the polarized parties.

The Change Question

The second unknown also concerns polarization in the broad American electorate. Has the level of polarization in the electorate *changed* appreciably in recent decades? More specifically, has polarization in the electorate *increased* and, if so, by how much, and when did it take place? Whereas the first question concerns the current level of polarization in the public, this question addresses how current polarization compares to the past. Examining different indicators of polarization in the public with different levels of inclusiveness and over different time horizons, some research finds polarization in the electorate has increased in recent years while others claim it is essentially unchanged.[53]

The Party Change Question

Shifting the focus from the electorate to polarization among political leaders of the parties and from questions of description to explanation, the third unknown is the reason or reasons for the increased polarization of the parties in government. Chapter 6 attempts to answer the party change question: Why have the political parties in government become more ideologically polarized? There is consensus that they have become more polarized, but why? There is no shortage of explanations offered for the increased polarization of the parties.[54] Among the many suspects are a partisan realignment, highly partisan and ideological presidents and congressional leaders, party-strengthening institutional changes in Congress, the rise of cultural or social issues, an increasing disparity in incomes, the politicization of the media (conservative talk-radio and a more liberal press corps), and reforms of the nomination process and the rise of political activists. Other suspected causes of increased party polarization include the greater flow of money into politics—especially from highly ideological groups and wealthy individuals at both ends of the spectrum—more effective partisan redistricting and the movement of voters into more politically homogeneous communities, and a growing history of "bad blood" between the parties on failed compromises on policies (from taxes to immigration) and crossing-the-line attacks on appointments (e.g., the Bork and Tower nominations). And this does not exhaust the list.

The Party Asymmetry Question

Chapter 7 addresses the question of whether the increased polarization of party elites has been asymmetric. More specifically, is the greater polarization of the parties the result of both parties moving away from the political center, or is it the consequence of the Republican Party becoming particularly conservative? Hare, McCarty, Poole, and Rosenthal find that "congressional Republicans have moved farther away from the center than Democrats" since the 1970s.[55] Thomas Mann and Norman Ornstein conclude that "the center of gravity within the Republican Party has shifted sharply to the right."[56] Has the increased polarization in Congress, in fact, been largely one-sided or is this conclusion only one side of the story, an artifact of the time frame in which polarization was examined? If Republicans have veered right much more than the Democrats moved left, why might this be the case and why have the parties remained as competitive as they are? If the Republicans became nutty right-wingers while Democrats were sensible centrists with a bit of a leftist tilt, one would have expected Democrats to win national elections routinely and handily—but they have not. Despite being a first party-term incumbent (an asset almost ensuring reelection), President Obama narrowly won reelection in 2012 and after the 2014 midterm elections Republicans gained a 54-46 majority in the Senate and their largest House majority in more than 80 years. Is the claim of asymmetric polarization mistaken and, if so, why?

The Median Voter Question

Chapter 8 examines a fundamental question of party polarization at the elite level: Why are the political parties polarized *at all*? According to the Median Voter Theorem, in seeking to win majority-rule elections in a two-party system, the parties' candidates should strategically move to the political center in order to capture the pivotal vote of the median voter. A party whose candidates remain positioned to the left or right of center cedes decisive political ground to the opposition. According to the strategy derived from the Median Voter Theorem, a centrist strategy extolled in practice as well as theory, the political parties as bands of political leaders should converge on the political center of the spectrum. Except for variations due to imperfect information, a multidimensional issue agenda, or a multimodal distribution of issue positions in the electorate, there should be virtually no party polarization. Yet, there is.

Despite the often-cited logic of the Median Voter, study after study has demonstrated a history in which the Democratic and Republican parties take divergent issue positions as organizations,[57] as activists,[58] as candidates in elections,[59] and as representatives and leaders in government.[60] So while chapter 6 addresses the timely matter of why the parties have diverged more as of late, chapter 8 tackles the age-old question of why thc parties diverge at all. Why don't parties surrender to the centrist siren call of the median voter? Are they simply caught out of position by the pull of the nomination process to the more extreme elements of their partisan base, or is there more to it?

Causes, Consequences, and Cures

Beyond the five questions about the unknowns of polarization raised so far, there are three remaining questions that broadly concern polarization within the democratic political system. These deserve to be grappled with even if they cannot be definitively answered. The first is the elephant-in-the-room question: Where does polarization come from? What are electorates and parties divided about? Why does the division take on the characteristics of a polarizing division— substantial, intense, and falling generally along ideological lines? The second question concerns the consequences of polarization. In what ways does polarization affect the democratic process, for good or ill? Polarization, particularly polarization of the parties, is generally thought to be dysfunctional. In the middle of the twentieth century, however, political scientists were complaining about just the opposite problem—the lack of distinctive, disciplined, and responsible parties. The final question of democracy and polarization is what, if anything, might be done or should be done about polarization of the electorate and the parties? Chapter 9 explores each of these three big questions.

CLARIFYING POLARIZATION

In the course of taking stock of what we know and don't know about polarization, six points emerge that should be kept in mind. Previous discussions of polarization have at times become sidetracked or have talked past each other because they were not attentive enough to these analytic concerns.

The first point is that we need to be clear that there is a basic difference between asking about the level of polarization and asking about change in the level of polarization.[61] These are related questions, but the answer to one does not entail the answer to the other. Polarization may or may not have increased, but whether it has or has not does not answer the question of whether the public or the parties are largely polarized. Discussions of polarization in the electorate, for instance, often drift from findings suggesting stability in polarization to unsupported claims of low levels of polarization.[62] One does not follow from the other. A driver may increase the speed of his car by 20 miles per hour, but this does not necessarily mean he or she is speeding. He or she may have only been going 10 miles an hour before hitting the accelerator. Conversely, slowing down by 20 miles an hour does not mean the driver is not speeding. He or she may have been driving 100 miles an hour before easing up on the accelerator. The level of polarization is not its change. And change is not its level.

The second point is that we need to be clear about what kind of polarization we are talking about. First-order polarization or polarization *without* grouping is a very different matter from second-order polarization (as in party polarization). As Fiorina contends, while the parties in the electorate have undoubtedly become more polarized than they were, the public (ungrouped by partisanship) might not have. The parties can become more polarized without the public becoming more polarized if immoderate citizens are more cleanly sorted out into more homogeneous parties. Analysts as well as citizens sometimes skip too freely between the two orders of polarization.

The third point to keep in mind is the difficult problem of obtaining, devising, or setting benchmarks for the level or change in polarization so that we can make sense of the evidence of polarization and properly interpret it. As Fiorina observes, "to some degree, polarization is a subjective judgment."[63] This is a serious problem. Without some kind of reasonable benchmark (and this could seem to be small; recall our shared DNA with bonobos), we will be left with the head-shakingly unilluminating and stultifyingly unsatisfactory answer that the polarization glass is not completely full, but neither is it completely empty. Ho hum.

The fourth point is that we should examine polarization among those who might plausibly make a political difference. With reference to mass polarization, it does not make sense to include the chronically nonpolitical in assessing polarization since they have chosen to opt out of the process, making their views of little consequence to the political system. One might be interested in examining separately this strata of the public for its potential impact should they ever become mobilized, but the views of those "in the game" or those who at some point could plausibly get "in the game" are of greater interest.

The fifth point is that there is an important distinction between actual opinions and our measurements of those opinions. The inclinations of voters toward political values and issues is different from their conscious thoughts about them, their thoughts are different from their expression of those thoughts, and how voters would choose to express their thoughts is different from how those thoughts might be imperfectly "captured" in responses to the pre-structured questions and answers on surveys. One would expect some slippage between the inclination to thought, thought to expression, and expression to measurement. There is communication friction, some loss in translation from the core thought to survey measurement (or a roll-call vote, for that matter). This is likely the case for everyone, but especially for those less absorbed by politics (part of the McClosky Difference). In short, we should be careful not to mistake our measurement difficulties for the cognitive shortcomings of voters.

The final point is that we should pay attention to the span of time covered in examining issues regarding the change in polarization. The availability of data may artificially restrict the time frame, causing us to miss the full polarization story. We should be alert to the possibility that a conclusion that polarization is unchanged over a certain period may be more about the limited period examined than the lack of change. A study of the change in polarization since 1980, for example, would simply miss any increase in polarization that might have occurred in the late 1960s and 1970s.

With the inventory of basic knowns and unknowns completed and a set of warnings and advisories in hand, we now turn to historical observations and theoretical expectations about polarization. How have observations about the nature and extent of conflict in American politics changed over time and what theories are available to explain the extent and development of polarization, particularly in the electorate?

CHAPTER 2

HISTORY AND THEORIES

As long as the reason of man continues fallible, and he is at liberty
to exercise it, different opinions will be formed.

—James Madison, *The Federalist*, Number 10[1]

The inventory of what we know and do not know about polarization
provides the initial groundwork for its examination. In this chapter,
that groundwork is completed by reviewing the history and theories
of polarization. The first part of the chapter offers a brief history of
research, thinking, and observations about political conflict since the
mid-twentieth century. What we know and might suspect about polarization are the result of many prior examinations of it. The second
portion of the chapter presents three theories about the development of polarization among elites as well as in the public.

Polarization in current American politics cannot be understood
without understanding its past—and not just polarization over the
last couple of decades. As the epigraph from James Madison attests,

both polarization in public opinion and concern about it are not new. A good deal of contemporary polarization research, however, unfortunately suffers from being too limited in the period of history it examines. In taking a somewhat longer view of American political history since the middle of the twentieth century, polarization appears to have developed in three phases. In the first, from the late 1940s to the early 1960s, both the parties and the electorate were not highly polarized. This changed in the mid-1960s (phase two). With a growing civil rights movement, intensifying anti-war protests, and an emerging counterculture, the nation divided. The electorate became highly polarized and not just on fleeting issues and passing leaders. The parties, on the other hand, remained heterogeneous, muddled, and not very polarized. By the late 1970s and early 1980s (phase three), the parties began to catch up with the highly polarized public. As the parties became more polarized in recent decades, an already polarized electorate grew more so—but the big change had occurred earlier.

The second portion of the chapter examines three theories of how recent polarization developed. Several theories have been constructed to make sense of polarization: where it comes from, why it is as extensive as it is, how and why it may have changed in various ways over the years. Though often implicit, two general strains of theories have dominated the debate about the development of polarization. A third theory is proposed here.

The first theory is the Emerging Polarization Theory. Its basic contention is that the political parties at the leadership and activist levels have polarized and that the electorate has followed their lead. A number of variants of this theory trace the polarization of the parties and the electorate to different sources, but they share a common claim that both the parties and the electorate have become highly polarized in the last few decades. Both were relatively unpolarized in the 1980s and both became highly polarized by the early 2000s. Polarization emerged.

The second theory is the No Polarization Theory. It claims the public was and remains largely centrist, that the belief the nation is highly polarized is a myth.[2] The political parties are more polarized at both leadership and ordinary voter levels, but the number of citizens holding strong non-centrist ideological views has not grown appreciably. This theory holds that the minority who are truly liberals or conservatives are now better sorted out into more homogeneous parties, but the American public remains a moderate public. There has been an increase in second-order polarization in the public (party polarization), but not in first-order polarization. Polarization in the public has not changed much and remains low.

The Revealed Polarization Theory, proposed here, is a third possibility. It claims that the electorate is and has been highly polarized since the late 1960s. Polarization had been masked and its consequences muted because of its poor representation by politically heterogeneous parties. The slow realignment of the parties left them lagging behind a public that had become quite polarized in and after the turmoil of the late 1960s. According to this theory, once polarization between the parties caught up with that of the public in the 1990s and early 2000s, the extent of the public's polarization became more evident. Polarized parties fueled further polarization in the public in recent years, but much of the change took place a good deal earlier.

The review of the history and theories of polarization turns first to the recent history of the polarization debate. How did the study of polarization evolve? What has been written about the nature of conflict in American politics over the years?

HISTORY

The Current Debate

The current wave of research on polarization in American politics might be traced back to the early 1980s. Initially, this work concentrated on only party polarization at the elite level. Among the first on the scene were Poole and Rosenthal and Nice.[3] Using interest group ratings, Poole and Rosenthal found increasingly polarized parties in the U.S. Senate. Quite separately and using an index of state ideological orientations within the political parties, Nice found that party polarization had increased in the composition of presidential electoral coalitions as well as in both houses of Congress. Binder, Fleisher and Bond, and several others established beyond a doubt that polarization between the parties in Congress has increased substantially since the late 1970s and, by virtually any metric, is now at a high level.[4]

While polarization at the elite level was largely a settled matter (though questions of its origins and symmetry remained in contention), polarization in the public was definitely unsettled. The controversy over the polarization of the public began with James Davison Hunter's *Culture Wars: The Struggle to Define America* in 1991 and the adoption of its polarization theme by firebrand conservative columnist Pat Buchanan in his highly controversial address to the Republican National Convention in 1992.[5] Responding to these claims with an exhaustive examination of survey data of the public's issue attitudes, Paul DiMaggio, John Evans, and Bethany Bryson found no increase in the public's polarization on political issues, though they did find evidence that the parties in the electorate had become more polarized.[6] The finding of significant second-order party polarization in the electorate is now well established,[7] but claims about first-order or general polarization in the public remain in dispute.

The controversy over the polarization of the American public was addressed head-on in Morris Fiorina's *Culture War? The Myth of a Polarized America.*[8] Building on the earlier findings of DiMaggio, Evans, and Byson, Fiorina and his colleagues (Samuel Abrams and Jeremy Pope) challenged Hunter, Buchanan, and the prevalent popular and journalistic view that Americans are highly polarized. According to Fiorina, not only is there no culture war in the United States, but the public remains "largely centrist."[9] Those in the electorate with non-moderate orientations are now simply better sorted or realigned into more ideologically distinct parties, made so through the influence of relatively small groups of ideological political activists (the "political class"), but this has not changed the essentially moderate character of the American public.[10] The sorting of non-moderates into more homogeneous political parties created a false impression of a more polarized electorate. Moreover, by Fiorina's reckoning, party polarization has damaged the quality of representation in the political system—creating a fundamental disconnect between highly polarized parties and a very moderate electorate.[11] In a follow-up review of the debate, Marc Hetherington concurs with Fiorina's claim that polarization in the public is a myth. The parties in the electorate are in many ways better sorted out between liberals and conservatives, but the evidence "turns up little evidence of popular polarization," according to Hetherington.[12]

This, however, did not settle the matter. Alan Abramowitz and others claim that polarization in the public is not a myth.[13] A large segment of the public is now politically engaged and deeply divided about political issues. Moreover, there is greater consistency or constraint in the public's positions on issues.[14] There has been an ideological realignment in American politics that has fueled a greater polarization of the American electorate.[15] The electorate has become both better sorted between the parties and more polarized since 1972.[16] In rebuttal and in looking at similar evidence, Fiorina concludes that "any evidence of increased polarization lies somewhere between nonexistent and slight."[17]

The Historical Baseline

The story of polarization in American politics, where it stands, and how we got here begins well before the recent flurry of research on the subject, well before Hunter's book or Buchanan's convention speech. The story begins well before the term "polarization" was applied to the political conflict shaping American politics. Elements of the story could go back as far as the founding and the discussion of the sources of faction in the *Federalist Papers*, or a few decades later in the heated battles over slavery leading up to the Civil War. A later start to the story might begin with the internal fissures (the ticking time bombs) of the Democrats' New Deal coalition in the 1930s. While each of these elements contributed to the current state of polarization, we can pick up the basic story in the late 1940s and 1950s.

The period from the late 1940s through the early 1960s was the calm before the storm. It was a period of relatively low levels of polarization in the public and between the parties. It was a period of growth and consolidation in America. Having survived the harrowing events of the Great Depression of the 1930s, World War II in the 1940s, the Korean War in the late 1940s and early 1950s, and even into a period of "Cold War" tensions with the Soviets, Americans were getting back to normal lives. The experiences, issues, and political leadership of the 1930s, 1940s and 1950s were unusually unifying and galvanizing for Americans. The nation experienced tremendous growth in virtually every way, from the economy to technology (e.g., television) to a "baby boom." Out of the trauma of the previous decades emerged a more united America. Political differences, though present (as always), were relatively mild. Seymour Martin Lipset referred to it at the time as "the current spirit of 'moderation' in politics."[18]

In contrast to current times, rather than inquiring about the reasons for polarization of the parties and the public, political observers and scholars of that day examined why Americans and their parties were *not* highly ideological, *not* very polarized. Though differences between party elites existed, as McClosky et al. and others documented, they were not severe.[19] The parties overlapped a good bit, with many conservative Democrats and liberal Republicans. The state of party polarization, or the lack thereof, is most evident in what scholars were saying about it at the time. In 1950, a special Committee on Political Parties of the American Political Science Association chaired by E. E. Schattschneider issued its report entitled "Toward a More Responsible Two-Party System." The report spelled out the deficiencies of less distinct, unpolarized parties and offered a series of recommendations about what might be done to achieve more responsible parties—effectively more polarized parties.

Both social theories of American political culture and empirical studies emphasized the relative absence of ideological divisions in the public. Among social theories addressing the exceptional centrism of American politics, two stand out.[20] In *The Genius of American Politics*, Daniel J. Boorstin contended that an "American Theory" inherited from our founding had long dominated American politics and made other ideologies superfluous.[21] Boorstin wrote that "the quest for the meaning in our political life has been carried on through historical rather than philosophical channels."[22]American politics was practical politics: differences over the means to achieve ends that we all agreed on, not differences over the ends themselves. Not the stuff of great polarization.

Two years later, in his highly lauded *The Liberal Tradition in America*, Louis Hartz also addressed the American consensus.[23] The absence of a feudal or class structure in America, according to Hartz, had led to the general adoption of classically Lockean liberal political principles and perspectives on individual rights and equality. No rigid class system meant no feudal tradition in politics, and the absence of a feudal tradition meant the absence of an opposition to it—no revolutionary or radical socialist tradition. This was the basis for the fundamental difference between American and European political traditions. Divisions exist in American politics, but (apart from the unique causes of the Civil War) they are tamely centrist and pragmatically addressed within a shared Lockean-liberal tradition.[24] No polarization here. We are all Lockean liberals.[25]

Empirical research on American politics at the time generally meshed nicely with these social theories. Most notably, both the classic study of *The American Voter* by Angus Campbell et al. and Philip Converse's seminal analysis of "The Nature of Mass Belief Systems in Mass Publics" described an electorate that was largely non-ideological.[26] This was consistent with other interpretations of that era that found a fairly centrist postwar America under President Eisenhower's "middle of the road" leadership. Samuel Lubell observed in *The Revolt of the Moderates* that "rarely in American history has the craving for tranquility and moderation commanded more public support."[27]

All was not entirely sweetness and light, however, and the extent of moderation as well as the general non-ideological character of the public might be easily overdrawn. Robert Lane demonstrated that "latent" or less consciously held and fully articulated ideologies were commonly held by Americans.[28] Significant political disputes existed, from battles over infiltration of institutions by communists to the early stages of the modern civil rights movement. Socioeconomic, racial, and religious differences continued to fuel political conflicts.[29] Moreover, the extent of political differences during this period may have been somewhat underestimated because of blurred party differences.[30] Even so, compared to other points in history, the overall tenor of the times was quite peaceful. These were the halcyon days of television's *Leave It to Beaver* and *Father Knows Best*. As Bob Newhart in his television character of Dr. Robert Hartley in the mid-1970s quipped about how America had changed: "That was during the '50s. I mean nobody had any problems in the '50s. You never had to worry about what Ike was going to do."[31] Comedian Mort Sahl joked that the choice voters faced in 1956 was between the "extremes" of Eisenhower's "gradualism" and Stevenson's "moderation."[32]

This all changed in the mid-1960s. Turmoil replaced tranquility.[33] America experienced social and political upheaval. Conflict over civil rights and then the Vietnam War left the nation deeply divided.

Stories of marches, sit-ins, protests, demonstrations, and riots in the streets filled the nightly newscasts, along with body counts from Vietnam. Inner cities burned. SDS (Students for a Democratic Society) organized war protests on college campuses and militant Black Panthers organized young inner-city African Americans. A generation gap, feminism, and the counterculture emerged. It was the hippies versus the hard hats and almost everyone had sympathies for one side or the other. A conservative movement quietly grew from the ashes of Goldwater's 1964 presidential defeat. The assassinations of Martin Luther King and Bobby Kennedy further inflamed passions on the left. Four student protesters were killed by National Guardsmen at Kent State University, and not long after, two more died at Jackson State. The New Left took on the establishment. It was the time of Woodstock and the chaos of the 1968 Democratic Convention. Vice President Agnew rallied "the silent majority" to rise in defense of "law and order" and traditional values. Not long after, Agnew resigned in disgrace. If all of that were not surreal enough, the era was capped off with the Watergate scandal, televised impeachment hearings, and the only resignation of a president in the nation's history. Political battles were pervasive. They even made their way into television sitcoms as blue-collar conservative Archie Bunker traded barbs with his new-politics liberal son-in-law in the show *All in the Family*. Things have not been the same since.

The mid-1960s to the mid-1970s were crowded years for Americans. The traumatic events of that period left the nation much more politically divided. The electorate became more issue-oriented and more ideological. The impact of issue preferences in presidential voting increased.[34] In *The Changing American Voter*, Norman Nie, Sidney Verba, and John Petrocik found a good deal more constraint in the issue preferences of voters beginning in the 1964 election, suggesting a more ideological outlook on politics.[35] Later analyses confirmed the electorate's increased ideological character.[36] In an often overlooked study of this period, Warren Miller and Teresa Levitan in *Leadership and Change* found a new form of the liberal-conservative division in the country, a new politics.[37] As they characterized it, the public had become divided between "the new liberals" and "the silent minority." Though one could well challenge aspects of this interpretation, in retrospect it seems clear that they were tapping into a more polarized and contentious electorate.

All was not so clear with the parties. Though the parties were increasingly pressured by their growing and impatient ideological wings, their polarization was slowed by several factors. The rich diversity or muddled centrism (depending on your point of view) of the parties was supported by the status quo reinforcing effects of congressional incumbency, the inertia of party identifications, and the historical absence of a viable Republican Party throughout the formerly solidly Democratic South. The centrist establishment of both parties also resisted, with varying degrees of success, the more polarizing influences of their newly strengthened insurgent wings.[38] As the parties dragged their feet in responding to the more polarized electorate, they entered an era of partisan dealignment or decomposition.[39] Some questioned whether a large portion of the electorate even considered the parties still to be relevant.[40] Though dealignment claims would later be seen as exaggerated, there is no doubt that partisanship was significantly weakened in this period.

The title and lead sentence of the American National Election Study's report on the 1972 election "A Majority Party in Disarray: Policy Polarization in the 1972 Election" neatly convey the disconnect between a highly polarized electorate and parties that had not yet realigned or sorted out that more polarized public: "The 1972 election marked the third time running that one of the major parties failed to cope with the polarization of policy demands among its supporters in the contest for the presidency."[41] A high level of polarization in the electorate that was not yet well matched with its partisanship led to a tidal wave of partisan defectors in presidential voting and the landslide reelection of a minority party president, Richard Nixon. The parties had not kept pace with a changing electorate.[42]

Historical Reconnaissance

This review of the history and study of American political conflict since the end of World War II is admittedly cursory. It is only the tip of the iceberg. It is not meant to stand as proof or even as evidence about how polarization developed. It should remind us, however, that questions and claims about polarization did not begin with the current debate. Far from it. Beyond that, the broadened perspective offered by this review suggests plausible answers to the questions that remain about polarization. The examination of theories that have been proposed to explain polarization may further advance these lines of questioning and the examination of the evidence in the following chapters.

The impression left by this excursion into polarization history is that polarization in the public and polarization between the parties have increased since the 1950s, that they increased at different times, and that the public became more polarized before the parties had been able to sort or realign themselves. Roughly speaking, polarization of both the first and second orders was relatively weak in the 1950s and into the 1960s. Polarization in the public increased a good deal in America's own "cultural revolution" of the mid- to late 1960s and into the 1970s. Polarization of the parties, in the electorate and among elites, seems to have developed in the late 1970s and into the 1980s. One might guess that polarization of the public and between the parties fed off each other in recent decades, with the electorate becoming slightly more polarized and the parties (having had a slower start) a good deal more so—but this is only loose conjecture. We now turn to tighter conjecture, the theories of polarization.

THEORIES

At this point we have a good idea of the questions about polarization—questions concerning its level and its development both in the electorate and among elites, both in general and between the parties. These are the unknowns. A review of history, sketches of rudimentary conditions as well as synopses of scholarship, also offers some clues into plausible answers to these polarization questions. The one remaining piece of groundwork to prepare prior to examining the evidence is the basic theories about polarization.

It would be easy for an examination of the theories of polarization to spiral out of control. Polarization, after all, concerns the formation of basic political preferences and the conflicts between them. This could be traced back to psychological responses to socioeconomic conditions, social networks, and socialization and, before you know it, to psycho-biology and DNA. I leave that to others. In the interests of keeping this inquiry manageable and keeping our eyes on "the ball," the theories examined here will be limited to the macro-level and will focus on questions about the first two unknowns: how polarized is the electorate and how has the extent of polarization in the electorate changed over time?

Theory is a grand term. Stripping away formalities, theories are essentially proposed general explanations of recurring phenomena. As used here, the theories of polarization are more about *what* happened rather than *why* it happened, and the application is to the current period of history rather than a broader generalization. This may have implications for more general understandings of polarization at different times and places, but the goal is to explain what happened to the level and change in political polarization in modern American history. Some may find this to be non-scientifically descriptive, but the presumption here is that we need to know what happened before we can hope to explain why it happened. Moreover, when we turn our attention in later chapters to party polarization, where we know what happened (it increased substantially), we will address the conventional theoretical "why" rather than "what" questions. For sticklers who remain queasy about how the term "theory" is being used, the term perspective or scenario may be substituted.

What are the plausible theories proposed of the level and change in polarization of the electorate in modern American politics? Two theories or scenarios dominate the debate and a third is proposed here. They differ over whether the electorate is now highly polarized and whether the extent of polarization has increased substantially in recent decades.

Emerging Polarization

The general journalistic view and a view often expressed or implicit in a good deal of scholarship is that political polarization in the public has grown substantially in the last several decades, that the extent of polarization is now quite high, and that this polarization is matched up quite tightly with partisanship so that party polarization expresses the sharply divergent views held in the electorate.[43] For any number of reasons, from expanding differences in religious beliefs, to increasing disparities in wealth and incomes, to the realignment of the parties and other factors, polarization has increased substantially and it is now at a very high level.

Many Americans seem to see things pretty much this way, at least with respect to the extent of polarization. In a November 2012 poll, Gallup asked respondents whether they thought that "Americans are united and in agreement about the most important values" or that "Americans are greatly divided when it comes to the most important values." The response was lopsided. More than two-thirds of respondents (69%) said they thought that Americans were greatly divided. Less than a third (29%) reported they thought Americans were generally united in their values.[44] The frequency of the "greatly divided" response was only slightly greater than it had been in either a 1998 *Washington Post* survey (66%) or the 1993 General Social Survey (63%).[45]

Though the idea that the nation (and not just the parties) has become more polarized in recent years is widely held, it is not so clear exactly when this change is supposed to have begun. The supposed emergence of polarization in the public must have preceded both Hunter's book and Buchanan's speech in the early 1990s, since they set off the current debate. Beyond this, the timing of the suspected onset of polarization in the electorate can be roughly estimated based on the timing of party polarization among elites. The polarization of the parties, according to this set of theories, reflects the polarization of the public. Since it is generally contended that political divisions occur first among political elites and then somewhat later spread to the mass public,[46] the suspected increase in polarization in the electorate must have occurred after the party polarization among leaders began to increase. If we take that to be when congressional party polarization began in the late 1970s, this would put the early rumblings of greater mass polarization perhaps in the mid-1980s.

The strength of the emergence theory would seem to be that it conforms to the public's prevailing impression about the level of polarization in the electorate as well as those of most observers of American politics. There is certainly a common sense that Americans are highly polarized, that political differences are unusually heated among average citizens. The last several decades have not been tranquil times politically.

There are, however, two points of possible weakness in this theory. The first is that the hard evidence of a substantial increase in polarization in the last couple of decades is ambiguous. Several analyses of differences in issue preferences as well as differences in declared ideological orientations suggest little, if any, increase in the last few decades.[47] This may be due to that fact that macropolitical changes tend to appear rather small, but other measurement issues (addressed in chapters 3 and 4) may also muddy the waters and there is evidence of greater consistency of preferences across a range of issues.[48] The second possible weakness in this theory is timing. It is unclear what event or circumstance since the late 1970s may have sent the public down the road to much greater polarization. Perhaps the polarization of party leadership had a sufficiently strong pull on the electorate to achieve this, but skepticism of this idea would be understandable. Finally, at this point and as observed in the last chapter, there is no established benchmark to indicate that the current level of polarization in the electorate is, in fact, high or, for that matter, low. It is a matter of degree and a high level or a low level of polarization is still in the eye of the beholder.

No Polarization

The second theory or perspective on polarization in the electorate has been quite clearly formulated by DiMaggio, Evans, and Bryson and by Fiorina, along with several of his colleagues.[49] After Hunter's book, Buchanan's speech, and the general adoption of the emerging polarization perspective in public discourse, the DiMaggio group's review of issue items in national surveys found no evidence of increased polarization. Building on this finding, Fiorina claimed that the sorting of ideologues into more homogeneous parties, along with the increased party polarization of elites that forced voters to choose between more extreme alternatives, fostered the false impression that the public was itself polarized when it was not. Apart from the neater sorting of liberals and conservatives into their respective party boxes, the predominant moderation of American politics was essentially undisturbed. According to this theory, second-order polarization between the parties has been mistaken for first-order polarization or general polarization in the public.

The main strength of the no polarization theory is the main weakness of the emergence theory: the evidence regarding an increase in mass polarization is spotty. As Fiorina summed it up, though the political class in America is clearly more polarized than it was, "a close examination of the general population finds little or no sign of a comparable increase in polarization."[50] The caveats concerning the magnitude of macropolitical changes of course apply and a closer inspection of the evidence in the following chapters will expose some serious problems with past examinations, but the ambiguous findings at this point are favorable to the view that the increase in polarization is much ado about nothing.

As with the emergence theory, the principal vulnerability of the no polarization theory would seem to be its claim that the electorate is largely unpolarized. This may reflect the hyperbole of using black-or-white language for a shades-of-gray phenomenon or the misapplication of elite standards of polarization or otherwise unrealistic standards (e.g., bimodality) for mass polarization. Beyond this, however, the claim of a nonpolarized electorate often reflects the unwarranted inference that findings of no change in polarization mean no polarization. Interpretations of the DiMaggio et al. analyses offer good examples.[51] Though DiMaggio et al. found no general *increase* in the dispersion of opinions on issue preference scales, these findings have been characterized as indicating "little evidence of polarization"[52] or "little in the way of polarization."[53]

In general, the major weakness of the no polarization theory is that, like the emergence theory, it lacks a benchmark for assessing what level of polarization should be considered to be high or low. Hetherington, for instance, observes as evidence of the electorate's moderation that "about 50 percent of Americans either characterize themselves as moderate or are unable to place themselves on the scale."[54] He implicitly assumes that a public equally divided between non-moderates and moderates or don't knows is largely unpolarized. Is it? Why? This count would also mean that about 50% of Americans characterize themselves as being either liberals or conservatives and who knows how many of the don't knows have ideological perspectives but lack familiarity with the terminology? From this perspective, the public might be regarded as fairly well polarized. In short, lacking a justifiable benchmark, any conclusion about the presence or absence of polarization is a highly subjective, mushy matter.[55] A second vulnerability of the no polarization theory is that it is left to explain why the two parties have polarized while the electorate they are trying to gain votes from has not. There are several possible answers to this conundrum (e.g., the influence of activist extremists), but the fact that it is raised at all for two highly competitive parties certainly complicates the "no polarization" story.

Revealed Polarization

Like the emergence theory, the revealed polarization theory concludes that the American electorate is highly polarized and was not always so. The theory departs from the emergence theory, however, in claiming that the electorate has been quite highly polarized for a long time. The polarization of the electorate is not a development of the last few decades. While the electorate's polarization may well have increased in recent years, it had become highly polarized long ago, most likely in the mid- and late 1960s.

Any increase in polarization of the electorate since the 1980s only added to its already high level. As the historical review described it, Americans in the 1950s had their differences but they were not highly polarized. The upheaval of the mid- to late 1960s, however, created deep divisions in values and political orientations. These differences did not fade away. They grew. They were less evident and more muted than they might have been because they were not well reflected in the heterogeneous political parties of that time. Incumbency, stable partisanship, and the absence of a viable southern Republican Party caused the parties to lag in their representation of the more polarized electorate. Once the parties began to polarize or sort themselves out in the late 1970s to early 1990s, rather than muting or masking polarization in the electorate, they revealed and accentuated it.

The two main strengths of the revealed polarization theory are that it comports with general perceptions that the public is polarized (like the emergence theory) as well as with the spotty findings regarding a significant increase in the electorate's polarization in recent decades (like the no polarization theory). Polarization of the electorate in recent times probably increased as the parties became more polarized, but this was not necessary to the assessments of polarization since the electorate's high level of polarization was a preexisting condition. Another strength of the revealed polarization theory is that it fits the history of partisanship—a relatively unpolarized electorate accepting relatively heterogeneous parties in the 1950s through mid-1960s (the highly partisan *American Voter* era), a more polarized electorate rejecting these same relatively heterogeneous parties in the 1970s (the weakened partisanship of dealignment), and a polarized electorate accepting more ideologically homogeneous parties from the mid-1980s to the present (restored partisanship).

As in the case of the other theories, the principal challenge for the revealed polarization theory is that of arriving at a sensible benchmark for determining what is and what is not a high level of polarization. A second and more easily addressed vulnerability of this theory is its claim that polarization in the electorate preceded the greater polarization of party elites. The prevailing view is that followers follow leaders.[56] As Fiorina puts it: "party sorting is largely a top-down process wherein the more visible and active members of a party, especially its elected officials and party activists, sort first and provide cues to voters that party positions are evolving."[57] However, in this case, the polarization of the electorate was not driven primarily by party realignment or sorting. It makes sense that voters do not respond to parties that have not yet transformed themselves (among elites), but party realignment is certainly not the only route to greater polarization among voters. In addition, there were strong historical reasons (the formerly Solid Democratic South) to expect that the realignment of the parties would have been considerably slowed down in this case, allowing change in the public to outpace it. And finally, as Layman and his colleagues observe, polarization in the public and among leaders probably are mutually reinforcing. It is not an exclusively top-down process.[58]

The three theories or perspectives on polarization may be clearly distinguished by their different answers to the two principal questions about polarization: the change question and the level question. The emergence of polarization theory claims that polarization in the electorate has grown a great deal in recent decades and that this level of polarization is now quite high. The no polarization theory disagrees on both counts. According to this theory, polarization in the electorate has not increased significantly and the electorate remains largely moderate and unpolarized. Finally, the revealed polarization theory claims that the electorate is now and has been quite polarized for many years. The electorate has probably become more polarized as the parties have become more polarized, but the principal point is that the highly polarized state of the electorate is not altogether new.

SIX CONTENTIONS

The next six chapters delve into the evidence pertaining to five of the unknowns of polarization: (1) its level in the electorate, (2) the change in this level in recent decades, (3) the reasons for increased party polarization, (4) the symmetry or asymmetry of party polarization, and (5) the reasons why the parties are polarized at all considering the powerful centrist pull of the median voter. In exploring these unknowns, the analysis must deal with many details and one could easily, as the old saying goes, miss the forest for the trees. So it may be helpful at this point, before we go poking at the trees, to very briefly lay out the six major contentions of the analysis—our forest.

The first contention concerns the direct evidence of polarization in the public. The direct evidence is flawed but instructive about the central questions of polarization when carefully examined. This direct evidence consists of the distributions of self-reported ideological orientations and issue attitudes. After considering various claims and charges that have been made about the quality of this evidence—dismissing some, putting some in perspective, and accepting some as substantial flaws in the data—and after devising benchmarks to evaluate properly the levels of polarization, the analyses of both the ideology evidence and the issue evidence arrive at essentially the same conclusions about the extent and change of polarization.

The second contention is that answers to the polarization questions should not rest simply on the direct evidence of self-reported ideologies and issue preferences. Polarization can also be effectively assessed with indirect or circumstantial evidence. As in the case of the prosecution of an accused criminal, when there may be lingering doubts about conclusions drawn from imperfect direct evidence, reliable circumstantial evidence can often be brought to bear on the matter. So too with polarization. Our knowledge about party polarization in government and the electorate, the extent and strength of partisanship, voter turnout levels, and even split-ticket voting offer multiple pieces of indirect evidence of polarization in the electorate. In every respect, the circumstantial evidence reaffirms the findings of the direct evidence.

The third and most important contention is that the direct evidence drawn from ideology and issue attitude data and a significant body of compelling circumstantial evidence indicate that the American electorate is highly polarized, has been polarized for many years, and has become significantly more polarized in recent times. It is not just the leaders and activists who are polarized, but normal voters as well. This does not mean that centrists have vanished. There are a great many centrists, but there are more non-centrists. Many are staked out on the political left and even more occupy the political right—and it has been this way for a long time. Most of those on the left and the right are not close to being fanatics, nor are many of them particularly sophisticated in their political thinking or articulate in its expression, but they do have greatly different worldviews that clash with those on the other side.

The fourth contention is an explanation of why the electorate's polarization was not apparent to many before the 1990s. Before that, many accepted the myth that the public was not highly polarized. This myth was sustained by the ideological heterogeneity of the parties. The muddled nature of the parties, owing largely to the historical absence of the Republican Party in the South since the Civil War, obscured and muted the extent of the electorate's polarization. Once the parties realigned (or sorted), the polarization of the electorate was highlighted and accentuated. The illusion of a mostly moderate public became difficult to sustain.

The fifth contention is that the increase in party polarization and the misperception of an asymmetry in party polarization are the results of an unusual staggered party realignment. The realignment of American politics from the New Deal party system of heterogeneous parties dominated by the Democratic Party to a competitively balanced party system with ideologically homogeneous parties began in the late 1960s and was not completed until the early 1990s, largely because there had not been a viable Republican Party in the South since the Civil War. The staggered nature of the realignment slowed and staggered the process of party polarization. Democrats moved to the left first and this was later followed by the Republicans moving to the right. Republicans moved even a bit further right in response to some growth in conservatism in the public (and some measurement issues further muddy the waters). If a narrow time frame is applied to the analysis, the staggered nature of the polarization dance (left foot first, then right foot) could be easily misconstrued as asymmetrical (missing the step to the left).

The final major argument of the book is an explanation of why party polarization exists at any level. Contrary to the expectation of the median voter theorem, the parties do not converge on the political center. To varying degrees, they polarize.[59] Why do the parties and candidates deviate from the median voter expectation? A number of possible answers have been considered, most commonly the pull of the nomination to the views of activist ideological zealots.[60] Though there may be a number of influences pulling away from the center, the principal answer is that winning the vote of the median voter does not mean that the median voter is the only voter who must be won over by a party. The median voter is a moving target. Increasing the turnout of a party's base effectively redefines the median voter closer to the party's base. Since turnout in the party's base is variable and depends on its satisfaction with the party's position, candidates cannot take the base for granted. Just as a party that is too extreme risks alienating centrists, a party that is too centrist risks turning off some of its more ideological supporters. They can easily abstain from voting if they feel their party's candidate does not represent their views well enough or if they perceive from a distance that the differences between a center-right and a center-left party are trivial. Strategically, a party's electoral fortunes may depend as much or more on motivating its base to turn out as it does with cultivating the support of fickle centrists. And this is a sure recipe for polarization.

With the foundation now in place, the questions of the extent and change in the American public's polarization can be addressed. These two questions are approached in different ways with different evidence in each of the next three chapters of part 2. Chapters 3 and 4 examine the direct evidence of polarization in the electorate: ideological evidence and issue preference evidence, respectively. Chapter 5 takes a very different approach, introducing indirect or circumstantial evidence of polarization.[61] Although their data differ in many ways (spoiler alert), the three analyses arrive at the same conclusion: Americans are highly polarized and their polarization has increased. The first leg of this tripod of evidence is established by the examination of ideological data in chapter 3.

PART TWO

THE POLARIZED
ELECTORATE

CHAPTER 3

IDEOLOGY AND POLARIZATION

This conflict over the proper limits of government has
intensified steadily until it has become the sharpest single
political divider in the country.

—Samuel Lubell, *The Future of American Politics*[1]

There are many conflicting claims about the extent and growth of
polarization in the American public. In this and the following two
chapters, these claims are put to the test (or, more accurately, tests).
This chapter evaluates the direct evidence of polarization drawn
from measures of ideological orientations. What does this evidence
indicate about polarization and its change in recent decades and
what is the quality of this evidence? Some serious reservations about
self-reported ideology as a measure have been raised. Are its critics or
the measure to be believed? In short, based on the direct evidence,
what claims about mass polarization should we trust?

Are Americans sharply divided in their politics or are they calmly gathered around a pragmatic political center? This is a tough question because the answer most probably lies somewhere in between. Americans are neither cantankerously polarized to the hilt nor blissfully of one mind. But the fact that Americans are not all at the outer edges of ideology or neatly clustered at the center does not mean that we can blithely split the difference and walk away thinking that the polarization questions are answered. We should be able to extract a more meaningful reading of polarization from the evidence.

IDEOLOGICAL DIFFERENCES

There is a long history of self-reported measures of political ideologies. Since at least the mid-1930s, surveys have asked respondents to declare their general ideological perspectives on politics as liberal or conservative.[2] Data drawn from these questions played important roles in public opinion research in the late 1960s,[3] but it was not until the early 1970s that surveys provided consistent question wordings offering response-options across the spectrum from liberal to moderate to conservative.[4]

Where better to begin an investigation of the polarization of the public than with what citizens themselves say about their own ideological orientations? After all, self-declarations are the basis for measuring the other major long-term political orientation of voters: individually in party identification and collectively in macropartisanship. The party identification of citizens is determined directly by asking respondents whether they think of themselves as Democrats, Republicans, independents, or something else rather than whether they routinely think or vote in a particular way or asking researchers how they would on some other basis classify a respondent's partisanship. The same measurement approach seems quite reasonable to follow with respect to ideology. Not all Republicans (or Democrats) think alike on all matters nor mean exactly the same thing in identifying with that party, and we would not expect that all conservatives (or liberals) are in lockstep either. Americans may not always label themselves correctly and no measure is without flaws, but the fact that individuals identify or associate themselves with a party or an ideology would seem highly credible, barring overwhelming evidence to the contrary.

Five Ideological Series

The direct evidence of ideological polarization is drawn from five highly respected national survey data series of ideological self-identifications. Each collected self-reported ideology data over a significant period. The five series include data from the American National Election Study (ANES), the General Social Survey (GSS), the CBS/New York Times polls (CBS/NYT), Gallup polls, and the National Exit Poll of voters conducted on election days. All have two important characteristics in common. Each series allows respondents to indicate whether they consider their views to be liberal or conservative, and each permits respondents to declare their views to be moderate or somewhere between liberals and conservatives.[5]

Beyond these common characteristics, there are many differences. The surveys were conducted over different intervals and in different years. The longest series is ANES. It has been conducted, for the most part, in conjunction with biennial national elections and extends from 1972 to 2012 (19 observations). The joint CBS and *New York Times* surveys have been conducted more frequently but at irregular intervals. Their ideology question was asked in 304 surveys conducted between 1976 and 2015. For the sake of comparability with the other series, the medians of these polls within calendar years are used to collapse the 304 surveys into 40 annual observations. The GSS series is from 1974 to 2014 (missing a few years) and has 28 annual observations. Gallup got a late start in settling on its ideological question. Its data span from 1992 to 2014 (23 observations). The shortest of the five series is the exit polls. It covers the ten presidential election years from 1976 to 2012. Overall, the combined series covers the years from 1972 to 2015 and consists of 120 annual observations.

The five series differ in several other ways as well. Each has its own distinctive question wording and sampling frame.[6] They also differ in their response options. CBS/NYT and the Exit Polls offer respondents three possible responses (liberal, moderate, or conservative). Others offer more gradations of liberal or conservative responses. Gallup's format allows respondents to place themselves on a five-point scale from "very liberal" to "very conservative." ANES and GSS present a seven-point scale (extremely liberal, liberal, or slightly liberal and the same on the conservative side). The five series also differ in how easily respondents can opt out of responding, with the ANES consistently generating the highest percentage of "don't knows" by explicitly offering respondents the "haven't thought much about it" option. Appendix A provides the question wording used in the five series.

Polarized Ideologies

What do these data reveal about ideological polarization in recent decades? What portions of these electorates were relatively polarized from one another? Polarization is measured here as the percentage of respondents claiming to be either liberal or conservative rather than moderate or not knowing their ideological orientation. A high percentage of liberals and conservatives would reflect a relatively polarized electorate. A high percentage of moderates or respondents unaware of their ideological perspectives would reflect a less polarized electorate. Figure 3.1 displays the combined percentage of liberals and conservatives (ideologicals) for each of the five series from 1972 to 2015.

As one would expect given the variety of question wordings, options offered, receptivity to "don't know" responses, and other differences as well as the normal sampling errors of surveys, there is variation across the series within each year. This is particularly the case in the 1970s and 1980s. In more recent years, the measures tend to converge. Some of the series start at higher levels of liberals and conservatives and others track greater changes in these levels over time. The GSS series is relatively flat in the high 50s. The ideological portion of the public was initially smaller in the ANES series and then grew at a higher rate. The CBS/New York Times and Exit Poll data fall in between.

Though they have their differences, the five different ideology series together support four important points about the extent and development of the public's polarization. First, at the outset in the 1970s and early 1980s, a large portion of the electorate already was fairly well polarized. At the low end of the range, ANES indicates that about 45% of Americans were neither moderates nor unaware of their ideological perspective. Generally about half the electorate in exit polls asserted liberal or conservative ideological orientations, and the CBS/NYT series normally found those declaring a liberal or con-

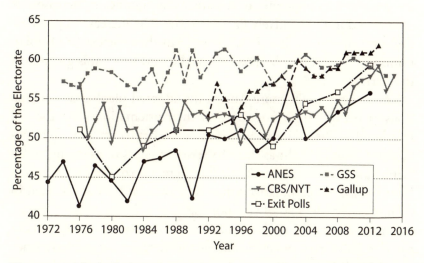

Figure 3.1. Ideologicals (Conservatives plus Liberals) in the American electorate, 1972–2015.

Note: The percentages are of all respondents. The data are from the American National Election Study, the General Social Survey, the CBS and New York Times Surveys, Gallup, and the national Exit Polls housed at the Roper Center.

servative inclination to outnumber moderates. According to the GSS measure, nearly three of every five Americans declared an ideological viewpoint. Taken as a whole, those asserting liberal or conservative perspectives constituted anywhere from 45% to 60% of Americans in the 1970s. Whether this should be interpreted as high or low is open to question—at least at this point. What is not open to question is that roughly half of Americans or more claimed a non-centrist ideological viewpoint as early as the 1970s. Contrary to a good deal of cavalier talk, *most* Americans were *not* moderates in the 1970s, probably no more than a bare majority were.

Second, the public has become more polarized and less centrist over time. In each series, the ideological portion of the electorate has grown. This is clearly visible in four of the five series, with the data plots moving to the upper right corner of the figure. A trend regression on each independent series as well as a pooled analysis of the five combined series, with the year as a trend variable, indicates for each data series a statistically significant upward trend in the ideological segments of the electorate. The details of the regression results are presented in appendix B. A statistically significant increase was even found in the relatively flat GSS series. The increase in polarization over time is weakest in GSS data, but then the extent of polarization in its earliest observations in the mid-1970s was greatest in that series.[7]

There is no doubt more Americans adopted ideological orientations or became more cognizant of their orientations over the last few decades. There can be questions over whether the growth in polarization was as slight as the GSS series suggests or as strong as the Gallup and ANES series indicate, but there is no question that Americans became more polarized than they were, at least as reflected in their declared ideological viewpoints.[8]

Third, though somewhat obscured by herky-jerky movements in the five data series, polarization has grown quite consistently since the 1970s. It has not been confined, as some might contend, to the contentious post-2000 period of the Bush II and Obama presidencies. Although the ideological clarity of more fully polarized parties may have pushed along polarization's increase in more recent times, the trend regression indicates that the public's polarization had increased significantly in the previous three decades and detects no substantial acceleration in this trend since 2000.[9]

Fourth, while there is some variation in the pervasiveness of ideological orientations measured by the different series in the 1970s and 1980s (though all indicated that a large share of the electorate were ideologicals) and variation as well in the degree to which polarization grew in the intervening years (though all find some growth), there is a general consensus that nearly three of every five Americans now associate themselves with either a liberal or conservative perspective. The spread of the percentage of ideologicals in the five series in figure 3.1 resembles a cone with a wide end on the left and a narrow end drawn to the upper right corner, approaching the 60% mark.

Based on a regression analysis of the pooled data from the five data series (the details of which can be found in appendix B), nearly half of Americans (49%) were either liberal or conservative in the early 1970s. This increased to about 56% by 2012. The ideological portion of the electorate expanded by approximately seven percentage points from the 1970s to the 2010s. This was accompanied, of course, by about a seven-percentage-point decline of non-ideologicals.

These are the self-declared moderates and those who would not or could not associate themselves with an ideological view. A majority of the decline among the non-ideologicals occurred among those indicating that they did not know how to characterize their political perspectives. This was about five of the seven-point drop. Whether these respondents had been ideologicals all along and only became aware of it in more recent years, or whether they (or their successors) developed a less centrist perspective in later years is unclear. What is clear is that they had been unable or unwilling to identify themselves as liberals or conservatives in earlier years and now, rather than claiming moderation, they report their general political perspectives to be either liberal or conservative.

In effect, the nation changed from one in which ideologicals and non-ideologicals were about at parity in the 1970s (still a large number of ideologicals) to one in which those reporting an ideological perspective outnumbered centrists by 12 percentage points (56% to 44%) in the 2010s. If we were comparing election returns, the former would be a dead heat and the latter a near-landslide. This is substantial change.

Some to the Left, More to the Right

A good deal of the increase in polarization in recent decades has been the result of more Americans claiming to be conservative. The portions of the electorate who report themselves to be conservatives and liberals are presented respectively in figures 3.2 and 3.3. Self-declared conservatives made up nearly 31% of the electorate in the 1970s according to figure 3.2. By the 2010s, they were nearly 35% of the electorate. In four of the five series, the increase of conservatives is statistically significant (see appendix B) and the increase just barely falls short of conventional significance levels in the fifth series (the exit polls). The change is greatest in the ANES series and weakest in the CBS/NYT data. The growing number of conservatives accounts for about four of the seven-percentage-point increase in ideologicals.

The percentage of self-reported liberals in the electorate is plotted in figure 3.3. As a comparison to the previous figure shows, except for the GSS series in the early 1970s in which they are near parity, conservatives otherwise substantially outnumber liberals. From 1972 to 1990, the mean conservative advantage over liberals was about ten

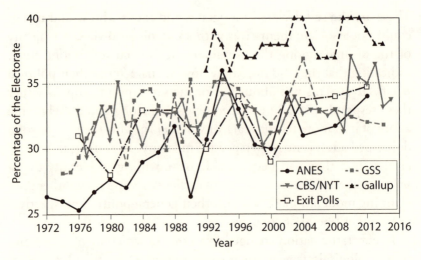

Figure 3.2. Conservatives in the American electorate, 1972–2015.

Note: The percentages are of all respondents. The data are from the American National Election Study, the General Social Survey, the CBS and New York Times Surveys, Gallup, and the national Exit Polls housed at the Roper Center.

percentage points. Since 2000, the mean gap grew to about 13 points. Though there was no discernible increase in the percentage of liberals in one series (GSS), the percentage of liberals increased slightly in two others (ANES and CBS/NYT) and more substantially in two series (Gallup and the Exit Polls). The pooled series indicates a significant increase of about two and a half percentage points in liberal ranks since the 1970s. The liberal trend is about two-thirds as large as the trend toward conservatives. In short, from the 1970s to the 2010s, Americans became less moderate and more polarized, with an increase in the ranks of liberals and a larger increase in the ranks of conservatives.

More Perspectives

A seven-percentage-point swing from the center to ideological views would seem to be a major political shift. (Recall the discussion in chapter 1 of small changes making a big difference.) A swing of this magnitude in either macropartisanship or the normal vote would certainly qualify as evidence of a realignment. In the distributions of ideological perspectives, however, the change does not look very

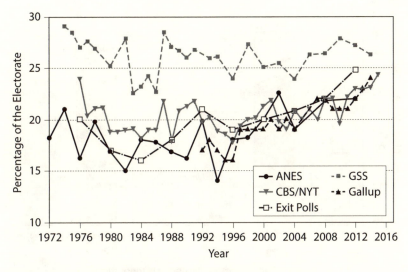

Figure 3.3. Liberals in the American electorate, 1972–2015.

Note: The percentages are of all respondents. The data are from the American National Election Study, the General Social Survey, the CBS and New York Times Surveys, Gallup, and the national Exit Polls housed at the Roper Center.

dramatic and the standard deviations of the 1972 and 2012 distributions are not very different.

The distributions of ideological views in 1972 and 2012 as reconstituted from the pooled regression analysis of the five ideological series are displayed in two histograms in figure 3.4. The difference in the two distributions is that the first (1972) is a bit more peaked in the center and the second (2012) is a bit more flattened. Despite the substantial seven-percentage-point shift away from the center, the 2012 distribution does not look much different from the 1972 distribution and is not remotely close to being bimodal or even flat.

The standard deviations of the two distributions comport with the visual impression. Coding liberals as zero, conservatives as one, and moderates in between at half a point, the standard deviation of the 1972 distribution was .35. The standard deviation of the 2012 distribution was only .37. After the seven-percentage-point movement out of the center, the standard deviation increased by a mere two-hundredths of a point (an increase of about 7% of the initial standard deviation). This ought to raise some eyebrows about relying

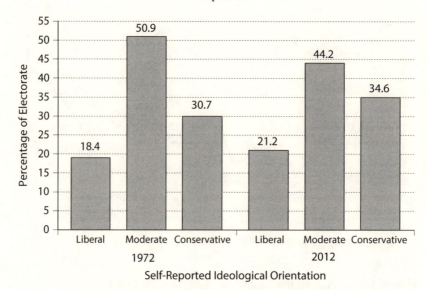

Figure 3.4. Self-reported ideological orientations, 1972 and 2012.

Note: The percentage of the electorate in each category was calculated from the pooled trend regressions reported in appendix B. The regressions included the year and a set of dummy variables for the survey organization. The median coefficient for the survey organizations (after including the baseline organization) was used in the calculations and, for comparability, percentages were adjusted to total to exactly 100%.

heavily on large changes in standard deviations in either ideological orientations or issue attitudes as evidence of increased polarization.[10] We know there was a shift of seven percentage points of the electorate out of the center to more ideologically polarized perspectives and that this is a substantial change by macropolitical standards, yet the standard deviation statistic barely budged and might be easily and erroneously dismissed as negligible.

Some additional perspective on polarization might be obtained by comparing the standard deviations in 1972 and 2012 to those of hypothetical extremes, perfectly centrist versus perfectly polarized. This is, in effect, a potential pair of benchmarks by which the actual extent of polarization can be gauged. This moves the polarization question beyond the inconclusive or hopelessly subjective state of being "in the eye of the beholder."[11] In the case of perfect centrism, an electorate composed of only centrists would yield a standard deviation of zero. In the case of perfect polarization, an electorate that was half on the right, half on the left, and empty in the center would yield a standard deviation of .50.[12] Based on the actual standard deviations of .35 in 1972 and .37 in 2012, the electorate is and has been more polarized than centrist. More precisely, the electorate was about 70% of the way to perfect polarization in 1972 and about 74% of the way in 2012.

This comparison of the actual distributions of ideological views in 1972 and 2012 with perfect centrism and perfect polarization assumes that these extremes were measured without error, and we know that this would not be the case. There is some degree of measurement error that would cause perfect centrism to appear to be somewhat more polarized than reality (moderate respondents misidentifying themselves as non-moderates) and perfect polarization to be somewhat less polarized than reality (ideological respondents misidentifying themselves as moderates). To take measurement error into account, the standard deviations of the two hypothetical extremes were recalculated after introducing a significant amount of error into the measurement. In the case of perfect centrism, a specified percentage of respondents were "misassigned" as ideologues. In the case of perfect polarization, the same percentage of ideologues were misassigned as centrists. Introducing an error of 20% of misassigned respondents produced standard deviations of .22 rather than zero for perfect (but mismeasured) centrism and .45 for perfect (but mismeasured) polarization. Even after introducing substantial errors into hypothetical extreme benchmark distributions, the 1972 electorate was about 58% of the way and the 2012 electorate was about 65% of the way toward the polarized end of the spectrum. Along with a simple count of ideologicals (liberals and conservatives) in figure 3.4, increasing from 49% in 1972 to 56% in 2012, these measures indicate the American public was already somewhat polarized in the early 1970s (about as polarized as not) and over the next four decades became significantly more polarized.

THE QUALITY OF THE EVIDENCE

The question now is whether these findings rest on credible data. What is the quality of this evidence? What is to be said for and against relying on the self-reported measures of political ideology for insight into the level and change of polarization in the electorate? How much confidence should we place in these findings? There is much to be said both for and against using the self-reported ideology measure to assess polarization. We begin by weighing the strengths of the evidence.

Strength of the Source

Perhaps the greatest virtue of the self-reported ideology measure and its use in evaluating polarization is its origin. Like party identification, issue preferences, and every other piece of information obtained from surveys of citizens, it is based on what respondents report about themselves, their thinking and their activities. The report of what a person willingly describes as his or her own ideological perspective deserves to be taken very seriously. Although respondents may not be well prepared to report accurately their opinions and beliefs on a survey, and surveys may not be constructed perfectly to draw out these opinions, there should be a strong presumption in survey research to accept at face value what respondents tell us about their thoughts and actions. One might question the very purpose of gathering survey data if responses were too easily set aside in favor of some fabrication of the researcher.

The weight of this presumption may be best appreciated in personal terms. Imagine that you reported on a survey that you were a liberal (or conservative, Democrat, Republican, hispanic, Catholic, Muslim, or anything else) and then found out that survey analysts, who had never met you or talked with you about your political views and thinking, who only knew you through your responses to a few questions on one survey, subsequently asserted that you had wrongly described your own thoughts! Unless the analysts had some extraordinary evidence to support their override, their attempt at mind reading might well be judged to be an extreme act of hubris. In Yiddish, the word is chutzpah.

Not all respondents, of course, are truthful or have accurate recall and not all survey questions facilitate accurate answers. On rare occasions, responses to surveys may warrant corrections or adjustments. There have been circumstances in which these self-reports have been overridden or adjusted, as in the case of voter validation studies of turnout[13] or the rescaling of party identification because of the ambiguity of the independent-leaning response categories,[14] or the unrepresentativeness of aggregate turnout and vote choice distributions,[15] but the evidence had to be overwhelming in each of these cases to justify deviating from the respondents' self-reports. In the cases of individual and aggregate turnout and aggregate vote choice, that overwhelming evidence was hard data, actual vote returns or voting records. In the case of party identification, the challenge was not to what respondents said. It was to how those responses were used to compose a scale. Otherwise, what respondents report stands.

A heavy burden of proof rests with those who would challenge a respondent's self-report of his or her ideological outlook. Given the psychological depth of an ideology (compared to more surface responses to current issues, for instance), this burden of proof would seem to be nearly unattainable. At the very least, any second-guessing of a respondent's characterization of his or her own political perspective must be approached with considerable trepidation.

Validity and Content

In terms of both validity and the reliability of the self-reported ideology measure, the measure appears to be on solid ground. If the measure gauges the respondents' underlying political perspectives as it purports to do, one would expect a strong association between the self-reported ideologies of respondents and their votes for ideologically compatible presidential candidates as well as their identifications with ideologically compatible political parties. Since there is a general consensus regarding the current polarization of the parties, we should see liberals generally voting for Democratic presidential candidates and conservatives for Republicans. Similarly, at the current high levels of party polarization, liberals should generally identify as Democrats and conservatives as Republicans. This is exactly what we find in 2012 ANES data. Among self-reported liberals, 93% identified with the Democratic Party and the same percentage voted for Democrat Barack Obama. Among self-reported conservatives, 81% identified themselves as Republicans and 83% voted for Republican Mitt Romney.[16] Since no one would contend that ideology is the *only* consideration in identifying with a party or voting for a candidate, these percentages are quite high. They provide strong evidence of the validity of the self-report as a measure of ideology. The slightly lower percentages for conservatives are understandable given that the

Republican Party is somewhat more conservative than the Democratic Party is liberal (more on this in chapter 7). The Republican Party may actually be a bit too conservative for some conservatives who have moderate tendencies.

Additional evidence that the self-reported ideology measure is meaningful is offered by the perceptions of the ideological orientations of the parties and the candidates. According to the 2012 ANES data, only 10% of respondents mischaracterized Barack Obama as a conservative candidate and only 11% claimed that the Democratic Party was conservative. Only about 14% claimed the Republican Party and Mitt Romney were liberal.[17] The apparent confusion about the application of the ideological terminology appears concentrated among about 6% or 7% of the respondents (fewer reported voters), most of whom had not associated themselves with either a liberal or a conservative viewpoint. The overwhelming majority of respondents applied it reasonably and consistently in describing the parties and the candidates. It would seem safe to assume that they applied the terms reasonably to themselves as well.

Those reporting ideological views in common tend to identify with the same ideologically compatible party and to vote for the same ideologically compatible presidential candidates, but what are the ideas that bind liberals together with other liberals and conservatives with other conservatives? What is the common content of these political perspectives? These are not easy questions to answer because there are numerous variants, degrees, and nuances to any ideology.[18] There is, however, as the chapter epigraph from Samuel Lubell suggests, one main thrust that binds each of them together and separates them from each other: the desired role, size, and power of the government.[19] This has been a perennial divide in American politics since Alexander Hamilton's advocacy of an energetic government was pitted against Thomas Jefferson's vision of a limited and restrained government. It is no accident that the iconic liberal president of the twentieth century, Franklin Roosevelt, presided over a huge expansion in the size and scope of government and the century's iconic conservative president, Ronald Reagan, declared in his 1981 inaugural address that "government is not the solution to our problem, government is the problem."[20]

The association of these different perspectives on government to self-reported ideological views is evident in responses to several questions posed in ANES surveys. Responses of self-reported liberals, moderates (and don't knows), and conservatives to a question about their general preference for change in the level of government services and spending are presented in table 3.1. Respondents were asked their position on a seven-point scale that ranged from a significant reduction to a significant increase in government services and spending. They also were given the option of indicating that they had not thought much about the matter. The precise wording of the question and the polar options may be found in the note to the table. The table reports the mean responses from *13* national surveys conducted in presidential and midterm elections from 1982 to 2012.

The distribution of responses in table 3.1 provides strong evidence of the validity of self-reported ideology. Ideological identifications matched up quite well with the expected responses about government services and spending. Liberals were three times more likely to favor an increase rather than decrease in government spending. Conservatives, on the other hand, were twice as likely to favor reductions as opposed to increases in government. From a different angle, liberals were more than twice as likely as conservatives to favor increasing government. Conservatives were almost three times as likely as liberals to favor sharp reductions in government. Less than a quarter of either self-described liberals or conservatives were out of sync—liberals for less government or conservatives for more government.

The strength of this evidence is particularly impressive in light of the number of problems with the services-spending question that may have weakened the relationship. The question's wording was leading (e.g., raising the specter of cuts in the highly supported policy areas of health and education). It failed to identify how spending increases would be funded. It was essentially a "free lunch" question. Since conservatives and liberals may agree on the need for more government spending for some purposes (national security, crime prevention, etc.) and less for others (foreign aid, welfare, etc.), an imperfect association with ideologies is to be expected. The nature of "more or less" spending questions also may invite responses reflecting perceptions of the current administration rather than ideological

TABLE 3.1. SELF-REPORTED IDEOLOGY AND PREFERENCES FOR CHANGES IN GOVERNMENT SERVICES AND SPENDING, 1982–2012

Self-Reported Ideology	Government Services/Spending Change Scale (%)			
	Increase a Lot	Same/DK	Reduce a Lot	Total
Liberal (18%)	52	31	17	100
Moderate/DK (51%)	34	48	18	100
Conservative (31%)	23	30	47	100
Total	34	39	27	100

Note: The entries are mean percentages. The data are from the ANES cumulative file and the preliminary release of the ANES 2012 Time Series Study. The percentages are the average of the 13 ANES surveys that included both questions since 1982. Self-reported ideology is VCF0804 in the cumulative file and "don't knows" are counted as moderates. The Government Services/Spending Scale is VCF0839, a seven-point scale. Responses 1, 2, and 3 were grouped as less spending. Responses 5, 6, and 7 were grouped as more spending. Responses 4 and 9 (Haven't thought much about it) were grouped as "same/don't know." The question wording was: "Some people think the government should provide fewer services, even in areas such as health and education, in order to reduce spending. Other people feel that it is important for the government to provide many more services even if it means an increase in spending. And of course, some other people have opinions somewhere in between … Where would you place yourself on this scale, or haven't you thought much about it?" The response poles were: "Government should provide many fewer services: reduce spending a lot" and "Government should provide many more services: increase spending a lot."

preferences. Some liberals might favor spending cuts if they think a liberal administration has been too free-spending and some conservatives might favor spending increases if they believe a conservative administration has gone too far in making cuts. Finally, the inevitable misassignments of some respondents near the border of the different response categories on either the ideology or the spending question undoubtedly blurs the association a bit between self-reported ideologies and preferences for changes in government spending and services. Yet, despite these measurement issues, the evidence reflects the expected wide gap between self-described liberals and conservatives.

Responses to a related ANES question about the size of government also support the measure's validity. The question asked whether respondents believed that "the less government, the better" or whether "there are more things the government should be doing." No middle option was offered. In the six ANES surveys conducted from 1990 to 2012, conservatives were more than twice as likely as liberals to associate themselves with "the less government, the better" alternative and liberals were twice as likely as conservatives to favor more government. As with responses to the services-spending question, the overwhelming number of self-reported liberals and conservatives held views similar to those reporting the same ideological outlook and each stood in sharp contrast to their ideological opposites.[21]

Beyond differences about the role of government, self-declared liberals and conservatives also have different priorities in their values. In a study asking respondents to rank seven political values, Jacoby found that liberals tended to assign greater importance to equality and economic security and conservatives tended to rate patriotism, social order, and morality more highly.[22] Differences in self-reported ideological perspectives reflect differences in fundamental political values. Combined with differences over the reliance on government, these findings indicate that self-declared ideologies are not empty labels.

Reliability

Regarding the reliability of the self-reported ideology, the 2012 ANES data indicate that self-reports of ideological orientations were quite consistent, at least during that campaign. The self-report question was posed to respondents both in the pre-election survey conducted from early September to early November and in the post-election survey from after the election to late January. One would not expect much real change in ideological views in this short period, so the stability of responses can reasonably be read as approximating the reliability of the measure. Responses were quite stable.[23] The stability correlation of the seven-point scale (with don't knows assigned to the moderate category) was .71 for all respondents and .77 for reported voters. Segmenting the electorate into three groups: liberals, moderates, and conservatives (again with the don't knows assigned as moderates), about 77% of respondents were stable. Another 13% were quite nearly stable, slipping one way or the other between the moderate and the slightly ideological categories. These might be fairly interpreted as respondents on the cusp of categories rather than confused about the terms.[24] Fewer than 11% of respondents changed their response by more than this shading.

Across a two-year time span, considering that we are likely to see some real individual change (as we do even in party identification), we see substantively the same picture. From 1990 to 1992, again using ANES data, 65% of respondents remained in the same general category (liberal, moderate or don't know, and conservative) and another 19% moved between the moderate or don't know categories and a slightly ideological category. Thus, about 84% of the respondents were essentially unchanged in their reported ideology. About 16% registered more than this minor amount of change. Some of this reflects normal measurement error, particularly when respondents are invited to opt out, and some reflects real change. The nation was becoming increasingly polarized. Self-described liberals increased by about two percentage points and self-described conservatives increased by three percentage points in the 1990 to 1992 ANES panel data. The bottom line is that the self-reported ideology measure appears to be reasonably reliable. There is a bit of shuffling by individuals between categories, but these are generally only minor shifts under the general liberal or conservative umbrellas or a bit of vacillation between a moderate (or don't know) or a slightly ideological designation.[25]

What is most important for the purposes of evaluating polarization is the reliability of the *aggregate* self-reported ideology measure. On this score, the news is even more positive. Between the pre-election and post-election ANES surveys in 2012, the distributions of liberals, moderates (plus don't knows), and conservatives hardly changed at all. None of the changes were more than 1.2 percentage points. Considering normal survey errors, this is negligible. In the 1990 to 1992 ANES panel data, differences were only slightly greater than within the 2012 election. Liberals and conservatives increased by 2.5 and 3.2 percentage points, respectively, between the elections (17.5% to 20.0% and 26.8% to 30.0%) while moderates and don't knows dropped by 5.6 percentage points (55.6% to 50.0%). Considering that some portion of these differences may have been real change, growing polarization, these data suggest that the aggregate self-reported ideology data are quite reliable. The over-time change in the aggregate self-reported ideology measure is quite comparable to the mean inter-election change in macropartisanship (3.2 percentage points) and even the mean error in the ANES presidential vote division (2.2 percentage points).[26] In short, the aggregate self-reported ideology measure is a reliable measure of the ideological divisions in the nation.

A Comprehensive Measure

The fourth strength of the self-reported ideology measure for assessing polarization is that it is a comprehensive assessment of a person's thinking rather than a pieced-together impression. Though it is true that most individuals are not very self-conscious of their general political values and perspectives and many are not comfortably conversant with the language describing ideologies, they are nevertheless best positioned to provide a general sense about where they are coming from on the political spectrum. Most cannot provide many details about their perspective—they are not political philosophers or psychologists or politicians after all—but there is a good chance that they can convey the gist of it. This is probably the best we can do.

The alternative to the self-report entails reconstructing a respondent's ideology from their responses to other survey questions. That is a very risky business. The many other questions posed in surveys would seem to barely scratch the surface of most people's political thinking. The self-summary of a person's political perspective is likely to correspond more closely to the reality of an individual's political outlook than a measure pieced together by others from a set of responses to a small battery of questions that may not correspond to how the respondent approaches politics or what political matters the respondent finds most important.[27]

CRITICISMS

There are compelling reasons to accept self-reported ideology as a meaningful measure of an individual's ideology and as an appropriate collective measure of the public's polarization, but the measure also has its problems.[28] Although criticisms of the self-reported ideology measure are varied, they amount to three related complaints. The first is that the American public is too politically unsophisticated to have real ideological perspectives. This criticism finds its roots in *The American Voter*[29] and in subsequent research on "mass belief systems" by Converse, Neuman, and others.[30] They found a great deal of instability in issue attitudes, low levels of political information and interest, and responses to open-ended questions about the candidates and parties were rarely indicative of a high level of conceptualization. Fewer than 16% of voters qualified by these standards for the designation of ideologues or near-ideologues. For everyone else, as Converse saw it, "assumptions of any liberal-conservative dimensions of judgment were most far-fetched."[31]

Despite its impressive pedigree, this criticism can be quickly set aside. While later research challenged the validity, reliability, and time–bound nature of these findings,[32] the criticism can be rebutted on more fundamental grounds. If ideologies are defined as core values about what is politically right and wrong (the definition adopted here), then having an ideological perspective does not demand highly sophisticated thinking. Highly structured and abstract thinking most probably does make one more conversant with ideological terms, but it is not a prerequisite for awareness of one's ideology, much less having an ideology. A sense about what is politically right or wrong can be based on thinking as sophisticated as philosophy or as unsophisticated as "gut instincts" (think "knee-jerk liberals" and "wing-nut conservatives"). It can be based on a wealth of information or next to none. Moreover, having an ideological perspective does not mean that it must guide all political evaluations, much less be articulated in responses to open-ended questions about candidates and parties who themselves may not have been particularly ideological (as the parties were in the 1950s). Many Americans are undoubtedly politically unsophisticated as the premise of the criticism contends, but this does not prevent these citizens from having meaningful ideological perspectives on political matters.

The second criticism is that citizens do not share a commonly understood and agreed upon idea of what it means to be a liberal or a conservative. The charge is that ideological labels mean different things to different people at different times. At its extreme, the criticism is that ideological labels (liberal or conservative) may not really mean much at all. They are merely symbols. Rather than reflecting some underlying way of thinking about politics, a self-report of having a liberal or conservative outlook is simply an indication of which symbol is considered more attractive. Of course, this is a radical view. A more realistic critique is that ideological identifications may not mean all that much either to the public's political inclinations or to the extent of its polarization if a common ideological label is claimed by those holding vastly different political perspectives.

A third and related criticism is that those purporting to hold an ideological view in common frequently differ in their attitudes about public policy issues and often deviate from the positions commonly associated with an ideological perspective. Are self-described conservatives really conservative if they take issue positions commonly characterized as liberal? Some self-professed conservatives, for instance, favor increased government spending on various domestic policy programs and purposes. Some interpret this apparent inconsistency as a flaw in the self-reported ideology measure. At an abstract level or merely symbolically, some people may think they are conservatives (or liberals) and report as much on surveys, but they do not exhibit the attitudes and preferences expected of conservatives (or liberals) at a practical or operational level.

Operational Ideology

Free and Cantril in the late 1960s were the first to notice the apparent discrepancy of professed ideology and issue preferences as a challenge to the self-report measure.[33] They noticed that a few self-reported liberals held conservative issue positions, but many more self-described conservatives adopted liberal issue positions. A good number of self-reported conservatives wanted to maintain or increase funding for education, public housing, and urban renewal and thought that the government should do more to reduce unemployment. These self-identified conservatives holding apparently inconsistent policy positions were labeled by Free and Cantril as "operational liberals."

Ellis and Stimson have updated and substantially extended Free and Cantril's interpretation of political ideology in the public.[34] Like Free and Cantril decades before, Ellis and Stimson found that many conservatives surprisingly supported *more* government spending for a wide range of purposes—from healthcare and education to mass transportation and the environment.[35] They constructed an index of operational ideology from responses to ten GSS questions asking respondents whether government was spending too much, too little, or about the right amount on ten different public problems. These included foreign aid, urban problems, crime, drug addiction, education, the environment, welfare, health, and "the conditions of blacks."[36] Anyone who favored increased spending rather than cuts on more problems (other than defense) was classified as an operational liberal. Operational liberals who reported that they thought of themselves as conservatives were classified as "conflicted conservatives."

An example of the kind of question that Ellis and Stimson use in their operational ideology index is an ANES question about preferences on changes in spending for dealing with crime.[37] Table 3.2 presents 2012 ANES responses of self-reported liberals, moderates, and conservatives to possible spending changes for anti-crime programs. The data demonstrate that a plurality of liberals, moderates, *and* conservatives favor devoting more resources to dealing with crime (though they might well differ over what "dealing" with crime entails as well as the source of the additional spending—including whether the additional spending might come from spending reductions elsewhere). Very few respondents of any ideological bent favor reductions in spending on anti-crime programs. Ellis and Stimson interpret the substantial percentage of self-declared conservatives favoring more spending on government programs, in this case anti-crime programs, as evidence of operational liberalism at odds with their symbolic attachment to the conservative label.

To demonstrate what they interpret as the robustness of operational ideology, Ellis and Stimson also examine responses to issues other than those involved with preferences about changes in government spending.[38] Whether the government should guarantee jobs for everyone is one such issue. Responses to the ANES version of that question in 2012 are presented in table 3.3. Liberals presumably would favor the government guarantee and conservatives would oppose it. As the table shows, a large majority of self-reported conservatives, as expected, opposed the proposed policy, while a plurality of liberals favored it. There were, however, some liberals adopting the expected conservative position and some conservatives taking the ex-

TABLE 3.2. SELF-REPORTED IDEOLOGY AND PREFERENCES FOR CHANGE IN SPENDING ON CRIME, 2012

Self-Reported Ideology	Preferred Change in Government Spending on Crime (%)			
	Increased	About the Same	Decreased	Total
Liberal (24%)	45	44	11	100
Moderate/DK (39%)	59	36	5	100
Conservative (37%)	47	42	11	100
Total	51	40	9	100

Note: The data are from the 2012 ANES study. The question wording is: "Next I am going to read you a list of federal programs. For each one, I would like you to tell me whether you would like to see spending increased or decreased. What about dealing with crime. Should federal spending on dealing with crime be increased, decreased, or kept about the same (kept the same)?"

pected liberal position. In this particular instance, a larger percentage of liberals (24%) strayed from the liberal line than conservatives (15%) from the conservative position. As this case demonstrates, there are a good number of individuals who hold issue positions that would appear to be contrary to or inconsistent with their self-reported ideology.[39]

Based on their evaluation of the associations between self-reported ideology and an array of both spending and non-spending issue positions, much like those examined in table 3.2, Ellis and Stimson conclude that, though "perhaps sincerely and deeply" identifying with the conservative label, nearly two-thirds of self-reported conservatives are actually misguided or "conflicted conservatives" who "support liberal public policies" and that "there is little evidence that conflicted conservatives are actually 'conservative' in any sense beyond self-identification."[40] Despite strong evidence to the contrary, such as that exhibited in table 3.1, Ellis and Stimson conclude that "Americans tend to want to call themselves 'conservative' while they advocate big government liberalism."[41] Put differently, and though they do not use the term, they essentially claim that as many as two-thirds of

TABLE 3.3. SELF-REPORTED IDEOLOGY AND PREFERENCES ON THE ISSUE OF GOVERNMENT GUARANTEED JOBS, 2012

Self-Reported Ideology	Government Guaranteed Jobs and Standard of Living (%)			
	Favor	Neutral	Opposed	Total
Liberal (25%)	46	29	24	100
Moderate/DK (38%)	36	29	35	100
Conservative (38%)	15	14	71	100
Total	31	23	46	100

Note: The data are from the 2012 ANES study. The question wording is: "Some people feel the government in Washington should see to it that every person has a job and a good standard of living. Suppose these people are at one end of a scale, at point 1. Others think the government should just let each person get ahead on their own. Suppose these people are at the other end, at point 7. And, of course, some other people have opinions somewhere in between, at points 2, 3, 4, 5, or 6. Where would you place yourself on this scale, or haven't you thought much about this?" Categories 1, 2, and 3 were grouped as favoring guaranteed jobs. Categories 5, 6, and 7 were grouped as opposing government guaranteed jobs. Category 4 was scored as neutral on the issue.

conservatives are really what might be called CINOs or "conservatives-in-name-only."[42]

These are bold claims. Some might say outlandish. There is no question that some people misidentify their political ideologies, but the idea that *two-thirds* of conservatives would be so confused seems implausible, especially in light of the considerable evidence of the self-reported ideology measure's validity. Many self-declared conservatives would no doubt be deeply insulted by the proposition that they were so ill-informed and misguided—or mesmerized by a shiny conservative label—that they could not accurately describe their own general political perspectives.[43] Still, as seemingly radical as the claims are, they are made by highly regarded scholars examining a good deal of professionally gathered survey data. They deserve to be taken seriously. The question is whether they should be believed.

Mountain or Mole Hill?

How serious are these critiques of the self-reported ideology measure? Do they discredit their use for assessing polarization in the electorate? More specifically, are the claims that Americans are really more "operationally liberal" while being "symbolically conservative," that is, liberal with a conservative veneer, well supported? Are these claims against self-reported ideology a formidable mountain or a concocted mole hill?

Based on the analysis that follows, the answer is that *none* of these criticisms, including the "conflicted conservative" and "operational liberal" claims, raise serious concerns about the basic declaration by respondents of their own political perspectives. There are variations in ideological outlooks, different degrees to which they are held, local variations, and various competing influences for how much they influence policy positions, but these variations and competing influences are just that and not evidence that the underlying political perspective is anything other than what respondents say they are, especially in light of the substantial evidence of the measure's validity and reliability.

First, it is a certainty that ideological labels mean different things to different people at different times. All liberals and all conservatives may not even prioritize their values in the same way.[44] This is to be expected. In itself, this does not amount to a challenge to the ideological concept or measure.[45] Any two conservatives in the public are likely to disagree over what it means exactly to be a conservative, just as any two conservatives (or, for that matter, liberals) in Congress are likely to disagree about what that ideological label requires. I would venture to guess that all Democrats (or Republicans) do not share the same idea of what it means to be a Democrat (or Republican) or that all Communists, Libertarians, or self-declared moderates are on the same page regarding their essential attributes. Beyond the political realm, all Catholics or Protestants or Jews or Muslims do not have exactly the same idea about what it means to be members of those religions. Any group affiliation, particularly those based on beliefs rather than on a physical characteristic, is likely to allow some ambiguity or variation in its membership criteria. Moreover, there

may be some significant variation in these definitions by time, region, and degree. What it means to be a liberal in 1950 in Mississippi
may be a good deal different from what it means to be one in 2015
in New York.[46] Any social group involves a somewhat moveable "big
tent." This variation does not mean that the grouping is an empty
symbol.

The Ellis and Stimson study illustrates the dangers inherent in
imposing a definition of what it means to be an adherent of an ideology and then attempting to reconstitute ideological attachments
from various attitudes and behaviors.[47] Their operational ideology
measure appears to assume that conservatism is reflected in the opposition to any increase at any time in government spending on a
broad array of domestic programs and that liberalism is observed in
the support for increased spending for these programs under any
circumstance (the assumption is reversed for defense spending). Respondents favoring an increase in spending in one area may qualify
as conservative, but only if they favor cuts in more programs. Many
die-hard, true-blue conservatives who favor limited, efficient, frugal,
affordable, and sensible government for truly public purposes, however, favor increased spending to improve the nation's health (e.g.,
cancer and heart disease research, infectious disease treatments), to
improve the nation's educational system (e.g., school vouchers, more
and better teachers), or to halt a rising crime rate (see table 3.2). From
time to time, they might even also have some reservations about the
need for ever higher defense budgets.[48] Are they any less conservative
because they want government to wisely spend more money to cure
cancer or keep the streets safe? Of course not. That a large majority
of self-described conservatives do not qualify as operational conservatives by Ellis and Stimson's litmus test might be better regarded as
evidence that the operational ideology measure is itself problematic
rather than that self-declared conservatives are not what they claim
themselves to be. To be clear, this is not to question the assumption
that conservatives favor less spending on domestic policies in general than liberals. They most certainly do. It is, however, to question
where the lines in spending are drawn between conservatives, moderates, and liberals, both in individual policy areas and in a collection
of policy areas. Conservatives do not always favor less spending than

the status quo on everything (other than defense) as the operational ideology index supposes.

Beyond variations in the meaning of ideologies, differences in the degrees to which ideologies are held and the contexts in which the opinions are given, and various complications in the construction of the operational questions, respondents professing an ideological perspective may stray from their ideologically expected position for many other reasons.[49] Even for highly committed ideologues, ideology is not the be-all and end-all. Other considerations often come into play in deciding where someone stands on an issue. Different perceptions, strategies, and priorities may lead people with strong ideological principles in common to take somewhat different policy positions on occasion. A conservative may have a personal commitment to reducing crime or fighting cancer or protecting the environment, for instance, and this may override, on occasion, a general and deeply held commitment to government frugality and restraint. Or, an ideological commitment may temper the extent of support for various spending priorities. In either case, neither the ideological nor public policy preference precludes the other. They can, and do, harmoniously coexist.

Elites and Operational Ideology

The problem of operational ideology, at least as formulated, is most glaringly evident in its failure to correctly classify ideological elites. This is a group for whom it should be most easily applicable (recalling the McClosky Difference from chapter 1). No one would seriously question that elected national Republicans in recent years have been quite conservative, perhaps uncompromisingly and stubbornly conservative.[50] If the operational ideology standard is meaningful, these unabashedly conservative Republicans should have substantially cut discretionary domestic spending when they controlled the levers of government. Between the 2002 and 2006 midterm elections, during the middle years of George W. Bush's presidency, conservative Republicans held this control. A conservative Republican occupied the White House. Clinton, Jackman, and Rivers estimated that President George W. Bush in his first term had been about as conservative as the most conservative members of the U.S. Senate, though some conservative pundits and his lack of vetoes suggested he might not have been that extreme.[51] Republican majorities also controlled both the House and the Senate (though short of a filibuster-proof Senate majority). A conservative Republican government, according to the operational ideology measure, should have produced substantial cuts in discretionary spending, but that did not happen. Contrary to these expectations, discretionary domestic spending actually rose by nearly $75 billion in four years, from $419 billion in fiscal 2003 to $494 billion in fiscal 2007. Over these four years of a conservative Republican government, discretionary domestic spending *grew* at an average annual rate of more than 4%.

The fact that operational conservatism is not reflected in the actions of unabashedly conservative elites is good reason to set aside the operational ideology measure. If conservative elites cannot clear the operational ideology hurdle to conservatism, we can hardly expect conservatives in the public to pass this test.

It is not that conservatives and liberals do not disagree generally about spending and the size of government; the evidence in table 3.1 indicates they do. However, there are some matters on which liberals and conservatives agree about the value of government involvement (e.g., the anti-crime issue in table 3.2), though they may still differ over how much more the government should spend and can afford to spend at any time and how those additional resources might be best spent.[52] What this suggests is that the purported operational measure of ideology is not a proper or useful measure of ideology and poses no serious challenge to the validity of the self-reported measure of political ideology.

The Double Standard

The case for self-reported ideological identification parallels the case for self-reported party identification. Each of the criticisms leveled at self-reported ideological identifications could just as easily have been leveled at self-reported party identification, yet the critics of the ideology measure do not suggest that party identification should be set aside, used with caution, or augmented by an assembled "operational party identification."

Like ideological identification, party identifiers often think and act contrary to what is expected of them.[53] Not all Democrats think alike. There have been southern conservative Democrats and northern liberal Democrats. There were Scoop Jackson Democrats, Gene McCarthy Democrats, and George Wallace Democrats. Some Democrats favored segregation and others opposed it. Some favored escalating the war in Vietnam and some favored immediate withdrawal. But, with all of this diversity, they all were Democrats. Even when they voted for Republican candidates, they defected from *their* party. They were not redefined as operational Republicans. Reagan Democrats were still *Democrats*. By the same token, whether Tea Party conservatives like it or not, RINOs are Republicans. There have been Goldwater Republicans and Rockefeller Republicans, but whatever stripe, they all were Republicans. Even Republican presidential candidates on some issues have strayed from expected Republican issue positions on occasion (e.g., John McCain on campaign finance reform), but they are certainly Republicans. While the diversity of opinions and actions internal to a party identification has been widely accepted, that internal group diversity of opinions and actions has been used to challenge the very credibility of ideological identifications.[54]

The double standard in the treatment of ideological and party identifications is not limited to their treatment with respect to opinion and behavior variations. Ellis and Stimson suggest that the election of liberal presidential candidates (Carter, Clinton, and Obama) raises suspicions about the self-reported ideology measure that indicates a conservative plurality.[55] How can liberals be in the minority, they ask, if liberal candidates win elections? Of course, the same question could have been asked about party identification, but was not. Like the liberal minority in ideological identification, the Republican minority in party identification has often won elections. Democratic party identifiers were in a large majority when Eisenhower won in 1952 and then again in a landslide in 1956 and when Nixon won in 1968 and again in a landslide in 1972. Though diminished a bit, a clear plurality of party identifiers were Democrats when Reagan won in 1980 and again in a landslide in 1984 and when George H. W. Bush won in 1988. These presidential election results did not precipitate a challenge to the measurement of party identification. The victory of a minority partisan group is just another deviating election, an election decided for reasons other than partisanship and not a valid reason to challenge the measurement of party identification. The victory of a minority ideological group, on the other hand, apparently is considered by some to be a good reason to doubt the ideological measure itself. Of course, it should not be. The election of a candidate from a minority ideology simply indicates that the election was decided by reasons other than ideology.[56]

There should not be a double standard for party identification and ideology. If the party identifications of straying self-described Democrats and Republicans are accepted at face value, then the self-descriptions of liberals and conservatives who occasionally deviate from the presumed ideological lines should also be accepted. Unless there is compelling evidence to the contrary, and the operational ideology measure falls far short of making that case, self-reported ideology should be considered to be a person's ideological perspective, just as self-reported party identification is considered a person's party identification. The ideological identifications of conservatism and liberalism for most Americans are claimed distinctions that carry with them important and real political differences—though not differences reflected very well in the operational ideology index. As a challenge to the self-reported ideology measure, operational ideology is a manufactured molehill, not a real mountain of concern.[57]

The bottom line is that self-reported ideology is a credible measure of the general political perspectives of Americans. There is solid evidence that a plurality, *not* a majority, of Americans are moderates (or don't knows) and their numbers have been on the *decline*. Many more Americans are conservative than liberal and though both ideological perspectives have been growing, growth has been a bit greater at the conservative end of the ideological spectrum than at the liberal end. The aggregate distribution of these perspectives indicates: (1) that Americans in the 1970s were already fairly well polarized, and (2) that the extent of polarization in the American public has grown significantly since that time.

CHAPTER 4

ISSUES AND POLARIZATION

The continuing fight—not sweetness and light—is the
hallmark of the American democracy.

—Samuel Lubell, *Revolt of the Moderates*[1]

Americans are highly polarized ideologically and have become more
so in recent years. This ideological polarization is important because
of its likely impact on everyday political conflict in society. The fundamentally different perspectives of liberals and conservatives on the
extent and purposes of government should spawn similar differences
on the nation's day-to-day policy issues. But the suspected effects of
abstract ideological perspectives on practical issue positions are just
that—suspected. The question is whether these suspected effects of
ideological polarization are realized in actual political divisions over
public policy issues? If the nation were simply polarized ideologically without it precipitating policy disagreements, as difficult as this
might be to imagine, ideological polarization would be a curiosity

without much consequence. The intensity and prevalence of conflicting views at the level of day-to-day real politics on policy issues is the basis for the great interest in polarization. Differences of opinions on the issues may cause tempers to flare, governments to shut down, and political conversations at workplaces, in pubs, and across dinner tables to become uncomfortable or even uncivil.

In this chapter, we turn to a second type of direct evidence of polarization in the public—issue polarization. As with the direct evidence of polarization observed in ideological differences, there are questions of what the issue evidence suggests about polarization and also about the quality of that evidence. What do differences in issue preferences reveal about the extent and growth of polarization in the public? Are polarized ideological preferences of the public reflected in polarized issue politics? And, if so, how extensively, on what issues, and has issue polarization increased along with the ideological polarization of the public? Finally, what is the quality of the evidence of polarization drawn from the public's issue preferences?

THE MYTH OF ISSUE POLARIZATION?

Most recent research on polarization in the public has examined differences on public policy issues. This focus is understandable. Issue preferences are more tangible than abstract ideologies and differences on the issues more directly affect levels of political conflict. The seminal work on issue polarization was conducted by Paul DiMaggio, John Evans, and Bethany Bryson in 1996 (henceforth the DiMaggio team) and updated by Evans in 2003.[2] The DiMaggio team undertook an exhaustive evaluation of the attitudes of Americans on the social issues measured in General Social Survey and American National Election Study since the early 1970s. They studied both the dispersion of social issue attitudes (measured by their standard deviations) as well as the interconnectedness of those attitudes.[3] Aside from the abortion issue, they found that attitudes on most social issues (and omnibus scales of social issues) had neither become more extreme nor more correlated with one another.[4] By this reckoning, public opinion on social issues had not become more dispersed or more constrained (intercorrelated). In their words, they found "little support for the widely held belief that Americans have become sharply polarized on a wide range of social and cultural opinions in the past two decades."[5]

Two limitations of the DiMaggio team's findings deserve note. First, their findings are limited to social issues rather than the full range of issues over which Americans might divide. Second, their findings concern only the change in social issue polarization rather than its level. They found no evidence that social issue polarization had increased significantly in recent years (the change question), but provided no evidence regarding the extent to which the public was polarized on social or any other issues (the level question).

Although their issue-constraint findings were rebutted by Alan Abramowitz, the DiMaggio team's general findings about the lack of increased polarization on social issues have been accepted and extended by several subsequent studies.[6] Using the DiMaggio team's findings as a springboard for their own analysis, Morris Fiorina and his collaborators concluded that "there is little evidence that Americans' ideological or policy *positions* are more polarized today than they were two or three decades ago."[7] Elsewhere, Fiorina and Abrams reported that public opinion research of issue attitudes "generally finds little in the way of polarization."[8] Marc Hetherington concurred with the no issue polarization verdict: "Fiorina quite convincingly shows that Americans' issue preferences have been and remain generally moderate."[9]

When joined with findings of substantial and growing ideological polarization, the purported findings of an absence of issue polarization (with the notable exception of Abramowitz's studies) raises some distressing questions. Contrary to the evidence of ideological polarization, are we to believe that Americans are *not* highly polarized and have *not* grown more so when it comes to their positions on practical matters of current public policies? Is it plausible that ideological perspectives have become disconnected from opinions about public policy issues? Are large portions of the public simply enamored of different ideological labels and fail to connect their ideologies to real policy issues? In *The Responsible Electorate*, the eminent political scientist V. O. Key wrote that "the perverse and unorthodox argument of this little book is that voters are not fools."[10] Was Key wrong? Are

American voters in fact fools who have become even more foolish in recent times as they have grown increasingly polarized ideologically while remaining largely centrists on public policy?

The answer to each of these questions is a resounding no. Americans are, in fact, quite polarized. They have become somewhat more so in recent years. Ideological labels are very meaningful for current politics. Liberals and conservatives have different political values, think that the world works differently, and disagree profoundly about public policy. Key was quite right: American voters are not fools.

The problem is not with the public, but with a variety of problems associated with analyzing polarization with issue preference data. Some of these problems involve analytical and conceptual flaws in assessing polarization. At its most basic level, the question of the extent of polarization is often confused with the question of whether polarization levels have changed. These are, however, quite separate questions and the answer to one is not the answer to the other.[11] Assessing the level of polarization in a meaningful way requires establishing some reasonable benchmarks, and this has not been done.[12] This analytical problem is a major but resolvable problem. Others are unfortunately less tractable.

Beyond serious analytic and conceptual problems are some severe data problems with using survey responses on issue questions to detect the level of polarization in the public and how it may have changed over time. Concerns regarding the quality of ideological polarization evidence pale in comparison to the quagmire of problems associated with the evidence of issue polarization.

Before delving into the details of this empirical thicket, we should examine some of the data regarding issue polarization. This may provide us with a better idea of what issue data reveal about polarization and some possible problems with those data. After this brief foray into the issue analysis of polarization we can itemize the many complications and pitfalls that might cause us to be cautious or even wary of issue polarization evidence—whether those data suggest polarization is great or small, growing or declining. On to the evidence.

EVIDENCE OF ISSUE POLARIZATION

The Elements

We should start with the basics. What is proper evidence of the public being highly polarized on public policy issues? To conclude that the public is highly polarized on policy issues requires evidence demonstrating considerable division of the public's issue preferences on important policy issues. There are essentially two elements to the evidence. First, the issue or issues in dispute must be important to a large segment of the public.[13] Widely different opinions on some minor issues would hardly count as the public being highly polarized. Second, substantial portions of the public must hold divergent views on these salient issues (or issue). The determination of just how divergent the views of the public are on the issue or issues requires the determination of some benchmark for comparison. Polarization is a matter of degree. The analysis of polarization is unsatisfyingly inconclusive if polarization is simply found to be high or low "in the eye of the beholder."[14] We can determine whether issue polarization has grown or declined over time using polarization at an earlier time as a benchmark, but to determine whether polarization is high or low at any single point in time requires an independent standard.

To the extent that there is evidence of a substantial portion of the public holding divergent preferences on an important issue or set of issues, there is some degree of issue polarization. Issue polarization does not require bimodality in preferences. This would only occur in the most extreme (and probably unrealistically so) cases of polarization. Issue polarization also does not require sharply different positions on multiple issues or on some overall average of issues, nor does it require that there are strong correlations among positions on multiple issues. When a single issue dominates politics, as the critical issue of slavery and its extension did prior to the Civil War and as the government's role in dealing with the economy did in the wake of the Great Depression, that is enough.[15] Whether Americans disagreed on other issues is irrelevant to polarization.

Of course, a single critical issue in one light may also be expressed as a number of more specific sub-issues in a different light. The general issue of slavery, for instance, might have subsumed issues about the slave trade, the speed or process in the abolition of slavery, issues regarding the treatment of escaped slaves, and other related matters. In modern American politics, the government's role in dealing with the economy can be seen as encompassing related issues of government regulation, tax rates, and the government's intervention in different economic spheres from energy policy to health policy, from support for alternative fuels to the manufacture and importing of incandescent light bulbs. Whether a single dominant issue finds expression in multiple sub-issues or whether a number of conceptually distinct issues collectively capture the nation's agenda, the association among these different issues also provides evidence of polarization. Issues that divide the nation in different ways (cross-cutting cleavages) tend to mute the polarizing conflict of the division as people find themselves with different compatriots on different issues. Issues that divide the nation in the same way (overlapping cleavages), in contrast, tend to deepen the divisiveness of those issues.[16] Social conflict becomes more sharply focused when the same political lines reappear across a number of issues.[17]

It is important to note that the correlation or sorting of opinions on some issues with opinions on other issues, like the sorting of issue opinions with party or ideological identifications, should not be minimized as merely a matter of appearance. The sorting of issue attitudes likely affects the extent of social conflict. Rather than a hodgepodge of shifting coalitions, more sorted issue attitudes establish political sides, a polarized "us" versus "them." Whatever differences exist on individual issues are collectively concentrated when the issue positions are correlated and, conversely, diffused when positions are unrelated from one issue to the next.

A simulation of three issue distributions demonstrates the collective polarizing impact of an increased correlation among attitudes on different issues. Table 4.1 presents the joint distribution of opinions between one issue (Issue A) and two other issues (Issue B and Issue C).

Issues B and C could also be considered as preferences on the same issue at two different times. In each case, simulated issue positions were created for 120 hypothetical respondents on seven-point scales, ranging from 0 for the most liberal position on an issue to 6 for the most conservative position. The distributions of opinions were

TABLE 4.1. POLARIZATION THROUGH THE SORTING OF ISSUES

Position on Issue A	Position on Issue B								Position on Issue C							
	0	1	2	3	4	5	6	Total	0	1	2	3	4	5	6	Total
0	0	4	2	0	2	0	0	8	2	2	2	2	0	0	0	8
1	2	2	2	2	2	2	2	14	2	4	4	0	2	2	0	14
2	2	2	4	8	2	2	0	20	2	2	6	6	2	2	0	20
3	2	2	6	16	6	2	2	36	2	2	4	20	4	2	2	36
4	0	2	2	8	4	2	2	20	0	2	2	6	6	2	2	20
5	2	2	2	2	2	2	2	14	0	2	2	0	4	4	2	14
6	0	0	2	0	2	4	0	8	0	0	0	2	2	2	2	8
Total	8	14	20	36	20	14	8	120	8	14	20	36	20	14	8	120

Congruent = 40 (33%)	Congruent = 52 (43%)
Incongruent = 24 (20%)	Incongruent = 16 (13%)
Congruent – Incongruent = 13%	Congruent – Incongruent = 30%
Correlation of attitudes on	Correlation of attitudes on
Issues A and B = .22	Issues A and C = .47

Note: Issue attitudes are scored on a seven-point scale from 0 (the most liberal position) to 6 (the most conservative position) with 3 being the "moderate" position. The distributions of opinions on each of the issues are identical, with a standard deviation of opinions of 1.58. Respondents with congruent attitudes on a pair of issues were on the left (0, 1, or 2) on both issues or on the right (4, 5, or 6) on both issues. Incongruents were on the left on one issue and on the right on the other.

identical and symmetric, centered on the moderate (scored 3) position. Each issue distribution has a mean of 3 and a standard deviation of 1.58. Though the issues have identical individual distributions, Issue A's association with Issue B ($r = .22$) is a good deal weaker than with Issue C ($r = .47$). As a result, more of our hypothetical respondents find themselves on the same side of the two issues in the pairing of Issues A and C than with Issues A and B. If we consider pairs of positions that are both on the left side (0, 1, or 2) or both on the right side (4, 5, or 6) of the scale as being congruent and positions crossing the scale as incongruent (e.g., a liberal position on Issue A and a conservative position on Issue B), a third of respondents (40 of 120) hold congruent positions and a fifth (24 of 120) hold incongruent positions on the weakly correlated Issues A and B. On the more strongly correlated Issues A and C, however, 43% (52 of 120) hold congruent views and only 13% (16 of 120) have incongruent opinions. We should expect that those who are consistently on one side of issue disputes will be more adamant about their views compared to those who find themselves sometimes agreeing with one side and sometimes with the other. As the number of those who are consistently on one side swells and as the numbers of those with a mixed bag of beliefs dwindles, polarizing conflict increases. In short, the sorting out of issues gives rise to polarization even when the distributions of positions on those issues are unchanged.

Two Issues

Are there large and increasing differences among the public on policy issues that are important to them? After setting aside the "more or less" questions because of the various problems discussed in the last chapter, two broad issue questions have been included in ANES studies since the early 1970s. Both concern the willingness of respondents to turn to the government to solve problems and provide services, the bedrock difference between the ideological outlooks on politics. Rather than survey a wide range of available data (that would, in any case, still leave a great many issues and policy preferences unmeasured), we will focus in greater depth on these two as issue exemplars.

The first issue concerns whether respondents think that "the government in Washington should see to it that every person has a job and a good standard of living." The question leaves to the respondent's imagination the lengths to which government should go in pursuing full employment, its funding sources, and what constitutes a "good" standard of living. The nongovernment option posed to respondents is that "government should just let each person get ahead on their own." This might be read either in absolutist terms as government doing nothing to encourage employment or as the government helping to create a pro-growth environment but stopping well short of guaranteeing everyone a good job.

The second issue asks about how extensive the government's role should be in paying for medical care. The liberal or pro-government policy option is support for "a government insurance plan which would cover all medical and hospital expenses." The smaller government policy option is that "medical expenses should be paid by individuals, and through private insurance like Blue Cross or some other company paid plans." Again, the details of either option are not discussed (and could not be in a question of reasonable length).[18] The question was prefaced by a reference to "the rapid rise in medical and hospital costs." Both the jobs question and the healthcare question are included in the small battery of questions examined by Abramowitz and Saunders and by Fiorina, Abrams, and Pope.[19] Positions on both of the issues as framed by the ANES questions were associated with individual reported presidential vote choices in each of the elections in which the issues were included from 1972 to 2008.[20] This suggests that these and related issues are of some importance to the electorate.

Table 4.2 presents the distributions of opinions on the government jobs issue and the government healthcare issue in the early to mid-1970s and more than three decades later in the mid-2000s. Seven-point scales used for both issues allow distinctions between those just slightly off-center from those with more extreme positions. In the interest of more robust evidence, mean responses in two pairs of ANES presidential election year studies (1972–1976 and 2004–2008) are reported for both questions. As in the ideology analysis, those who reported they had not thought much about the issue (don't knows) are scored as centrists (4s on the 1 to 7 scale). The more liberal response to both issues calls for greater government involvement.

Attitudes about the government guaranteeing jobs and a good standard of living for everyone are presented in the top panel of the table. In perusing the distribution of opinions in the early and mid-1970s, about a third of Americans were centrists (or don't knows) on this issue and this rises to better than half (56%) when those just slightly off-center are added to the mix. Thirty-some years later, fewer are dead-center on the issue, but about the same percentage of respondents (55%) are located in the middle three response categories. The standard deviation of the distribution is essentially unchanged (around 2.0). On this issue, as the options are presented, opinions appear to be no more polarized than they were in the early 1970s.

Opinions regarding government supported health insurance, at least as of 2008 (prior to the enactment of Obamacare), also fail to support the claim that polarization increased. In the 1970s, less than

Chapter 4

TABLE 4.2. POLARIZATION OF POLICY VIEWS ON TWO ISSUES, 1972–1976 AND 2004–2008

Issue	Years	Seven-Point Issue Preference Positions (Percentages)							Standard Deviation
		Liberal			Mod-erate	Conservative			
		1	2	3	4 & DK	5	6	7	
Guaranteed Jobs and Standard of Living	1972–1976	12	5	9	35	12	9	18	2.0
	2004–2008	10	8	11	28	16	14	12	1.8
	Change	−2	+3	+2	−7	+4	+5	−6	−.2
Healthcare and Insurance	1972–1976	23	7	6	30	6	6	22	2.3
	2004–2008	19	12	12	26	13	10	9	1.9
	Change	−4	+5	+6	−4	+7	+4	−13	−.4

Note: The data are from the indicated ANES studies and were calculated from VCF0806 and VCF0809 of the ANES Cumulative File. Only respondents answering the self-reported ideology question (including "don't knows") were included. The distributions are the mean percentages of the two indicated election year surveys. Don't knows are treated as moderates and combined with those responding in the middle of the issue scale (coded 4). The question wordings are: JOBS: "Some people feel that the government in Washington should see to it that every person has a job and a good standard of living. Others think the government should just let each person get ahead on his/their own. And, of course, some other people have opinions somewhere in between. Where would you place yourself on this scale, or haven't you thought much about this?" HEALTHCARE: "There is much concern about the rapid rise in medical and hospital costs. Some feel there should be a government insurance plan which would cover all medical and hospital expenses. Others feel that medical expenses should be paid by individuals, and through private insurance like Blue Cross or some other company paid plans. And of course, some people have opinions somewhere in between. Where would you place yourself on this scale, or haven't you thought much about this?" The correlation between the two issues was .29 in the 1972 and 1976 elections and .43 in the 2004 and 2008 elections.

a third of Americans were perfectly centrist on the issue (30%) and over 40% were more broadly moderate. In the first decade of the 2000s, however, about half of Americans were in one of the three middle positions on the issue. The biggest change from the 1970s to the 2000s was the double-digit decline in those most strongly advocating the conservative position. The standard deviation actually dropped slightly from the earlier to the later period, suggesting that polarization had not increased.

The issue polarization story, however, is not simply a matter of differences on individual issues, as table 4.1 illustrated. Polarization is a phenomenon concerning conflict among people and this is not the same thing as attitude conflicts on isolated individual issues. Attitudes on issues may be more or less polarizing depending on whether they line up to reinforce differences or cross-cut one another to diffuse differences.[21] Though opinions on the two issues examined did not become perceptibly more extreme over time, differences on these issues were more often held in common. They were reinforcing. *The correlations of views on these two issues increased significantly from the mid-1970s ($r = .29$, 1972–1976) to the mid-2000s ($r = .43$, 2004–2008).* This was roughly on the order of the hypothetical cases constructed for table 4.1.[22]

These findings suggest that though opinions on individual issues may not be any more dispersed than they had been in earlier years (as the DiMaggio and Fiorina teams found), they are positively correlated and have become somewhat more so (as Abramowitz and Saunders found).[23] This greater overlap of issue opinions may have intensified whatever conflict there was on these issues.[24] This might be termed polarization through the clarification of issue conflict, rather than the birth of new conflict on individual issues.

Still, the question remains whether there was significant conflict on these individual issues to begin with. If we merely witnessed more highly correlated but generally *centrist* opinions, it would *not* indicate that the nation was highly polarized.[25] One would have a fairly neatly and mildly divided nation. A high level of polarization requires that the correlated (or sorted) opinions themselves be non-centrist. As with the examination of ideological polarization, we need benchmarks in order to properly interpret what this evidence reveals about the extent of issue polarization and how it may have changed.

Benchmarks

Are Americans highly divided or substantially unified in their positions about the government providing jobs, a good standard of living, and health insurance? The distribution of opinions in table 4.1 indicates standard deviations of about two (1.8 to 2.3 more specifically) for both issues whether in the 1970s or 2000s, but how should this be interpreted? Are standard deviations of about two big or small? Is this evidence of a nation largely polarized or largely centrist? To answer this question in any meaningful way requires benchmarks, some independent metrics. As in the analysis of ideological polarization, benchmarks for issue polarization can be constructed by setting out polar opposite cases: a nonpolarized, perfectly centrist nation versus a completely divided, perfectly polarized nation. The benchmarks are the theoretical minimum and maximum levels of issue polarization. These idealized polar cases can then be made more realistic by introducing some random measurement error into them. The dispersions of the observed data distributions can then be compared to the dispersions of the nonpolarized and polarized constructed distributions.

Table 4.3 presents the polarization benchmarks for seven-point issue scales. The no polarization condition is presented in the top panel of rows and the complete polarization condition is presented in the bottom panel. Each panel includes three variations on the condition: measured without error, measured with random errors or misreports for 20% of respondents, and finally with random errors for 30% of respondents. In the most extreme case of no polarization, everyone is in the middle category (category 4). In the most extreme case of complete polarization, half the nation is off to the far left position (scaled 1) and half to the far right (scaled 7). With 20% of the cases mistakenly assigning themselves to the "wrong" issue position (that is, a numbered position that does not best reflect their actual opinion), the centrist category is depleted by 20 percentage points in the perfect nonpolarization case and the extreme categories in the complete polarization are each reduced by ten percentage points. The adjacent categories increase in number, but at diminishing rates. Smaller errors should be more common than larger errors.

TABLE 4.3. ISSUE POLARIZATION BENCHMARKS

| Condition | Measurement Error (% misassigned) | Seven-Point Issue Preference Positions (Percentages) | | | | | | | Standard Deviation |
| | | Liberal | | | Mod-erate | Conservative | | | |
		1	2	3	4 & DK	5	6	7	
No Polarization	None	0	0	0	100	0	0	0	0.0
	20	0	3	7	80	7	3	0	0.6
	30	1	5	9	70	9	5	1	0.9
Complete Polarization	None	50	0	0	0	0	0	50	3.0
	20	40	7	3	0	3	7	40	2.8
	30	35	9	5	2	5	9	35	2.7

Note: Each row totals to 100%. The midpoints between no polarization and complete polarization standard deviations would be 1.5 when there is no measurement error, 1.7 with 20% misassigned (measurement error), and 1.8 with 30% misassigned (measurement error).

Under the unrealistic conditions of flawless measurement, the standard deviations of the seven-point issue scales range from a value of zero when perfectly centrist to a value of three when divisions are at their maximum. Introducing some realistic amounts of error raises the standard deviations for nonpolarized conditions and lowers it for highly polarized conditions. The midpoints between the polar conditions rise from 1.5 points without measurement error to 1.8 when 30% of the respondents are a bit off the mark.

With the benchmark boundaries serving as a guide, it is now possible to provide a meaningful answer to the question of whether the polarization glass is more full than empty or more empty than full. Comparing the observed dispersion measures in table 4.2 to the benchmark standards in table 4.3, and assuming that the issue scales accurately reflect public opinion (unfortunately, not an easy assumption to grant, as will be explained shortly), the public appears to be more polarized than not on these two issues. Even assuming a 30% misassignment measurement error, all of the standard deviations are at or above the 1.8 point midpoint between no polarization and complete polarization. These individual issue differences may be magnified collectively by the increasingly positive correlations among them. The issue polarization glass is, thus, more full than empty—that is, if these data are to be believed. This is the question to which we now turn.

THE ISSUES WITH ISSUE POLARIZATION

The evidence of polarization drawn from the attitudes about different issues is riddled with problems. This is especially unfortunate since so much of the research on polarization has relied heavily on these data. This review addresses five of the major problems with the issue evidence of polarization.[26] Broadly speaking, two might be thought of as presenting analytic problems and three can be broadly defined as measurement problems. The analytic problems concern how issues come and go on the political scene and how the meaning of those issues often changes. Capturing the essence of conflict over political issues involves trying to hit a moving, evolving, and sometimes disappearing target. The measurement problems include the small range of all possible issues that are measured, the fixed framing of issues and position options offered on surveys, and the well-known substantial measurement errors associated with responses to issue items. Some of these problems affect assessments of the extent of polarization in the public. Others affect the detection of how much polarization may have changed over time. Some affect both.

The problems with issue attitude data in measuring polarization are considerable. Overall, these problems should cause us to be somewhat skeptical of conclusions about polarization that rest on simple evaluations of issue position scales. Though there are some sophisticated scaling techniques that may address some of these problems, ultimately they must rest on tough assumptions and they can improve upon flawed data only so much.[27]

Time Bound

One of the major problems confronting the use of issue attitudes in tracking the level of polarization over time is the intrinsically short-term nature of contemporary political issues. Issues are about the problems and proposals that occupy the nation's attention at a particular point in time. They come and they go (even if they sometimes remain on a survey). An issue may be hotly salient one year and anachronistic a few years later. Their time-bound nature creates some obvious comparability problems for tracking any change in polarization over the decades.

Though general policy areas like the economy and national security may routinely find their way onto the national agenda, the particular issues and policies in dispute in even these policy areas are short-lived. The public may have been highly divided over Taft-Hartley or the Tennessee Valley Authority in the late 1940s, but these issues would generate only blank stares and no news coverage today. The list of "here yesterday and now long gone" domestic policy issues is lengthy: meat shortages, Medicare and the Great Society programs, wage and price controls, desegregation of schools, open housing laws, urban unrest and rioting, busing to achieve integration, gas lines, Watergate and the Nixon pardon, the Equal Rights Amendment, stagflation and the misery index, the Kemp-Roth tax cuts and budget deficits, the Clinton impeachment, and prescription drug plans. Obamacare divides the nation today, but it was not around ten years ago and may not be around as an issue (at least in its current form) ten years from now.

Like domestic issues, many foreign and defense policy issues have had "use by" dates that expired long ago. Military conscription, containment of the Soviet Union, Korea and General MacArthur, the missile gap, Kemoy and Matsu, the Bay of Pigs, Vietnam, apartheid and South Africa, hostages in Iran, Nicaragua and the Sandinistas, development of a neutron bomb, the Strategic Defense Initiative, Bosnia, the Gulf War, the Afghanistan and Iraq Wars and the list goes on. What were highly contentious issues to the public at one time might not now even generate a glimmer of recognition.

The short life span of many issues is evident even in public opinion surveys. Even after broadening issue wording to make it less time-specific, ANES has dropped a number of issue scales over the years. It stopped asking about the segregation-desegregation issue after 1978, about open housing after 1976, about busing to achieve integration after 1984, about foreign relations with Russia after 1988, about both urban unrest and the pace of civil rights progress after 1992, and about school prayer in 1998. Some issues have come and gone on the ANES surveys even more quickly. Issue questions about policies against inflation and campus unrest appeared in the 1972 study and were gone by the next election.

The short-term nature of issues creates problems for assessing the level of polarization in the public and is even more problematic for determining how that level may have changed. When the same issues are not the same from one decade to the next, polarization must be gauged by opinion differences on the issues deemed salient in each period, and these have not necessarily been asked in all periods. To determine how polarization has changed over time, opinion differences on different issues must be compared. The lack of constancy in salient issues across time raises the problems of comparing "apples and oranges."

Context Matters

A second problem with the issue evidence of changing polarization is that the same issue may mean different things about political conflict in different contexts.[28] An opinion judged to be quite liberal at one time may be considered moderate or even conservative at a later time or vice versa. The literal consistency of an issue question's wording does not guarantee the consistency of what a response to that issue question means in a different context.

A few examples illustrate the point. An extreme case is the comparison of views about the abolition of slavery at different points in history. Before the Civil War, an abolitionist position generally would have been considered to be quite radical. Today it would just be considered weirdly obvious. Same position, different meaning. In the 1940s and 1950s, opposition to racial segregation was a liberal position; but by the 1980s it was a position so widely accepted that pollsters stopped asking about it. Again, same position, different meaning. In the early 1970s, supporters of the proposed Equal Rights Amendment were considered fairly moderate, but by the mid-1980s it had become a decidedly liberal position. What an issue position reveals about social conflict can sometimes change very rapidly. In the early 2000s, support for civil unions for homosexual couples was a liberal position. Liberal Democratic President Barack Obama favored civil

unions until months before his reelection in 2012. By that time, support for civil unions was the position staked out by conservatives. Political conflict on the issue, however, did not subside as conservatives
became more accepting of civil unions. Quite the opposite. Demands
for acceptance of gay marriage shifted the debate in ways that would
not be reflected by responses to a fixed question.

The importance of context to many of the issue questions may be
most clearly seen in the huge changes in attitudes toward increasing
or decreasing defense spending in the 1980s.[29] Table 4.4 provides the
details of the attitudinal shift and the shift in the context in which
the attitudes were expressed. The ANES survey item asked whether
prospective voters favored greatly increasing or decreasing defense
spending. In 1980, a sizeable majority favored increased defense spending and only one in ten favored cuts. Four years later, pretty much
the same electorate was quite evenly divided between increasing and
decreasing commitments to defense. Reading this outside of context
(as the operational ideology measure does), it might appear that a
large portion of the electorate had made "an about face," turning away
from the conservative position in support of a military buildup to a
more liberal or perhaps moderate reticence about more defense spending. Had the public changed its mind about its support of national
defense so much so quickly? No, as the bottom two rows of the table
plainly demonstrate, circumstances had changed a great deal. After
four years of extracting a "peace dividend" from the Pentagon's budget under the Carter presidency, many saw defense as underfunded.
Then, after four years of a military buildup in the Reagan presidency,
calls for reductions nearly tripled and those favoring further increases
were cut in half. Did the voters' thinking change? No, the circumstances changed. The difference is in the circumstances and not in the
thinking of the voters. Unfortunately, survey responses to issue items
are too often used out of context, and whether views are moderate or
extreme depends upon the context in which they are expressed.[30]

In determining their positions on the issues, most Americans adapt
to the political reality of their day and to conditions as they see them.
Their views reflect what they think might be politically possible and
what current real-world conditions might require. These contexts,
however, often change and sometimes change quite quickly (see the
gay marriage issue), even as issue question wordings and position

TABLE 4.4. ATTITUDES ABOUT INCREASING OR DECREASING DEFENSE SPENDING, 1980 AND 1984

Preference for Defense Spending Change	Percentage of Respondents	
	1980 After President Carter's Term	1984 After President Reagan's First Term
Greatly Decrease	10	28
Same or Don't Know	30	41
Greatly Increase	60	31
Total	100	100
Defense Spending	Percentage	
Mean Annual Growth in Constant (1972) Dollars	1.6%	6.0%
As % of GNP over presidential term (change)	Drop from 5.5% to 5.2% (−0.3%)	Increase from 5.2% to 6.4% (+1.2%)

Note: The wording of the ANES question is as follows: "Some people believe that we should spend less money on defense. Others feel that defense spending should be greatly increased. Where would you place yourself on this scale, or haven't you thought much about this?" The greatly decreased spending category includes responses 1, 2, and 3. The greatly increased spending category includes responses 5, 6, and 7. The same or don't know category includes responses coded 4 and 9.

options on surveys remain unchanged. Issue attitudes often evolve in response to the political or policy environment, but the issue evidence read literally does not. Issue attitude data may be consistent in a very literal sense across time, but this consistency may be superficial, failing to capture opinion differences because the issue itself has changed.[31]

Tip of the Iceberg

The time-bound nature of contemporary issues and the context-dependent nature of their meaning for political conflict are considerable problems facing the tracking of issue polarization over time, but there are also a number of practical problems with issue position data. The first of these is that the issue positions measured on surveys are only a small fraction of the wide range of issues considered important by different segments of the public. The number of surveyed issues has expanded with the proliferation of polls, but it still represents just the tip of the issue agenda iceberg.

The numbers tell the story. ANES began asking about Americans' views regarding public policies on seven-point scales in its 1972 election study. Though ANES examines some issues (e.g., abortion policy) in different formats, responses to the seven-point issue items are commonly used to assess polarization. Eight seven-point issue scales were asked in 1972. The issues ranged from Vietnam withdrawal to taxes to campus unrest. In ANES presidential year studies since then, normally six to nine seven-point issue scales have been included.[32] The ANES cumulative file includes 12 seven-point issue scales that have been asked frequently enough to merit inclusion.

To put these numbers in perspective, they can be compared to the number of different issues that voters mention in response to what they considered to be the most important issues facing the nation. After cleaning up the code of responses to this question in 1988 by eliminating about 170 responses, ANES identified about 130 distinct issues. The list might be further whittled down to take into account issue similarities. This would still leave about one hundred different issues. These run the gamut: farm subsidies, minimum wage, taxes, immigration policy, foreign investment, productivity, national defense, foreign policy issues dealing with various hot spots, the arms race and nuclear weapons, the military draft, the space program, budget deficits, welfare reform, campaign finance, narcotics, pollution, energy policy, abortion, women's rights, crime, poverty, civil rights, terrorism, gay rights, healthcare, and unemployment. The list goes on and on. A list of issue-related responses to open-ended questions about what voters like or dislike about the candidates and parties is not quite as long, but still many times more than the number of seven-point scaled issues included in ANES surveys.[33] Fiorina reports that a Pew poll conducted in 2006 found that at least 40% of Americans at that time considered 18 different issues to be "very important."[34] Is the small subset of all issues asked about on the seven-point issue scales representative of all the other issues voters have on their minds? We do not know. They were not measured.

Question Construction

Perhaps the biggest drawback to issue polarization data is the fact that issue questions on surveys employ a pre-defined frame of each policy issue with a pre-defined pair of policy options.[35] In many policy disputes, there are differences about how the issue is seen or even what the issue is essentially about, as well as what the policy options are. The framing of an issue varies from person to person in real life, but not on surveys. A single issue frame and a set of policy options, while necessary for a survey from a practical standpoint, are subjective impositions on respondents. Responses to issue preference questions on surveys are notoriously sensitive to both question wordings and the policy options offered. As a result, issue preference responses may indicate as much or more about the way in which the issue and options were framed and worded as they do about the real issue preferences that they purport to measure.[36]

Decisions about the structuring and phrasing of issue questions and policy options offered to respondents may have substantial implications for assessing polarization. If the issues are posed in a particularly inflammatory way, polarization may appear greater. They may accentuate conflict. If worded in less controversial ways, the public might appear more moderate. They might highlight moderation. The alternative preferences offered may also make a big difference. More extreme or unpalatable alternatives might drive respondents away from the poles and to the center (smaller standard deviations). By the same token, when more reasonable or pleasant options are offered to them, respondents may gravitate to the poles (higher standard deviations).

The problems associated with issue question wording can be illustrated with one of the frequently asked questions over the years in ANES studies. The "Urban Unrest" issue was asked beginning in 1968 through 1976 and then again in 1992. The question ANES posed to prospective voters before these elections is as follows:

> There is much discussion about the best way to deal with the problem of urban unrest and rioting. Some say it is more important to use all available force to maintain law and order—no matter what results. Others say it is more important to correct

the problems of poverty and unemployment that give rise to the disturbances. Where would you place yourself on this scale, or haven't you thought much about this?

Respondents were offered a seven-point scale anchored at the 1 position with the policy option of "Solving problems of poverty and unemployment" and at the 7 position with the policy option of "Use all available force." They were also provided the option of simply indicating that they had not thought much about the issue.

Did most respondents think about the subject of urban rioting in these terms? Was this the way they saw the alternative public policies available on the issue? It is hard to say in retrospect, but easy to see some serious problems with the question and the proposed policies. First, who would be against solving poverty and unemployment? Must those favoring a crackdown on rioters oppose correcting or solving (eliminating?) the problems of poverty and unemployment? A middle position suggests a bit of each, but it is not difficult to imagine strongly favoring *both* options, and this view would not be conveyed by a middle position. Second, is it accurate to characterize the views of those wishing for a firm response to rioters to be in favor of "all available force"? This might easily be read as endorsing some draconian measures. "All available force" might mean martial law or the imposition of a police state. Third, one might question whether the suggested possible implications of each policy are balanced. Looming over the hard-line option is the disturbingly ominous "no matter what the results" possibility. The soft-line option, on the other hand, lightly supposes that "solving poverty and unemployment" (a neat trick that has proven elusive) will eliminate the causes that gave "rise to disturbances" (burning down city blocks are "disturbances"?). The point is that constructing issue items for surveys is an art not always practiced very artfully, and question effects are difficult to separate from whatever real opinions (and polarization or moderation) might be intermingled with them.

This problem may make gauging the level of issue polarization especially difficult. Depending on how the issue question is posed, what premises are suggested, and what policy options are allowed, public opinion can appear more polarized or more centrist than it really is.

Issue Response Instability

A major problem in assessing issue polarization is that issue data have been notoriously plagued by attitude instability and random measurement error. In panel survey data, issue attitude responses jump around fairly freely when the same issue question is posed at different times. A good deal of this movement suggests response instability rather than a pattern of real change. This noise in issue measurements has been attributed to a combination of vaguely focused or partially formed respondent attitudes on various issues (nonattitudes) and problems in forming survey items that accurately and reliably measure those issue attitudes.[37] Robert Erikson succinctly made the point: "responses to opinion items are unreliable."[38] More recently, Ansolabehere, Rodden, and Snyder found that multiple measures of issue preferences can greatly reduce measurement error to reveal substantially greater attitude stability and structure.[39]

Substantial instability in responses to isolated issue questions on surveys is certainly understandable. Few respondents are deeply immersed in politics (recall the McClosky Difference). Politics and political issues are well down the list of life's priorities for most. When presented with a long survey of political questions they are not prepared to answer, and presented with issue questions and alternatives they may not have thought much about recently or thought about in the same way that the survey presents the issue and alternatives, the best we might reasonably hope for is an honest but rough top-of-the-head reaction.[40] Even the issue responses of the better educated and more politically sophisticated are no more stable than those less educated and less politically attuned.[41]

Whatever its source, whether it be survey or respondent limitations or a mix of the two, response instability has consequences for the use of issue attitude data in discerning polarization levels and its change. Because of the noise or random component in issue attitude responses, more moderate publics appear to have more dispersed opinions than they really do. Recall the increasing standard deviations with increases in random error introduced in the three scenarios presented in table 4.3. Centrists look less centrist as their responses stray from the center. On the other hand, again recalling the same table, random error makes true extremists look less extreme.

Random error in their responses moves their responses away from the poles toward the center of the spectrum and attenuates the correlations among issue responses.[42] Together these measurement problems would make a polarized public appear somewhat less polarized than it is.

What are the consequences of random errors in issue responses for assessing polarization in the public? For the determination of the level of polarization, random issue response errors add a greater measure of uncertainty and detract from the usefulness of the evidence. It muddies the waters. For the determination of changes in polarization levels, the consequences are more interesting. Because of random errors in issue responses, changes in polarization are more difficult to detect and appear smaller than they are in reality. The instability of issue responses causes moderate publics to appear more polarized than they really are and polarized publics to appear more moderate than they really are. Put differently, random response errors have the effect of biasing issue evidence against finding change in polarization levels. This bias is unlikely to be so severe that polarization change goes undetected, but it may help to explain at least some of the difficulty encountered in detecting an increase in polarization in recent decades.[43]

THE IDEOLOGICAL CONNECTION

Despite the many reasons to be wary of issue evidence of polarization and the obstacles to obtaining a clear view of polarization using issue data, the findings of issue polarization comport fairly well with those of ideological polarization. Like the ideological polarization findings, the issue polarization findings (despite their many problems) indicate that Americans have been fairly well polarized for some time and have grown more so. Though issue preferences (or at least survey responses) on the government jobs and healthcare issues did not grow more dispersed over time, comparisons to the benchmarks indicate that they were fairly well polarized to begin with and that an increase in the constraint or sorting of these issues into greater alignment with each other is evidence of an increase in issue polarization.

The findings of the ideological and issue evidence of polarization when examined in tandem buttress one another. Americans are divided over ideologies and on many issues. Moreover, they are divided in the same way on both ideology and the issues. Americans are not only better sorted out by their positions on different issues, their sorting more closely corresponds to their self-declared ideologies.[44] An underlying ideological polarization appears to be reflected in the polarization of issue attitudes. Self-described liberals are more likely to differ from self-described conservatives on a host of issues. While issue positions, ideologies, and party identifications have long been somewhat aligned, especially among the more politically sophisticated, their alignment for many had been fairly weak.[45] Their correspondence is now significantly stronger and more common.[46]

Views about the government jobs and healthcare issues illustrate the ideological connection. Table 4.5 presents the evidence of the now greater overlap of issue positions with their associated ideological perspectives.[47] Consistent liberals are those who favored a government insurance plan on the healthcare issue and favored government guaranteed jobs and a good standard of living on that issue. Consistent conservatives are those who favored private insurance plans and individuals being responsible for their own employment and living standards. Inconsistent conservatives and liberals took positions on these issues that were considered consistent for the opposite ideological perspective. A third group, not included in the table (but easily computed from those who are), held a middle position or no position on the issue.

At least with respect to the two issues related to government intervention on jobs and healthcare, from the mid-1970s to the mid-2000s, it became more common for those with an ideological perspective to have issue attitudes in sync with that outlook. This was true of both liberals and conservatives and on both the healthcare and jobs issues. By the same token, issue positions at odds with ideological perspectives became less frequent across the board. In the cases in which this decline was slight (conservatives), the frequency of inconsistency was low at the outset. From the early 1970s to the mid-2000s, mean correlations between ideologies and issue preferences increased from .27 to .35 on the jobs issue and from .26 to .38 on the healthcare issue.

These findings support and augment the findings of ideological polarization presented in chapter 3. Not only has the percentage of Americans expressing non-moderate ideological perspectives increased

TABLE 4.5. CHANGE IN THE CONSISTENCY OF IDEOLOGICAL ORIENTATIONS AND ISSUE PREFERENCES, 1972–1976 AND 2004–2008

	Consistency of Self-Reported Ideology and Issue Preferences (Percentage of Respondents)				
	Healthcare Issue				
	Liberal on Issue		Conservative on Issue		Correlation of
Years	*Consistent*	*Inconsistent*	*Consistent*	*Inconsistent*	Issue Preference with Ideology
1972–1976	57	24	49	26	.26
2004–2008	66	11	55	24	.38
Change	+9	−13	+6	−2	+.12
	Guaranteed Jobs Issue				
	Liberal on Issue		Conservative on Issue		Correlation of
Years	*Consistent*	*Inconsistent*	*Consistent*	*Inconsistent*	Issue Preference with Ideology
1972–1976	42	31	60	15	.27
2004–2008	47	24	68	14	.35
Change	+5	−7	+8	−1	+.08

Note: The "consistent" and "inconsistent" designations refer to whether the self-reported ideology was in the same direction as the issue preference. See the note to table 4.2 for the details about the two issues. The percentage of ideologues taking neither an ideologically consistent nor inconsistent issue position (a moderate position or a don't know response) are the omitted category for both liberals and conservatives.

in recent decades, but those liberals and conservatives are more likely to espouse support for issue positions consistent with their broad political outlooks. For various reasons, there still are some who hold apparently inconsistent issue attitudes, but their numbers are smaller than they had been. Despite the many problems that plague issue attitude data, the extent and growth of issue polarization is in evidence. The direct evidence from ideological and issue data tells the same story: Americans are highly polarized, they have been quite polarized for some time, and they have grown more so in recent decades.

CHAPTER 5

CIRCUMSTANTIAL EVIDENCE

E pluribus discordia

Polarization has become the defining characteristic of modern American politics. Americans are so entrenched in opposing political camps, it sometimes seems the two sides quarrel about everything—from constitutional rights to the weather (the climate change debate). The extent of polarization is evident in both self-reported ideology and issue attitude data. The fact that the issue analysis corroborates the ideology analysis should bolster confidence in these findings. Both indicate a highly polarized public and both indicate a public polarized along the same lines.

Although all the direct evidence points in the same direction, some concerns about the quality of that evidence may remain. Self-reported ideology data have come under substantial critical scrutiny, most notably from Ellis and Stimson.[1] Though it appears that these data are fundamentally reliable and valid, they are not perfect and some may retain reservations about them. Issue attitude data, widely used in examining polarization, are even more problematic. Even though the direct evidence supports consistent conclusions about polarization, the problems and claims about it still may leave some uncertainty about the findings.

This uncertainty may be alleviated by the circumstantial evidence of polarization. Beyond the "eyewitness" direct testimony of self-reported ideology and self-reported issue attitude data, with all of their flaws (overrated or not), there is circumstantial evidence of polarization. In legal parlance, circumstantial evidence is "evidence which inferentially proves the principal fact by establishing a condition of surrounding and limiting circumstances, whose existence is a premise from which the existence of the principal fact may be concluded by necessary laws of reasoning."[2]

Circumstantial evidence might be regarded as indirect evidence. If it can be demonstrated that a possible answer to a polarization question (e.g., the nation is mostly moderate) is *inconsistent* with undisputed facts, the possible answer should be considered implausible (or reasons to dispute the "undisputed fact" must be raised). By the same token, if it can be shown that a possible answer is *consistent* with undisputed facts, the plausibility of that answer should be enhanced. Like direct evidence, circumstantial evidence can vary in strength. Circumstantial evidence that may be more tangential to the question, on the one hand, may only slightly tip the scales. Circumstantial evidence central to the question in contention, on the other hand, can compel a verdict. In essence, circumstantial evidence provides a "reality check" of the findings.

What circumstantial evidence can be brought to bear on the two questions of public polarization: the relative question of whether polarization has increased and the absolute question of whether polarization is at a high level? Happily, since polarization is at the center of American political life, there are many undisputed political circumstances that may provide clues to the polarization puzzles. We begin by introducing these into evidence.

THE EXHIBITS

Though much about political polarization is in dispute, many political characteristics related to polarization are not. Eleven facts about American politics, past and present, provide the basis for several dif-

TABLE 5.1. EXHIBITS OF THE CIRCUMSTANTIAL EVIDENCE OF POLARIZATION

Exhibit	*Generally Stipulated Evidence*
A	Parties in the Electorate Are Highly Polarized in the 2000s
B	Parties in the Electorate Were Not Highly Polarized in the 1960s and 1970s
C	Most Americans Are Partisan (identify to some degree with a political party)
D	Partisanship Increased in the mid-1980s
E	Partisanship Decreased in the early 1970s
F	Parties in Government Are Highly Polarized in the 2000s
G	Parties in Government (post–1920s) Were Not Highly Polarized until the 1980s
H	Turnout Increased in the 2000s
I	Turnout Declined in the 1970s
J	Split-Ticket Voting Declined in the 1990s and 2000s
K	Split-Ticket Voting Increased in the 1970s and 1980s

ferent pieces of circumstantial evidence of polarization. These exhibits A through K are summarized in table 5.1. They concern the levels and changes of party polarization in the electorate, partisanship in the electorate, party polarization in government (among leaders), voter turnout, and split-ticket voting.

Party Polarization in the Electorate (Exhibits A and B). Although there may be some quibbling about just how far party polarization in the electorate has gone and though prior research lacked benchmarks to gauge its level, it is widely agreed that the major political parties in the electorate are now highly polarized. There is also a consensus that party polarization in the electorate has increased and that the parties were not highly polarized from at least the 1940s to the 1980s. According to ANES data (excluding don't knows), about a quarter of Democrats in 1972 were self-described liberals. Forty years later that had nearly doubled, from 26% to 49%. At the same time, conservative ranks in the Republican Party grew from less than half of the party in 1972 to three-quarters in 2012 (42% to 74%). The Democrats are now a fairly homogeneously liberal party. Republicans are now a homogeneously conservative party. To be sure, neither is pure. Both have a more centrist-oriented wing and they will never attain the homogeneity levels of elites (the McClosky Difference), but the gulf between the parties in the electorate is a chasm, at least as political differences in the mass public go. "There is widespread agreement," according to Layman, Carsey, and Horowitz, "that the Democratic and Republican parties in the electorate have become more sharply divided on ideology and policy issues in recent decades."[3] Other studies reaching this conclusion have already been reviewed in chapter 1.

Most Americans are Partisans (Exhibit C). ANES surveys administered in the 16 presidential elections from 1952 to 2012 indicate that about 11% or 12% of respondents were pure independents, identifying with neither the Democratic Party nor the Republican Party. In the 2012 study, that number was 14%. Typically, about another 22% (24% in 2012) initially indicate they are independent of the parties, but report in a follow-up question they are closer to or lean toward either the Democrats or the Republicans. Research on party identification has concluded that these independent leaners are really partisans who were initially reluctant to admit to their partisanship.[4] Among reported voters, the number of true independents is even smaller, typically about 8%. In short, better than 85% of Americans and 90% or more of voting Americans are to some degree either Democrats or Republicans.

Changes in Partisanship (Exhibits D and E). While the extent of partisanship in the electorate has generally been quite high, it has varied. No characteristic in American politics has been as thoroughly probed and tracked as party identification. That rich line of research indicates partisanship was quite strong in the 1950s and through the mid-1960s, declined beginning in the early 1970s, and rebounded beginning in the mid-1980s.[5] In the presidential election years from 1952 to 1964, sometimes called "the golden age of partisanship," typically about 36% of ANES respondents called themselves strong Democrats or strong Republicans. In the period of party decline or dealignment from 1968 to 1980, strong party identifiers dropped to about 26%. In the most recent four elections (2000 to 2012), the ranks of strong party identifiers increased to about 33%.

Party Polarization in Government (Exhibits F and G). The polarization of the parties in government (more specifically in Congress) and its increase since the 1980s was established in chapter 1. Poole and Rosenthal's DW-NOMINATE roll-call scores for the parties in Congress tell the story.[6] The parties were quite heterogeneous and relatively unpolarized from the late 1920s to the mid-1980s. Since then, they have become more highly polarized. Poole and Rosenthal report that "polarization in the House and Senate is now at the highest level since the end of Reconstruction."[7]

Changes in Voter Turnout (Exhibits H and I). Like partisanship, turnout in American politics since 1950 declined and then rebounded. Measured as the percentage of the voting eligible population who voted for president, turnout was relatively high in the 1950s and 1960s, declined in the 1970s and 1980s, and then increased to nearly its previous levels in the 2000s.[8] The mean turnout in the five presidential elections from 1952 to 1968 was 62%, never dropping below 60%. Turnout then dropped about five percentage points in 1972 to about 56% and bottomed out in 1996 at 52%. Except for the 58% turnout in the 1992 election, often attributed to the unusual showing of third party candidate Ross Perot, turnout never exceeded 56% in this period. Over the eight presidential elections from 1972 to 2000, the mean turnout was 55%. Since then, turnout levels have rebounded to nearly their prior levels. In the three presidential elections since 2000, according to data obtained from Michael McDonald's United States Election Project, turnout averaged 60% of the eligible population.[9]

Changes in Split-Ticket Voting (Exhibits J and K). Split-ticket voting followed a similar (but inverted) pattern to that of voter turnout and partisanship. Measured as the percentage of major party presidential voters who voted for a different party's candidate in House elections, ticket-splitting was low in the 1950s and 1960s. According to ANES data, the mean percentage of major party presidential voters who split their tickets in the five elections from 1952 to 1968 was 14%. Split-ticket voting then increased substantially in the 1970s and 1980s. In the five presidential elections from 1972 to 1988, this doubled to an average of 28%. Split-ticket voting has declined to nearly its previous levels in elections since then. In the six elections from 1992 to 2012, split-ticket voting averaged 17%. In 2012, it was only 10%. Overall, from 1952 to 2012, split-ticket voting levels increased quite a bit and then declined quite a bit.[10]

The Arguments. With these 11 facts about modern American politics now introduced into evidence, they will be used to construct arguments that are either consistent with or inconsistent with different claims about polarization in the public. A highly polarized public should be expected to react to some political developments differently than a weakly polarized or centrist public. If the parties have changed in ways that a highly polarized or a weakly polarized public likes or dislikes, then this approval or disapproval should be reflected in a number of ways by the public (stronger or weaker partisanship, higher or lower turnout, more or less ticket-splitting). Those approving of how the parties have changed should be more likely to find one of them worthy of a strong identification. They should also find turning out to vote for one of them worthwhile and supporting across-the-board rather than casting a split-ticket. Disapproval for party changes should have the opposite effects on partisanship, turnout, and ticket-splitting. Are the uncontested facts about American politics consistent with a public that is highly polarized or with one that is largely centrist?

THE ARITHMETIC OF POLARIZATION

The first circumstantial evidence argument is based on the polarization of the parties in the electorate (exhibit A) and the pervasiveness of partisanship (exhibit C). The question posed from these facts is this: if the parties in the electorate are now highly polarized (or sorted) and if virtually all Americans are partisans, how can the public itself not be highly polarized? The answer is that they cannot be. If the two premises are true, *it is logically impossible for the public not to be highly polarized.* Given the two conditions, the public must be polarized at least to the same extent as the parties in the electorate are polarized.[11] There may be some slippage, owing to the small percentage of independents, but the parties encompassing nearly the entirety of the public cannot be highly polarized without the public also being polarized to nearly the same extent. The arithmetic of polarization does not add up any other way.

After simplifying the issue for the moment by setting aside polarization's interval nature, there are four hypothetical conditions of party polarization (or any other second-order or group polarization)

TABLE 5.2. FOUR HYPOTHETICAL SCENARIOS OF PUBLIC AND PARTY POLARIZATION

Polarization Levels		*Public Polarization*	
		High	Low
Party Polarization (aka Sorting)	High	Possible	Impossible
	Low	Possible	Possible

Note: This assumes that the entire public is divided between the two parties.

and public polarization. These are displayed in table 5.2. It is possible for both the parties and the public to be highly polarized (upper left cell) or for both the parties and the public to be relatively unpolarized (lower right cell). It is also possible for the public to be highly polarized while the parties are relatively unpolarized (lower left cell). Finally, and this is the scenario of principal interest, the fourth scenario would have the parties being highly polarized but not the public (upper right cell). When the public is entirely composed of partisans, and it is close to that (assuming the classification of "leaners" as partisans is appropriate), this scenario is an impossibility. The parties can be less polarized than the public, but the opposite is not possible, at least not possible when the public is composed entirely of partisans.

Let's walk through the argument that the parties cannot be highly polarized without the public itself being highly polarized—when the public is completely partisan.[12] If the public is composed almost entirely of partisans and the partisans in the two parties differ to the degree that the parties are considered highly polarized (or sorted), then the overall public which is equivalent to the combination of the two groups of partisans also must be highly polarized using the same standards applied to the two groups of partisans. The parties in the electorate can only divide up what is in the public to divide up. The parties can reflect the polarization in the public well or they can reflect it poorly, but the parties cannot reflect something that is not in the public to begin with. The amount of polarization in the public restricts the amount of polarization that is possible between the parties.

The logic of this is displayed in the three panels of figure 5.1. The first panel represents a public composed of 30% liberals, 40% moderates, and 30% conservatives. The second panel divides this public into two fairly homogeneous and polarized parties of equal size. All of liberals and half the moderates are in a left-dominated (60% to 40% liberal to moderate division) Democratic Party. All of the conservatives and half the moderates are in a right-dominated Republican Party. If these parties are polarized, and they reflect numbers not too far off reality (high on the liberal side and low on the conservative side, but close to the count of current moderates), then the public (panel A) is polarized. The only difference is the organization of the ideologues into the parties. Take down the party boxes and we are dealing with the same people and their same political differences. Applying the same standards, if the parties in panel B are highly polarized, the public in panel A is polarized.

The association between party polarization and the polarization of the general public is not a two-way street. The public must be polarized if the parties are, but the polarization of the public does not depend on the polarization of the parties. As a comparison of panels A and C indicate, the parties may be quite unpolarized within a highly polarized public. The parties in panel C, in sharp contrast to those in panel B, are entirely unpolarized. The two parties in panel C have the identical mix of ideological perspectives. Rather than the differences in the public being organized *between* the homogeneous parties of panel B, they are organized *within* the heterogeneous parties of panel C. The ideological sorting or realignment that would take place in moving from the heterogeneous parties of panel C to the party polarization of the more homogeneous parties of panel B does not require an *increase* in public polarization (the general distribution of ideologies is the same in each panel) but it does require that the public be highly polarized. Ideological differences cannot be sorted into separate parties (or by any other set of groups) unless they first exist in the general public. Party polarization cannot be constructed out of thin air. If the public of panel A were unpolarized, the party polarization of panel B could not exist. There would not be enough people with conflicting views to organize into two polarized parties. As the punch line to an old Maine joke goes: "you can't get there from here."[13]

Panel A: The Public

L	L	L	M	M	M	M	C	C	C
L	L	L	M	M	M	M	C	C	C
L	L	L	M	M	M	M	C	C	C
L	L	L	M	M	M	M	C	C	C
L	L	L	M	M	M	M	C	C	C
L	L	L	M	M	M	M	C	C	C
L	L	L	M	M	M	M	C	C	C
L	L	L	M	M	M	M	C	C	C
L	L	L	M	M	M	M	C	C	C
L	L	L	M	M	M	M	C	C	C

Panel B: Highly Polarized Parties

Democrats   Republicans

L	L	L	M	M	M	M	C	C	C
L	L	L	M	M	M	M	C	C	C
L	L	L	M	M	M	M	C	C	C
L	L	L	M	M	M	M	C	C	C
L	L	L	M	M	M	M	C	C	C
L	L	L	M	M	M	M	C	C	C
L	L	L	M	M	M	M	C	C	C
L	L	L	M	M	M	M	C	C	C
L	L	L	M	M	M	M	C	C	C
L	L	L	M	M	M	M	C	C	C

Panel C: Unpolarized Parties

Democrats

L	L	L	M	M	M	M	C	C	C
L	L	L	M	M	M	M	C	C	C
L	L	L	M	M	M	M	C	C	C
L	L	L	M	M	M	M	C	C	C
L	L	L	M	M	M	M	C	C	C
L	L	L	M	M	M	M	C	C	C
L	L	L	M	M	M	M	C	C	C
L	L	L	M	M	M	M	C	C	C
L	L	L	M	M	M	M	C	C	C
L	L	L	M	M	M	M	C	C	C

Republicans

Figure 5.1. The public polarization limits on party polarization.

Note: Distribution of ideologies: 30% liberal (L), 40% moderate (M), 30% conservative (C).

The arithmetic of polarization should settle the issue about whether Americans are highly polarized, but there is more circumstantial evidence to consider.[14] While the arithmetic of polarization analysis revolves around party polarization *in the electorate* (as well as the near-completeness of the public's partisanship), at the center of the next body of evidence is the increased polarization of the parties *in government*.

THE EFFECTS OF MORE POLARIZED PARTIES

The most important change in modern American politics has been the substantial increase in the polarization of the parties in government (exhibits F and G). From at least the 1930s to the late 1970s, the parties in Congress were ideologically heterogeneous and relatively unpolarized. This often gave rise to assembling a legislatively success-ful "conservative coalition" of Republicans and Southern Democrats. Since the early 1980s, this has changed dramatically. The parties have become much more polarized. Party polarization has grown so great that it has been judged to be "at the highest level since the end of Reconstruction."[15] One would reasonably expect this change in party polarization would cause voters to react quite differently toward the parties and their candidates. A predominantly moderate public would be expected to react one way to this change and a highly po-larized public would be expected to react quite differently.

An increase in the polarization of the parties in government, mov-ing from very heterogeneous moderated parties to more ideologically unified parties, would be generally welcomed by a highly polarized public, but would make a moderate public feel disconnected and poorly represented by either of the parties. This should have import-ant observable political consequences. Three of the consequences of changing party polarization have been itemized among the exhibits: changes in turnout, in partisanship, and in split-ticket voting.

It is important to note at this point that this is not to suggest that anyone necessarily likes polarization itself, either in the public or between the parties. Most Americans, whether they are moderates, liberals, conservatives, or something else, do not like polarization. Some people like a good argument, but many more are made quite uncomfortable by conflict. Moreover, everyone would prefer for others to agree with them as much as possible. Welcoming party polarization is not about the polarization and the conflict it generates, but about having a party that represents your views to your satisfaction, whether you are on the right or the left.[16] Ideologically homogeneous polarized parties do this more frequently for liberals and conservatives. More moderate heterogeneous parties better reflect the views of centrists. In terms of the representation of their political perspectives, the move from heterogeneous to more homogeneous parties, essentially from less polarized to more polarized parties, should please liberals and conservatives and displease moderates.

The well-established premise that the parties in government are highly polarized and the three possible macropolitical reactions to it (changes in turnout, partisanship, and ticket-splitting) are the basis for a battery of three tests of opposing claims about public polarization: that the public is largely moderate or that it is highly polarized. In general terms, given that the parties in government have become considerably more polarized, are changes in turnout rates, in the strength of partisanship, and in split-ticket voting rates more consistent with the public being highly polarized or with the public being substantially centrist? Which piece best fits the puzzle of American politics?

The form of the argument is this: if two premises are true, one regarding the increased polarization of the parties in government and a second involving the polarization of the public (or lack thereof), then we should expect to observe changes in the political behavior or attitudes of the public (turnout, partisanship, or split-ticket voting) in response to the increased polarization of the parties.[17] If the expected change in the public's behavior or attitudes is observed, then it is circumstantial evidence that the premise regarding the public's polarization is true (barring something else having intervened). However, if the expected change in the public's behavior or attitudes is not observed or there is change in the direction opposite to that expected, then something is wrong. Either one or both of the premises were untrue, something else intervened, or there was an error in the observation of the expected behavior or attitudes. The change in party polarization in government is very well documented, as are the changes in turnout, partisanship, and split-ticket voting and, while there are a great many possible influences on turnout, partisanship, and ticket-splitting, it seems improbable that any of these would have the same impact on all three developments at the same time.[18] Thus, it would appear that any failure to observe the expected changes in public behaviors and attitudes must be considered as circumstantial evidence that the premise regarding public polarization was false. That is the general logical structure of the arguments. Now to the specifics.

Assuming a Moderate Public

What if it were true that the American public was and remains largely unpolarized? How would such a moderate public respond to the substantially more polarized political parties? In general terms, a largely moderate public would be expected to respond poorly to political parties that abandoned the political center to adopt more ideologically non-centrist positions. The views of moderates would not be very well represented either by a predominantly liberal party or by a predominantly conservative party. They might be expected to register their displeasure with the offered choices in one or more of three ways.

First, a moderate public facing the choice between candidates of more polarized parties might be expected to turn out to vote at lower rates than it had. Voting turnout is affected by a great many factors, but one important factor is how well potential voters think their views will be represented by one of the candidates or parties. In an individual-level study of voting and non-voting, John Zipp concluded that "if one has a clear choice among the candidates (is not indifferent) and one's policy preferences are close to at least one candidate (one is not alienated), one is much more likely to vote."[19] Adams, Dow, and Merrill and, more recently, Leighley and Nagler confirm these alienation and indifference effects on turnout in later elections.[20] If the parties have moved out to the wings of the ideological spectrum while the public has remained in the middle, fewer people should find themselves close enough to either party to make it worth their while to turn out to vote.

Second, if the public is moderate and the parties have gravitated to more ideologically distinct positions, fewer should maintain strong bonds to the parties. As with turnout, psychological identifications with either of the parties should reflect, in no small part, how well people think a party represents their views. As party policies drift further to each end of the spectrum, many in the political center might feel disconnected from the parties.[21] With partisanship strongly affected by the experience voters have with the parties, this should take a toll on the party identifications and loyalty of moderates.[22] The number professing strong party identifications should decline.

Third, if the public is moderate and if the ideological distance between the parties' policies has grown, there is good reason to suspect that moderates might attempt to achieve more centrist policies by attempting to balance Democrats and Republicans in government against each other, encouraging them to compromise. The logic of policy-balancing voting is to cast a split-ticket in the hopes that policies are neither as liberal as liberal Democrats might like nor as conservative as conservative Republicans would favor.[23] As the parties in government move further to each ideological end of the spectrum, the appeal of the policy-balancing argument should increase with moderates. In short, a moderate public and increasingly polarized parties in government should add up to increased split-ticket voting.

Assuming a Highly Polarized Public

What changes should be expected from the substantially increased polarization of the political parties in government *if* the public was and remains highly polarized or grew even more polarized? In contrast to a predominantly moderate public, a highly polarized public should welcome more ideologically coherent parties. A highly polarized electorate, even if not measuring up to the polarization levels of elites (recall McClosky and random measurement errors in surveys), would be dissatisfied with tweedledum and tweedledee centrist parties, but might work up some enthusiasm for parties that reflected their outlooks and opposed the other party's contrary views. As with a moderate public, these reactions should be reflected in changes in turnout, partisanship, and split-ticket voting. The expected changes in these political behaviors and attitudes are diametrically opposite to those expected from a moderate public.

Increased polarization of the parties in government should cause a highly polarized electorate to turn out to vote at a higher rate, to identify more strongly with a party, and to be less inclined to split their tickets. Turnout in a highly polarized public should increase with parties offering more polarized alternatives. More potential voters in a polarized electorate should find one of the parties to be close enough to their views that it is worth the effort to support it with their votes. Moderate parties, on the other hand, would leave some liberals and some conservatives on the sidelines feeling that neither party truly represented their views or was vote-worthy. The logic behind increased partisanship is similar. Liberals and conservatives may find it difficult to commit strongly to pale liberal and pale conservative parties, but this reticence should change, with liberal and conservative parties expressing more consistently strong convictions. Finally, in the old days of heterogeneous parties, liberals and conservatives would be more likely to find some stray conservative Democratic candidates and liberal Republican candidates to support at the congressional level, thus producing split-tickets. With more polarized parties offering more consistently liberal Democratic and conservative Republican candidate options, liberals and conservatives in the electorate should have less reason to stray from a straight party vote and ticket-splitting should decline.

Which Piece Fits the Puzzle?

The unquestionable increase in the polarization of the parties in government from the 1970s to the 2010s should have produced one set of changes in turnout, partisanship, and ticket-splitting from a moderate public and just the opposite from a highly polarized public.[24] A moderate public would have been displeased by the change. A polarized public would have been pleased. Each would have reacted accordingly. Are the changes in turnout, partisanship, and ticket-splitting in the face of increasingly polarized parties those of a largely moderate public or of a highly polarized public? Which view of the electorate fits with the other pieces of the American political puzzle?

In each of the three key tests of public reactions (turnout, partisanship, and ticket-splitting) the public reacted in ways *expected of a highly polarized public* and *precisely opposite to what would be expected of a largely moderate public*. Table 5.3 summarizes the three tests for the two public polarization scenarios. First, the observed increase in turnout (exhibit H) was expected from a highly polarized electorate and not from a moderate electorate. In fact, turnout was expected

TABLE 5.3. SIX TESTS OF PUBLIC POLARIZATION USING CIRCUMSTANTIAL EVIDENCE, 1970S–2010S

Response to the Polarization (Sorting) of the Parties in Government				
Behavior or Attitude Response to Changed Party Polarization	*Expected* Change from 1970s to 2010s If the Public Were:		*Actual* Change	Was the Change Consistent with a Highly Polarized Public or a Relatively Unpolarized Public?
	Substantially Moderate, Relatively Unpolarized	Substantially Ideological, Highly Polarized		
Strength of Partisanship	Lower	Higher	Higher	Highly Polarized
Voter Turnout	Lower	Higher	Higher	Highly Polarized
Split-Ticket Voting	Higher	Lower	Lower	Highly Polarized

to decline in a moderate electorate. Second, the observed increase in partisanship (exhibit D) was expected from a highly polarized electorate and not from a moderate electorate. In fact, partisanship was expected to decline in a moderate electorate. Finally, the observed decline in the rate of split-ticket voting (exhibit J) was expected from a highly polarized electorate and not from a moderate electorate. In fact, split-ticket voting rates were expected to increase in a moderate electorate.[25]

In each instance, the electorate reacted as though it were highly polarized, and in each instance it not only failed to react as a moderate public would have been expected to have reacted, but reacted in precisely the opposite way. There were declines when increases were expected. Increases when declines were expected. This circumstantial evidence, all six tests, is unequivocally consistent with the public being highly polarized and inconsistent with the claim that the public was and remains largely centrist.[26] Judging by how they have reacted to the greater polarization of the parties in government, even with the general aversion to the sharper conflict this entails, Americans seem more pleased than displeased with the change. More have found a party that they can identify with strongly, that is worth turning out to vote for, and that is worthy of a straight ticket ballot.

More of the Puzzle Solved

Evidence of any sort becomes more credible if it fits with facts or helps explain phenomena beyond that of immediate interest, if it fits an even bigger picture. The circumstantial evidence of turnout, partisanship, split-ticket voting, and polarization of the parties in government may help to explain American politics beyond the question of public polarization levels since the 1970s. It also may explain *when* the public became highly polarized, why partisanship and turnout declined in the 1970s, and why split-ticket voting increased at about the same time.

Based on the well-established increase in the polarization of the parties in government that began in the late 1980s, we were able to deduce from the electorate's increase in turnout and partisanship and its decrease in ticket-splitting that the public is highly polarized. The public is more in sync with the newly polarized parties. Turnout and partisanship rose and split-ticket voting declined. However, prior to these post-1970s changes, these three barometers of satisfaction with the parties had moved in the opposite direction. From the 1950s and 1960s to the 1970s and 1980s, turnout dropped (exhibit I), partisanship declined or dealigned (exhibit E), and split-ticket voting nearly doubled (exhibit K). Throughout this period, the parties in government remained ideologically heterogeneous, largely unpolarized. So if there was no change in the party polarization, what precipitated the consistent change in all three of our barometers: turnout, partisanship, and split-ticket voting?

Following the rationales used to evaluate this circumstantial evidence for our current politics, the movements in each of the three barometers suggest that the public in the 1950s and 1960s had been more in sync with the parties than it was in the 1970s and 1980s. The party polarization in government did not change in this period, so the polarization of the public must have changed. A fairly moderate public of the 1950s and into the mid-1960s appreciated the heterogeneous parties of that era. However, by the late 1960s and early 1970s, the public had become much more polarized—though its parties had not kept pace. There is an abundance of anecdotal evidence to this effect, some of which is recounted in chapter 2. But here we have some hard evidence, albeit circumstantial. Convulsed by Vietnam, a civil rights movement, a feminist movement, and an expansive culture war of sorts, the moderate post–World War II public of the 1950s morphed into the contentious and more polarized public of the late 1960s. Many in this more polarized public reacted as though they felt the moderate parties of the day no longer represented them very well. The ranks of independents and non-voters grew (though neither by as much as was thought at the time) and many Americans more freely defected from their parties in casting their congressional and presidential votes.

THE DEVELOPMENT OF POLARIZATION

The evidence just presented is circumstantial, but it should carry a great deal of weight. Its elements (the exhibits) are all highly confirmed by a great deal of prior independent research. While every measure is imperfect, few social science measures have been more thoroughly vetted than those used to measure turnout, partisanship, and split-ticket voting. Whatever flaws might remain in these at the individual level should be of less concern when they are *aggregated* as they are here, and even less of a concern when the *changes* in their aggregate levels are examined, as they generally are here. The measure of the polarization of the parties in government (Congress) also has been very carefully crafted and examined. Though there are some concerns about its comparability over time (discussed more fully in chapter 7), it and alternative congressional ideology measures agree that the parties in government have become more polarized.

Adding to the credibility of this circumstantial evidence is that one parsimonious explanation, the correspondence or lack of correspondence between polarization in the public and polarization of the parties, in government as well as in the public, takes us a long way toward explaining changes in turnout, in partisanship, and in ticket-splitting. It does so not only for recent times (the 2000s), but for the 1970s as well. The polarization explanations of turnout, partisanship, and ticket-splitting could not be any simpler. Changes in the correspondence of party and public polarization caused appropriate changes in each of these behaviors and attitudes. In turn, these changes help us pin down what we were not sure about—the degree to which the public was polarized.

This is not to suggest that other factors did not affect changes in turnout, in partisanship, and in rates of ticket-splitting. They unquestionably did. Among these other possible influences are: demographic changes in the electorate (the age effects of the baby boom generation and the increase in ethnic and racial minorities), the appeals of presidential candidates and the records of presidential performance, rule changes (the Twenty-Sixth Amendment to the U.S. Constitution, which extended the suffrage to those over 18 years of age, and the proliferation of presidential primaries leading to enhanced powers for party activists), the flood of money into campaigns, and the many changes in communication technologies. All of these and other factors probably mattered separately to changes in turnout, partisanship, and ticket-splitting, but a single common cause is likely to have been the driving force behind the three key changes. The strong common cause is the degree to which the parties reflected the extent of polarization in the public—*the correspondence of polarization between the parties and polarization within the public*. The changes in turnout, in partisanship, and in ticket-splitting when combined with our knowledge of how polarization of the parties in government changed allow us to track the development of the public's polarization. The puzzle has come together.

Three Stages

The circumstantial evidence strongly suggests that the development of polarization in American politics since the 1950s proceeded in three stages. The essential aspects of these and their approximate years are presented in table 5.4. The dates associated with the stages are approximate since the transitions developed over time. Changes did not happen either to the parties or to the public overnight and, as chapter 1 reminds us, polarization is a matter of degree, and other influences may have affected its development as well.

The first stage of polarization in modern American politics is the post–World War II period up through the mid-1960s, prior to the tumult of the Vietnam War protests and the growth of the associated counterculture of the late 1960s. Having come through the Great

TABLE 5.4. THE DEVELOPMENT OF POLARIZATION IN AMERICAN POLITICS SINCE 1950

Polarization Level	Period of Polarization Development		
	1950–1964	1968–1988	1994–Present
Parties in Government	Relatively Unpolarized	Relatively Unpolarized	Highly Polarized
General Public	Relatively Unpolarized	Fairly Well Polarized	Highly Polarized

Note: The designated times are approximate. Polarization is a matter of degree and changes in it take place gradually. As such, the designation of times and levels of polarization are used here to simplify developments.

Depression, World War II, and then the Korean War and brought together by the Cold War with the Soviets, Americans were fairly well unified and wary of ideologies. They wanted what President Warren Harding decades earlier had called "a return to normalcy." They got that with President Eisenhower. There were controversies: Senator Joseph McCarthy's hunt for domestic communists and his excesses in that pursuit, a growing civil rights movement, and other differences, but it was generally a period of political calm, consolidation, and a return to normal life. V. O. Key summarized it nicely: "In the 1950's, the era of Eisenhower, a period marked by few dramatic acts of executive initiative in domestic politics, a mixture of consensus and indifference about political issues seemed far more characteristic of the population than did conflict."[27] Americans were relatively unpolarized and so were their parties. Turnout was fairly high, many identified strongly with one of the political parties, and most voters cast straight party-line ballots.

All that gave way to the turbulence of the mid- to late 1960s. Vietnam and war protests, civil unrest and rioting in the cities, marches and rallies, showdowns over racial integration, the hippies versus the hard-hats, the assassinations of the Reverend Martin Luther King, Jr. and Senator Bobby Kennedy, the debacle of the 1968 Democratic convention in Chicago, the shootings at Kent State and Jackson State, the list goes on. It was a jolt and many subsequently moved to the left and others to the right. As destabilizing as these events were, they were magnified further by demographics. The post–World War II baby boom generation came of political age. They had not been through the galvanizing experiences of the Great Depression and World War II. The New Left and the counterculture bloomed and set off a backlash. The public became much more polarized.[28] Their parties, however, remained the mix they had been for many decades. There were Rockefeller Republicans and Goldwater and later Reagan Republicans. Democrats came in various stripes, from McGovernites on the left to Alabama Governor George Wallace's Southern Democratic segregationists.[29] The result of this disconnection between public and party polarization was that turnout dipped, partisanship declined somewhat, and split-ticket voting soared.

The gradual or staggered realignment of the parties, with many southern conservative Democrats in Congress being replaced with southern conservative Republicans, and non-southern liberal Republicans being replaced by non-southern liberal Democrats, brought the polarization of the parties in government into line with the public's polarization. The process took a long time and faced many obstacles (more on this in the next chapter), but the result was a more coherent, if sometimes dysfunctional, polarized political system. The public appeared more placid, however this was not because the divisions of the 1960s had subsided but because those divisions were now represented. There was a new normal. Turnout increased, the ranks of strong party identifiers rose while "pure" independents declined, and fewer voters split their tickets.

These three stages in the development of polarization correspond quite closely to the findings of three landmark studies of American voting behavior. The electorate of the late 1950s was portrayed in the seminal *The American Voter* as highly partisan, but non-ideological and holding uncorrelated issue attitudes.[30] *The Changing American Voter* found a less partisan but more ideological electorate in the 1970s.[31] Finally, *The American Voter Revisited* portrayed an electorate in the twenty-first century that was at once more partisan than it had been in the 1970s and more ideological than it had been in the 1950s.[32]

Bottom-Up Polarization

This account of the development of polarization in three stages contradicts the conventional wisdom that political change is a top-down process, that the mass public changes only in response to changes at the leadership level.[33] This was not the case throughout more than the last half century of American history. The circumstantial evidence as well as the direct evidence indicate that the polarization of the public *preceded* the polarization of the parties in government (elite polarization).

The reasons for this bottom-up rather than top-down sequence of change will be explored at greater length in the following chapters, but we cannot leave this conclusion without briefly speculating on why and how the public was ahead of party leaders in becoming more polarized. In this instance, the views of the parties in government lagged behind those in the public for three reasons. First, elected party leaders had a vested interest in staying elected by preserving the status quo and they were able to preserve the status quo and slow the pace of change by using their considerable advantages of incumbency. Second, for historical reasons dating back to the Civil War and Reconstruction, there was no viable Republican Party in the South. Many conservative white Southerners were willing and able to vote for Republican presidential candidates, but the absence or weakness of state and local Republican Party organizations in the region prevented or inhibited that carrying over to congressional voting—leaving many southern conservative Democrats in office into the 1980s and early 1990s. Finally, though voters are less attentive to politics than leaders and are thus sometimes less easily moved, this is offset by the fact that voters are also generally less burdened by prior partisan commitments. If moved to change, and that does not come easily or often, voters can change without having to shed quite as much baggage.

REVIEWING THE EVIDENCE

Having examined in chapter 3 the direct evidence of polarization drawn from self-declared ideological orientations, in chapter 4 the direct evidence drawn from issue attitudes, and now the several different kinds of indirect or circumstantial evidence of polarization, it is time to pull these findings together to determine what the totality of the evidence indicates about the theories of polarization. Which macro-level polarization theories are supported by these findings and which are not? How polarized is the electorate and how has this changed over time? Since nearly all prior research on the polarization of the public has addressed the change question rather than the level question, we address the change question first.

The Change Question

What evidence indicates that the public has become more polarized in recent decades and what evidence indicates that there has been no appreciable change in polarization? The evidence that there has been no change in polarization is limited to the observed lack of a general increase in the standard deviations of the public's attitudes on issue scales. Extreme positions on issues such as the two exemplar issues examined in chapter 4 are no more frequent in recent times than they had been. This comports with the DiMaggio team's and Fiorina team's findings. Despite the many serious problems with issue attitude data, this has served as the foundational evidence that polarization in the public has not grown.

On the other side of the ledger, the ideology evidence drawn from five different data series finds that polarization in the public has grown significantly since the early 1970s. Though the dispersion of issue attitudes has generally not increased, the sorting or correlations among those opinions has increased a good deal. This comports with the findings of Abramowitz and Saunders.[34] The evidence of the growth of issue polarization in recent decades is in the sorting of people into coalitions of aligned issue preferences rather than the adoption of more extreme issue attitudes. Moreover, the correlations of issue attitudes and ideological orientations indicate that they generally divide the nation along the same lines. Finally, though much of the circumstantial evidence has not spoken to the question of a change in polarization, the extension of that evidence to the pre-1970s period does speak to it. It indicates that there was a significant change in the polarization of the public in the late 1960s and early 1970s, before much of the direct evidence considered here was available.

Has the public become more polarized in recent decades? Yes. The only evidence to the contrary is that opinions on policy issues have not become more extreme. This should be considered in light of the various problems with issue attitude data; but, more importantly, the greater overlap of attitudes on different issues provides positive evidence of greater polarization.

All of the other evidence regarding polarization change indicates that the public has grown more polarized.

The Level Question

Lacking benchmarks by which to determine polarization levels, previous research sidestepped the issue of whether polarization levels should be considered high or low (though they frequently slid into making claims about it). Several polarization benchmarks were established in chapters 3 and 4. In considering both the ideology and issue evidence, benchmarks of deviations from the ultimate levels of polarization and moderation were established and these were adjusted for the reality of random measurement errors. In the consideration of circumstantial evidence, implicit benchmarks were established using the consensus about party polarization, both in the electorate and between the parties. These benchmarks provided leverage to assess whether current levels of polarization in the public are high or whether the public is largely moderate.

What did the evidence indicate about the current level of polarization in the public? All of the evidence examined indicates that Americans are now highly polarized. In terms of ideologues compared to moderates, the American public looks more like a perfectly polarized public than a perfectly moderate public. More precisely, the benchmark analysis of ideological identifications indicates that Americans are approximately two-thirds to three-quarters of the way between a nonpolarized nation and a completely polarized nation. Though the importance of the sorting of issue attitudes (as opposed to the dispersion of attitudes on isolated issues) complicates the analysis of issue attitude polarization, it essentially corroborates the ideology findings. All of the circumstantial evidence also indicates a highly polarized public. Since an overwhelming number of Americans are partisans, the public must be considered highly polarized if the parties in the electorate are considered highly polarized. With the parties in government becoming more polarized, changes in turnout, in partisanship, and in ticket-splitting were in each instance the reactions expected of a highly polarized public and diametrically opposite to those expected of a generally moderate public.

In short, the American public is quite highly polarized. Moreover, these findings are about the polarization of the entire public, not just the most politically engaged portion of it. The entire public includes voters and people who might have seriously thought about voting, as well as those who are chronically nonpolitical. The latter two groups are commonly underrepresented in all surveys, but they are included (except in the Exit Polls that were part of the evidence in chapter 3). If we were considering the polarization of actual voters and those who stood some realistic prospects of voting, estimated polarization levels would be even higher.

Polarization in America has reached the point that its effects go beyond people holding sharply divergent political views. Many on both sides now find it difficult to fathom how reasonably intelligent people can reside at the other end of the ideological spectrum.[35] Those on the other side are often dismissed as insincere, misinformed, stupid, delusional, or worse. Their views are derided as impervious to evidence and immune to reason. This goes both ways. Many liberals vilify conservatives and many conservatives disparage liberals. With opponents thought to be living in their own parallel and inferior universe, it is easy to see why exchanges often become uncivil or fruitless and why many choose to avoid discussions across the ideological divide. Polarization levels are high, often uncomfortably high.

Revisiting the Theories

In chapter 2, three theories of public polarization were discussed: emerging polarization, no polarization, and revealed polarization. To review, the main thrust of the emerging polarization theory is that polarization has increased. The no polarization theory claims that the public was not highly polarized and remains substantially moderate. The revealed polarization theory contends that the public has long been highly polarized and that this had been masked by the lack of ideological clarity between the previously less polarized parties.

Which of these theories is supported by the evidence? Two are strongly supported: the emerging polarization and the revealed polarization theories. The public has been polarized since the late 1960s, polarization of the public became more clearly evident with the polarization of the parties, and the public's polarization increased further in recent decades as the polarized parties organized along more clearly ideological lines. The evidence does not support the contention that the public is substantially moderate and that polarization is an illusion. The accumulated evidence indicates that Americans are highly polarized.

The American public was fairly polarized in the 1970s and became more so over the last four decades. These findings do not rest solely on the self-reported ideology evidence examined in chapter 3, or solely on the evidence of more highly correlated issue preferences discussed in chapter 4, or even on the battery of deductive tests of varied circumstantial evidence reviewed in this chapter. Each in their separate and very different ways was convincing, but it is the fact they all arrived at the same conclusion that is ultimately the most compelling basis for the polarization findings. Together, they are the clincher.

There have always been divisions in American politics. In the past, these many conflicts have divided the nation in many different ways. This pluralistic arrangement generally dampened, a bit, the intensity of any single conflict. This has changed. The divisions that in the past had divided the nation in different ways have increasingly come to divide the nation in the same way. Ideological perspectives, preferences on a range of issues, and partisanship have come together—not perfectly, but substantially—to create a highly polarized political system.

PART THREE

THE POLARIZED PARTIES

CHAPTER 6

WHY ARE THE PARTIES MORE POLARIZED?

The Times They Are a-Changin'

—Bob Dylan[1]

Americans are highly polarized and so are their political parties. Differences between rank-and-file Democrats and Republicans are great and differences between the parties' leaders are even greater. In Congress, according to an analysis of roll-call voting from 2005 to 2012, every Democrat was to the political left of every Republican.[2] In the electorate, according to the 2012 ANES, among Democratic party identifiers, liberals outnumbered conservatives by 3.5 to 1 (45% liberals to 13% conservatives). Among Republican party identifiers, conservatives outnumbered liberals by more than 16 to 1 (70% conservatives to 4% liberals). Republicans were seven times more likely than Democrats to support the activist-conservative Tea Party movement (50% to 7%). At both levels, ideological differences between the parties are now huge.[3]

This was not always the case. The parties in government had been characterized as insufficiently distinct to provide voters with a real and accountable choice, the possibility of a responsible party government.[4] The broad-based parties were ideologically blurry from at least the 1930s to the 1980s. In the electorate, the parties were broad and overlapping coalitions, each spanning much of the ideological spectrum.

Why did this change? How did the parties become more polarized? Although the full answer to this question is complicated, involving the reasons why the parties previously had not been highly polarized, the short answer is that the parties became more polarized because of a staggered partisan realignment that began in the 1960s and ended in the 1990s, and because the public that the parties represent became more polarized.[5] Most of this chapter is devoted to recounting the story and presenting the evidence of the staggered realignment and the impact of the public's increased polarization, but several other explanations for increased party polarization have also been raised. So, before moving on to the realignment and public polarization explanations of increased party polarization, these alternative or competing explanations should be discussed and the reasons for my setting them aside explained.

WHAT DIDN'T POLARIZE THE PARTIES

Aside from the realignment and public polarization explanations, five major explanations for increased party polarization have been suggested. The theories contend that the increase in party polarization can be traced to: (1) more effective partisan gerrymandering, (2) increasing income inequality, (3) ideologically motivated party activists, (4) an ideologically driven political media, and (5) polarizing presidents. Arguments and evidence have been marshaled for and against each of these theories elsewhere. Without rehashing each case, the reasons are reviewed for concluding that each of these theories falls short of being the *principal* reason why party polarization in both government and the electorate increased since the 1980s.

Gerrymandering

The gerrymandering explanation of increased party polarization is that the redistricting process has become so technologically advanced that incumbents are more securely protected in districts redrawn to keep them in office, thwarting any serious challenge by the opposition. Electorally secure incumbents are then free to vote as they wish. This generally allows more ideologically extreme voting. Making general elections perfunctory events also has the effect of elevating the importance of primaries. This pushes representatives to further extremes to preempt being outflanked within their own party. The Tea Party, in particular, has gained leverage from threatening incumbents with being "primaried" or challenged for renomination by ideological purists in the party.

The major problem with the gerrymandering explanation of increased party polarization is that it offers only an explanation of increased polarization in the U.S. House. It does not account for the increased polarization in the Senate, in other offices (federal and state), or among partisans in the electorate. Party polarization is a much broader phenomenon than gerrymandered redistricting could possibly explain. For this and other reasons, gerrymandering is clearly not the driving force behind the growth of party polarization.[6]

Income Inequality

For decades now, the rich in America have been getting richer and the poor poorer.[7] Nolan McCarty, Keith Poole, and Howard Rosenthal argue that this increasing income inequality is behind increasingly polarized parties.[8] Economics are a potent political force. To the extent that economic self-interests of the "haves" and "have nots" diverge, each may turn to the party they feel best defends their interests—however, the evidence indicates this has not increased party polarization.

Whether some have different views about which party best serves their economic interests, or see those interests differently, or hold broader principles overriding economic self-interests, or are concerned about matters beyond their economic self-interests, the empirical associations of incomes, ideological perspectives, and partisanship are weaker than often presumed. As Bryan Dettrey and I have demonstrated, "even with the increased levels of income inequality, there is a good deal of ideological and partisan diversity even at the extremes of the income distribution."[9] In the 2012 ANES, among those with family incomes in the bottom third of the income distribution, 19% were liberal Democrats as might be expected, but about as many (18%) were unexpectedly conservative Republicans. The rest were moderates, independents, or held mixed attachments (e.g., conservative Democrats). Lest one think that these are poor misguided or misled souls, the weakness of the supposed economic self-interest drive is evident among the rich (and more educated) "misguideds" as well. Although conservatives outnumber liberals among the top quintile income category of voters, about a quarter of these high-income voters are liberals.[10] Increases in income inequality are not the cause of increased party polarization in the electorate. As Walter Lippmann observed long ago, contrary to economic determinism, political views do not follow neatly from a person's position on the economic ladder.[11]

Ideological Activists

A frequently claimed explanation of increased party polarization is that ideological activists within the parties have had a greater role in steering the parties and have used their influence to pull the parties toward the ideological poles.[12] Fiorina and Abrams argue that these members of the "political class," political activists and campaign contributors along with their allied media cheerleaders (more on them shortly), have steered the parties to the extremes for their own purist ideological purposes.[13] The opening of the nomination processes through primaries and caucuses resulting from the party reforms of the late 1960s and early 1970s shifted internal party nomination powers from the professional party organizations and bosses to the activists. The party organizations had been single-mindedly focused on winning elections and reaching out to average voters in the political center. In contrast, party activists and those financially backing campaigns were more interested in a party's ideological purity.[14]

Is a major shift in power from pragmatic party organizations to more ideologically driven activists behind the increase in party polarization? There are good reasons to doubt that the empowerment and growth of an activist political class had a great deal to do with the parties becoming more polarized. First, if the parties in the electorate and among leaders were ideologically diverse in the 1950s and 1960s, why were the activists any different? They weren't. They were ideologically diverse as well. Though the college student antiwar, counterculture left is the stereotype of party activists, there is evidence that activists come in all stripes. For instance, former segregationist Governor George Wallace of Alabama received nearly as many votes nationally in 1972's Democratic primaries as the party's eventual nominee George McGovern (23.5% to 25.3%). Governor Wallace finished first in five of the 21 primaries held that year, including in Florida, Maryland, and Michigan. McGovern finished first in seven.

While many believe that ideological activists captured the parties and pulled them to the extremes, ideological activists have been around and wielding a good deal of power as long as parties themselves and, though party reforms and a more open nomination process provide them with a bigger public platform, the evidence is that they have *not* pulled the national parties to electorally tenuous extremes. In most presidential nomination contests, the establishment or moderate candidate has been nominated over the insurgent or more sharply ideological opponent. From 1972 (the first post-reform election) to 2012, there have been 16 seriously contested major party nominations. This excludes the perfunctory nomination of six incumbent presidents and one nomination in which it was unclear which candidate was the establishment candidate (the Democrats in 1980). Of the 15 nominations in which one or more establishment-moderate candidate competed with one or more activist-backed ideological candidate, the establishment- moderate candidate was nominated 12 times and the activist-backed hopeful was nominated only three times.[15] Activists may be loud, but they have not captured either of the parties—at least as measured by their success in nominating their preferred candidates. Moreover, two of those three activist-backed nominees (Reagan in 1980 and Obama in 2008) went on to win the general election, suggesting further that activists have not been pulling their parties toward unelectable extremes. In short, though activists on occasion have pulled both parties out of the electable mainstream, the parties have *not* become generally more polarized because activist extremists have had their way.

Partisan Media

In the penultimate scene of the classic movie *Casablanca*, the German Major Strasser is shot by the movie's reluctant hero Rick. When the police arrive moments later, a patriotically awakened Prefect of Police casually instructs them to "round up the usual suspects."[16] For virtually every problem and development in modern American politics, you will find the media in the lineup of "the usual suspects." The growth of party polarization is no exception. Blaming the messenger never goes out of style. The media are easy targets. In this instance, however, they are quite plausible targets. Since much of what Americans learn about politics is filtered through the media, a highly partisan media may be more than mere bystanders in the rise of party polarization.

Since the late 1980s, the segment of the news and opinion media with strong ideological perspectives has grown quite a bit. Talk radio and cable news networks with definite ideological views have developed large audiences and have become an important player in national political discourse. Much of this growth is on the political right (Rush Limbaugh, Fox News, and others), in response to what many regard as a left wing tilt of the establishment press, but there are some overt media proponents on the left as well (MSNBC, Democracy Now, and others).

Has this partisan media led to the greater polarization of the parties? It may have contributed to party polarization and helped to direct ideologues to their more hospitable parties, but the partisan media has not been the principal force in increasing the polarization of the parties (or, for that matter, the public).[17] Ironically, the obvious ideological thrusts of the partisan media may have reduced its potential polarizing effects by triggering selective exposure, producing likeminded audiences.[18] To a great extent, the partisan media preaches to the choir. As a result, those who tune in are invigorated and reinforced in their views by the ideological message they came to hear.[19] Ideologically congruent audiences get what they came for—the comforting and inspiring validation of the like-minded. The partisan media may intensify the views of those within the ideological bubble, but is ill-suited for drawing in those not already so predisposed.

Like the political parties, the news and opinion media recognized and responded to the potential audience of a highly polarized public. The process by which the parties became more polarized was well under way before the new partisan media got off the ground (Rush Limbaugh's national talk show launched in 1988 and Fox News in 1996). Given the wide and expanding range of choice in available media outlets and perspectives, it is far more plausible that partisan ideologues provided an audience for a new partisan media than it is that a new partisan media transformed neutral audiences into polarized partisans.

Polarizing Presidents

Some have suggested that one or more recent presidents pursued policies that polarized the electorate and the parties in government. In particular, President George W. Bush has been portrayed as a polarizing president—"a divider, not a uniter."[20] Gary Jacobson called him "the most divisive president in modern history."[21] The evidence for this claim is the wide divide between the president's partisans and the opposition partisans in their approval ratings for the president.

The evidence, however, also indicates that a widening partisan gap in presidential approval ratings is not peculiar to the Bush presidency. According to Gallup, the party gap in approval ratings for President Obama in the fourth year of his first term was just as wide as it had been for President Bush in the fourth year of his first term.[22] Each of President Obama's first four years in office was among the top eight years of party divisions over a president. According to Gallup's numbers, aside from G.H.W. Bush's term, there has been successively greater party polarization in presidential approval ratings since the 1980s.[23] Partisans were more polarized about Clinton than Reagan and more polarized about G. W. Bush than Clinton. As of January 2016, according to Gallup's numbers, partisans were even more divided about Obama (a 70% gap) than they had been about G. W. Bush (a 61% gap).[24] Through seven years in office, President Obama averaged an approval rating of 83% from Democrats and only 13% from Republicans.

It does not seem plausible that successive presidents in recent times have independently decided to perform their jobs in progressively antagonistic ways. Two possibilities are far more plausible. First, the performance of presidents has been judged by increasingly polarized partisans. In effect, recent presidents are the object of polarization, not its cause. Second, if recent presidents have pursued more polarizing policies, it may be because they were nominated by and elected by partisans who were already highly polarized.[25] From this standpoint, presidents are a conduit for increasingly polarized party politics, not an independent cause of it. In either case, the greater polarization of the parties is not so much about presidents as it is about public opinion.

The Agitators

Ideologically committed activists, campaign contributors, partisan media, and party leaders (including presidents) undoubtedly have helped to push polarization along, giving compelling and often strident voices to both sides. They have helped to bring to the surface and to shape the public's latent ideological inclinations. They have helped to direct ideological Americans to those with whom they are in common cause, including the parties. In their different ways, each has also inflamed the passions of polarized views, sometimes at the expense of reasonableness and civility. They have fueled the polarization fires.

Although certainly contributing to polarization, from a broader perspective, these ideological advocates—from placard-waving activists to the partisan media to elected leaders—have been "the middle men" of increased polarization. They are intermediary forces that had themselves grown out of the greater polarization of both the public and the parties. They are at once the products and the facilitators of increased polarization, but not the original driving forces behind it.

THE CAUSES

So what *has* caused the once relatively unpolarized parties to become so highly polarized? There are two interrelated causes: party realignment and the increased polarization of the public. First, over a period of several decades, the parties realigned or became re-sorted along more ideological lines.[26] This staggered realignment process changed the balance of power between the two parties from one in which the

Democrats had clearly dominated the Republicans to a very competitive party system. The realignment process changed the two ideologically diverse parties into two ideologically distinct parties.

Party realignments are rare in American politics.[27] There have only been a half dozen in more than two centuries of American history. They are basic and enduring changes in the relative electoral power of the parties and this often entails changes in the composition of the parties and the issues that divide them. Realignments define a new "normal" in American politics.[28] While every realignment produces substantial shifts in the normal balance of power between the parties, each has developed quite differently from the others—a fact that has seriously vexed those seeking generalizations about them. The staggered realignment of the latter half of the twentieth century (roughly 1958 to 1994) is no exception.

The staggered realignment was very unusual in several respects. Unlike the New Deal realignment that took about six years to complete, the staggered realignment took place over several decades. It showed up first in presidential voting in the late 1960s, then in party identifications in the mid-1980s, and finally reached completion in congressional elections in the 1990s. It shifted power toward the Republicans and competitive balance, but the Democrats were its initial beneficiary. The realignment is often associated with political change in the South (away from Democrats and toward Republicans), but its initial movements were in non-southern states (away from Republicans and to Democrats), particularly in New England and Mid-Atlantic states. It was very much a two-step dance: one step toward liberal Democrats, then two steps toward conservative Republicans. Unlike realignments that displace one cleavage issue with another, the staggered realignment was simplifying. It merged one set of issues (racial issues) with the dominant set of issues associated with the New Deal's views of government responsibilities and powers. Finally, rather than replacing one majority party with another, the staggered realignment replaced the New Deal party system dominated by the Democrats with a party system in which the Democrats and Republicans were near parity. This was not your great-grandfather's realignment.

The fundamental reason for these unusual twists and turns was that the New Deal party system contained within it the remnants of the post–Civil War Reconstruction party system: moderate to liberal Republican areas in the North and a "Solid South" of conservative Democrats. A realignment does not instantly wipe away the past. Even with the New Deal realignment, there remained major institutional (no southern Republican Party) and cultural ("Yellow Dog Democrats") impediments to the natural partisan divisions between liberal Democrats and conservative Republicans. The New Deal party system had established a big Democratic majority coalition, but it was also a fragile, unsettled, and ultimately unsustainable coalition of antagonistic voting blocs. It finally crumbled and was slowly replaced in the staggered realignment by a much more ideologically coherent, internally stable (if still contentious) and nationally competitive party system.

A second cause of more polarized parties is the more polarized public. Just as the parties were unusually unpolarized in the New Deal party system because of the complicating historical legacy of Reconstruction, the public had been unusually unpolarized in the 1950s and early 1960s because of the galvanizing historical legacy of the Great Depression and World War II. The temporary political quiescence of the post–Depression, post–World War II public gave way under the pressure of the political upheaval of the 1960s and the coming of age of new generations of voters who had not been bonded together (and politically exhausted) by the events of the 1930s and 1940s. Competitive parties could not long ignore the newly polarized public of the 1960s and 1970s. A polarized public would eventually be represented by similarly polarized parties—and eventually they were.

A FRAGILE PARTY SYSTEM

Before reviewing the development of the party realignment that precipitated the increased polarization of the parties, it is important to understand what preceded it. The increased polarization resulting from the staggered realignment is attributable, to a great extent, to the weak party polarization of the New Deal party system. Formed in the 1930s in the wake of the Great Depression, the New Deal party system contained within itself, to appropriate a phrase from Karl Marx, the seeds of its own destruction. The Democrats' New Deal coalition was an uneasy alliance. Its dissolution and realignment into a more polarized party system was only a matter of time.

The fragility of the Democrats' New Deal majority was evident even before the 1930s realignment. The Democratic Party was bitterly divided even in the nineteenth century and grew more so in the first decades of the twentieth century. The party was deeply divided between its rural southern and western fundamentalist Protestant and populist wing (the William Jennings Bryan faction) and its urban northeastern ethnic Catholic wing (the Al Smith faction). Its southern and western Protestant wing was nativist and advocated the prohibition of liquor. Its northern wing included many recent Catholic immigrants and opposed prohibition. The two wings were more naturally adversaries than allies. It was a cultural mismatch. Although generally liberal, the party included a fair number of moderates and even some conservatives on economics and matters of government responsibilities. The big division among Democrats, however, was over racial issues. On race, the party's strong southern conservative contingent and its non-southern wing of moderates and liberals were diametrically opposed to one another.[29]

As the population of Catholic immigrants grew, conflict between the two wings intensified. Internal party battles boiled over in the 1920 and 1924 national conventions. The two wings openly battled in platform fights over planks on prohibition, self-government for Ireland, and condemnation of the Ku Klux Klan, as well as over the presidential nominations. It took 44 ballots of delegates in 1920 to nominate James Cox as the party's candidate and a record 103 ballots in 1924 to nominate John W. Davis.[30] The deep rifts within the pre–New Deal Democratic Party certainly contributed to the party losing three consecutive presidential elections in landslides (1920, 1924, and 1928). The party's New Deal majority coalition was built on a party with a cracked foundation.

The contentiousness of politics within the Democratic Party's coalition was on display from before its creation to its ultimate dissolution. Though Democrats dominated American politics from the 1930s to the mid-1960s, the party was always a fractious and disparate coalition of groups.[31] Within only a few years of its formation in the 1930s, President Franklin Roosevelt openly campaigned in Democratic primaries against fellow Democrats who had opposed parts of his New Deal program. FDR's attempted purge of southern conservative Democrats in the 1938 midterm elections was unsuccessful, but it was only one battle in a longer internal party war.[32] Democratic divisions reached another peak in the 1948 presidential election. Mainstream Democrats nominated President Harry Truman, but southern Dixiecrats bolted in support of South Carolina's Governor Strom Thurmond and Democrats on the far left bolted to support former Vice President Henry Wallace. The patching of the coalition to elect Truman was only temporary. After coming very close to splitting the southern popular vote in 1952, President Eisenhower became the first Republican to win a majority of the two-party vote in southern states since the 1872 election.[33] About a quarter of Democratic party identifiers defected to vote for Eisenhower in the 1952 and 1956 elections.[34]

The Democrats' internecine battles were so common that they became fodder for now familiar jokes. Humorist Will Rogers claimed: "I'm not a member of an organized party, I'm a Democrat." Fifty years later, Representative Mo Udall would tell audiences that if Democrats were to form a firing squad, they would form it in a circle. The Democratic Party majority was a fragile patchwork in constant need of reassembly. At some point that would no longer be possible.

THE SEQUENCE OF THE STAGGERED REALIGNMENT

The First Step

Edward Carmines and James Stimson in their 1989 classic study of *Issue Evolution* discovered what might be regarded as the Rosetta Stone of modern American politics.[35] It identified the highly unlikely 1958 midterm election as the beginning of the end for the Democrats' New Deal majority, as the event largely responsible for precipitating a major realignment in American politics. What is peculiar about 1958 and the three elections that followed (particularly 1964) is that their immediate effects favored Democrats, but their long-term consequences favored Republicans. These elections of the late 1950s and early 1960s upset the delicate balance within the Democratic coalition that had allowed it to survive the 1938 purge, the 1948 bolts, the defections to vote for Eisenhower in the 1950s, and many other internal skirmishes.

The political climate of the 1958 midterm election, during Eisenhower's second term, strongly favored the Democrats. An economic recession had begun in the fall of 1957 and carried into 1958.[36] Real GDP declined by four percentage points in the final quarter of 1957 and devastatingly plunged another ten percentage points in the first quarter of 1958.[37] Already holding a 234-seat majority in the House, Democrats added another 49 seats in the midterm. This gave them an unusually large majority of 283 seats, 65 seats more than necessary for control. Democratic gains in that year's Senate elections were even more impressive. They went into the election with a bare majority (49 Democrats to 47 Republicans) and came out with 15 more seats (64 Democrats to 34 Republicans). Two of the additions were the result of Democrats being elected from the newly admitted state of Alaska.

The Democratic Party's large gains of 1958 were supplemented in the next few elections, particularly in Lyndon Johnson's 1964 landslide defeat of conservative Republican Barry Goldwater less than a year after the assassination of President Kennedy. After 1964, Democrats dominated with 295 seats in the House and 68 seats in the Senate. Democrats' congressional numbers were critical to kicking off the realignment not only because Democrats greatly outnumbered Republicans, but because liberal Democrats now greatly outnumbered conservative Democrats. The standoff between conservative and liberal Democrats, especially over civil rights issues, was no more. With liberal Democrats greatly outnumbering conservative Democrats, there was nothing immediately in the way of internal party politics as well as national public policy taking a turn to the left. With two exceptions (one being a detour), all else in the realignment followed, almost like a row of dominoes tipping one after another. Democratic gains from 1958 to 1964 put in motion a series of changes begetting changes until the new hyper-competitive party system was completed in the 1990s and nurtured further sorting and polarization in the decades that followed.

The events and consequences in this 30-year staggered realignment are complex, but can be boiled down for our purposes to a sequence of eight steps. The first of these was the direct result of Democratic Party's congressional super-majorities and the landslide election of Lyndon Johnson. As Carmines and Stimson documented long ago, civil rights legislation prior to the mid-1960s had been on hold because of a standoff between racially liberal Democrats and their conservative fellow partisans.[38] LBJ and the super-majority of liberal Democrats elected between 1958 and 1964 changed that. Along with the cooperation of some racially liberal Republicans, the Democrats passed landmark civil rights legislation. The otherwise liberal Democratic Party had become transformed from the conservative party of racial issues to the liberal party, period. The Republican Party was outflanked on racial issues and became the more conservative party, not just on the New Deal issues of the welfare state, but on everything. The issue-space had been simplified. The cross-cutting issues of race no longer cut across the parties. This was a critical step in the realignment. Though still internally diverse, the parties' prevailing positions were now ideologically consistent across the full range of issues.

Step Left, Step Right

The second step accompanied the first. With congressional Democrats moving on civil rights legislation, African Americans became more highly mobilized and their loyalty to the Democratic Party soared. This provided a significant boost to the Democratic vote in 1964 and beyond. The African American two-party presidential vote for the Democrats increased from 68% in 1960 to 94% in 1964.[39] The reported turnout of African Americans jumped from 53% in 1960 to 65% in 1964.[40] Since African Americans held generally liberal political views, their greater mobilization and attachment to the Democrats moved the party a bit further to the left. The sorting had begun.

With the Democratic Party under the sway of its liberal wing, moving forward on civil rights legislation, and attracting greater support from African American voters, conservative southern white Democrats felt more estranged than ever from the national party. Republicans seized their opportunity. In what became known as the Republicans' "Southern Strategy," the presidential campaigns of Republicans Barry Goldwater in 1964 and Richard Nixon in 1968 sought to make inroads in what had long been the Democrats' "Solid South."[41] They met with some success. Despite being trounced nationally in Lyndon Johnson's 1964 landslide, Goldwater carried five southern states, and despite Alabama Governor George Wallace's third-party candidacy that captured five southern states in 1968, Nixon managed to win the other southern states with the single exception of Texas. Republican inroads in the presidential voting of white southerners, however, were not immediately matched with gains below the presidential level. That would be a long and arduous process. This accounts, in large part, for the realignment being as prolonged as it was.[42]

Even though Republicans by the mid-1960s were the more conservative party on all issues, racial issues included, there was substantial resistance to breaking conservative white southerners of their generations-old habit of supporting Democrats over Republicans. The resistance was both cultural and institutional. Culturally, the party of Lincoln and later Reconstruction had long been unwelcomed in the South. Republicans faced a public raised with the idea that it would be better to vote for anyone or anything, up to and including a yellow dog, than for a Republican (hence, "Yellow Dog Democrats"). Being a Republican was almost unthinkable. Unlike the fairly rapid movement of African American voters toward the Democrats by mobilization (step two), the movement of conservative southern whites toward the Republicans (step three) developed slowly through the conversion of some Democrats into Republicans and through generational replacement as older cohorts of conservative Democrats were replaced by younger cohorts of conservative Republicans.

As an institution, the Republican Party was weak to nonexistent in the South since the party's founding before the Civil War. There was virtually no Republican Party infrastructure throughout most of the region.[43] Democratic primaries were effectively the election. If you wanted your vote to make a difference, you were a Democrat. The Democratic Party was a political monopoly. If you had political ambitions, you were a Democrat. Being a Republican locally was a dead end and the entrenched Democratic Party establishment across the South had no interest in seeing it otherwise. Not a single Republican was elected to the Senate from a southern state from 1912 (the first year senators were popularly elected) to 1964.[44] In 1960, only 7 of the 106 House members representing the 11 states of the South were Republicans.[45] Even into the 1980s, the coattails of Republican

presidential candidates running strongly across the South were routinely wasted because many congressional Democrats were reelected
without even a token Republican challenge.[46]

The Republicans' institutional problem in the South was most
evident in southern state legislatures—the farm teams for developing candidates. In 1960, a mere 3.5% of southern state legislators were
Republicans. By 1980, their numbers had grown, but to only 17%.[47]
Democratic officeholders were not about to relinquish their offices
without a fight and, using the many advantages of their incumbency
and keeping their distance from their more liberal colleagues, many
were able to fend off Republicans for many years.

Building a southern Republican Party from scratch was painfully
slow, but it was crucial to the realignment and to the polarization of
the parties. The gradual movement of conservative white southerners out of the Democratic Party and eventually into the Republican
Party would contribute to party polarization in two ways: by the
subtraction of conservative white southerners, the Democrats became more liberal, and by their addition, Republicans became more
conservative.

A Polarizing Generation and Times

Unlike the first three steps of the realignment, the fourth step was
independent of those that preceded it. It was the political impact of
the "baby boom" generation and the divisive events of the 1960s.
Baby boomers, born after the end of World War II and into the early
1960s, were coming of political age in the late 1960s and 1970s. As
their name suggests, it was a big generation, a demographic bulge in
the nation's age distribution. Unlike their parents' generation, boomers had not been unified by the crises of the Great Depression, World
War II, and the Cold War with the Soviets. They had not become
politically galvanized. They brought with them the growth of the
counterculture (sex, drugs, and rock 'n' roll), engagement in civil rights
and Vietnam War protests, college unrest from demonstrations to
administration building takeovers, confrontational political activism,
New Left politics, and the generation gap.

As a cohort, baby boomers were disproportionately liberals and
Democrats. They played major roles in the campaigns of Senators

Gene McCarthy and Bobby Kennedy in 1968 and in the presidential nomination of Senator George McGovern in 1972. They played a role in the fiasco of the Democratic National Convention in Chicago in 1968 and members of their cohort were victims at Kent State and Jackson State. Their political commitments were fueled by these events, and by the assassinations of Bobby Kennedy and the Reverend Martin Luther King, Jr., and the seemingly unending and futile war in Vietnam and its toll on American lives. Some were hippies or later yippies, some were in SDS (Students for a Democratic Society), and some were Black Panthers. Most boomers, however, were not radicals or even extreme liberals. As in any generation, there was a good deal of political diversity, but the political divisions grew and were real. It was caricatured as the hard-hats versus the hippies, Archie Bunker versus Meathead on the popular *All in the Family* television show of the period, but behind the stereotypes were real differences. For good or ill, the baby boom generation and the political events of its time changed the nation's political culture. The nation and to some extent the parties (apart from the lagging South) became more polarized.

Dealignment and Detours

The fifth step in the realignment, a product of the four that preceded it, was the party dealignment from the late 1960s into the early 1980s. Party dealignment (aka party decline or decomposition) was the weakening of the electorate's attachments to the political parties. At the time, many observers speculated that the party system's decline was permanent, that political parties in American politics had become irrelevant in an era of increasingly candidate-centered campaigning.[48] The widely acknowledged dean of the Washington press corps, *Washington Post* reporter and columnist David Broder, wrote *The Party's Over.*[49] After the 1960s, fewer Americans professed strong identifications for either party, more claimed to be independents, split-ticket voting increased, third-party activity increased (Wallace in 1968, McCarthy in 1976, and Anderson in 1980), and, most tellingly for the matter of party polarization, fewer Americans held positive views about one party and negative views about the other. According to Martin Wattenberg's analysis, between 40% and 50% of ANES respondents were "positive-negatives" in the 1952, 1956, and 1960 elections. In the next four presidential elections (1972 to 1984), their numbers dropped to between 27% and 31%.[50]

While some interpreted dealignment as the demise of parties in modern American politics, this was far from the case. In retrospect, the decline in partisanship was real, but had been somewhat exaggerated and, rather than a permanent characteristic of a new political order, the weakening of partisanship was a transitional phase in the realignment of the parties. A major reason for its exaggeration was the misinterpretation of "independent leaners" as independents. As noted in chapter 5, these "independent leaners" in virtually every important respect think and behave like partisans and not like "pure" independents.[51] Since there had been significant growth in the 1970s of those reporting to be in the "independent leaning to the Democrats" and "independent leaning to the Republicans" categories, counting these Americans as independents inflated the extent of dealignment.

The dealignment, however, was not entirely a misinterpretation of a measurement. It was real and substantial. Measuring the strength of the electorate's partisanship as the percentage of strong party identifiers minus the percentage of pure independents, partisanship in the overall electorate dropped from about a 30% net level in the 1950s and early 1960s to about a 10% net level in the early and mid-1970s.[52] This was a major development, but even in the depths of the dealignment, the electorate remained more partisan than not.

There are three reasons why the dealignment was temporary, a phase in the realignment. First, the conversion and generational replacement of Democrats into Republicans required a good deal of time. People do not abandon important lifelong self-identifications easily or quickly.[53] Second, as already noted, the building of a viable Republican Party in the South was a lengthy process.[54] Finally, many elected Democrats were able to fend off Republican challengers through the many advantages of incumbency, from credit-claiming and constituency service to helpful gerrymandering and well-heeled campaign financing.[55] A good number of these Democrats, particularly in the South, held on to their seats for decades after the national Democratic Party had grown out of sync with the more conservative views of their constituents.

Dealignment amounted to a delay in the polarization of the parties. The public had become substantially more polarized than the parties but, because of the unique institutional problems for Republicans in the South and the often successful efforts of incumbent Democrats in holding Republican challengers at bay, the polarization of the parties below the presidential level lagged behind. There was a disconnect, and the dealignment reflected it. As Stephen Craig observed, the differences between the parties were not pronounced enough for the more polarized electorate.[56] Though the presidential candidates presented "a choice, not an echo," as the Goldwater campaign put it, the parties below the presidential level had remained ideologically heterogeneous. As a result, many liberals did not yet feel sufficiently well represented by the Democratic Party and many conservatives felt the same about the Republican Party. Craig keenly observed that the dealignment coincided with a substantial increase (from 48% in 1968 to 62% in 1980) in Americans agreeing with the statement that "parties are only interested in people's votes but not in their opinions."[57] As Carmines, McIver, and Stimson found, among independents having characteristics that might have predicted a Democratic or Republican party identification ("unrealized partisans"), they found that "Unrealized Democrats are consistently more conservative than Democrats while Unrealized Republicans are more liberal than Republicans."[58] Many of the conservative unrealized Democrats would eventually find a home in the Republican Party and many liberal unrealized Republicans eventually would settle in as Democrats.

Beyond the realignment delays associated with partisan conversions, generational replacement, and dealignment, two events also delayed the realignment: Watergate and the Carter presidency. Both were speed bumps in the movement to a more competitive and polarized party system. The Watergate scandal in the 1972 presidential campaign, its cover-ups, and the congressional investigation and impeachment hearings leading to the eventual resignation of Republican President Nixon in August of 1974 (and then his pardon by President Gerald Ford), gave many second thoughts about moving to the Republicans. The 1976 election of President Jimmy Carter, a former Democratic governor of Georgia, also slowed the realignment process. Regarded at the time as coming from the more moderate southern wing of the Democratic Party, Carter's election would for a short time stall Republican inroads in the South. Carter carried ten of the eleven states of the Confederacy in 1976, but only one (his home state of Georgia) four years later.

The Reagan Revolution

The seventh step in the staggered realignment was the 1980 and 1984 elections of President Ronald Reagan and the solidification of the realignment in a significant aggregate change in party identifications. After the delays and detours of the 1970s, the realignment was back on track and the political system was well on its way to a new normal. Coming out of the conservative wing of the more conservative party, President Reagan further clarified the ideological differences between the parties. Though not a rigid ideologue, President Reagan might be regarded as the first clearly conservative president since Calvin Coolidge left the office in 1928. With ideological differences between the parties sharpened and many becoming more comfortable with the idea of voting Republican, the Democratic Party's dominance of party identification in the electorate was substantially reduced.[59] When Reagan defeated Carter and Anderson in 1980, Democratic Party identifiers outnumbered Republican Party identifiers in the ANES by 19 percentage points. Reagan's victory that year depended on the votes of many conservative "Reagan Democrats." When Reagan was reelected four years later, the difference was only 9 percentage points. The change was not temporary. When Reagan left office in 1988, the party identification gap was only 7 percentage points.

The shift in party identification toward the Republicans and competitive balance was an important indicator (albeit a lagging indicator) that a new, more competitively balanced and polarized party system was developing and that partisan dealignment had been a temporary phenomenon. The realignment, however, even in the early 1990s remained incomplete. Republicans were now competitive in presidential elections. They had won five of seven presidential elections between 1968 and 1992.[60] Democrats, however, continued to dominate congressional elections. Democrats had Senate majorities in all but six of the 34 years from 1960 to 1994 and controlled the House for 40 consecutive years. They gained control of the House in the 1954 midterm election and maintained their majority through eight presidencies and the first half of President Clinton's first term. Some interpreted this as evidence that a realignment had not occurred or that it was a "split-level realignment" or a "two-tier electoral system," a presidential election level realignment, but otherwise a candidate-centered dealignment.[61]

The Congressional Step

The eighth step in the realignment was taken on Election Day 1994, the midterm election of President Bill Clinton's first term. It was the final act of a realignment process that had begun 36 years earlier in the 1958 midterm. Presidential voting habits had changed. Aggregate party identification divisions had changed. But change had come slowly to congressional elections. It finally arrived in 1994. When the dust settled on the 1994 midterm, Republicans had gained ten Senate seats (including one party switch) and 54 House seats. They held majorities in both chambers of Congress. There were 230 Republicans and 204 Democrats (and one "other") in the newly elected House and 53 Republicans and 47 Democrats in the Senate. Representative Newt Gingrich became the first Republican Speaker of the House since Representative Joe Martin handed the gavel over to Representative Sam Rayburn four decades earlier. Subsequent elections proved that the Republicans' gains of 1994 were not a fluke. Republicans won House majorities in nine of the eleven national elections from 1994 to 2014. The 1994 election was the long-delayed congressional breakthrough of the realignment.

There have been many interpretations of why Republicans fared so well in 1994. Most focus on the events leading into the election, but these fall well short of explaining the magnitude of Republican gains. President Clinton's presidency had a rocky start, especially on his national healthcare proposal, but his approval ratings were not dismal going into the midterm (the low- to mid-40% range). The Republicans' "Contract With America" package of proposals was innovative and attracted a good deal of attention, but it was hardly momentous enough to produce such a dramatic and lasting swing. What did have the seismic impact was the completion of the realignment—the development of the Republican Party in the South, the passage of old-line southern conservative Democrats both in and out of office, along with their succession by a new generation of southern Republicans.

Indicative of the Republicans taking root in the South was their growing numbers in the region's state legislatures. Their numbers grew from less than 4% in 1960 and only 17% in 1980 to more than 30% in 1992. The road to 1994 had been paved.

A REAL REALIGNMENT

The staggered realignment was unusual in so many ways and took so long to complete that it is often misunderstood. Two misunderstandings stand out. First, because of its slow development, unlike the relatively speedy New Deal realignment, some have questioned whether the realignment actually occurred and, even more basically, whether the concept of partisan realignment remains meaningful in modern American politics.[62] Second, because the last and most dramatic change took place in the South among white southerners, the realignment is often regarded as a southern rather than a national realignment. There is plenty of evidence, however, that the realignment was quite real and very national in scope—and it left the nation with two highly polarized parties.

The evidence of the realignment's impact is presented in table 6.1. Through the eight steps of the realignment, there were three consistent indications that the balance of power between the parties had shifted from the Democrats being clearly the majority party to the parties standing at nearly equal strength. Presidential voting habits changed first and most easily, requiring neither a change in psychological identifications nor the parties' institutions. The vote shift occurred around the 1968 election.[63] The median Democratic presidential vote dropped by about 4 percentage points from the nine elections before 1968 to the twelve elections since then.[64] Though only about half the magnitude of the 1930s realignment, it is nevertheless a major change in the parties' baseline vote. Typical elections changed from a 54 to 46 split favoring the Democrat to a 50-50 toss-up.

Aggregate party identification (macropartisanship) changed more slowly through the conversion and generational replacement of Democrats with Republicans. Partisan change by individual changes in identifications or through the passage of generations less encumbered by old attachments involved lengthy transitions. It was not until 1984 that the new and more competitive balance of party iden-

TABLE 6.1. THE STAGGERED REALIGNMENT'S CHANGE IN RELATIVE PARTY STRENGTH, 1932–2014

The Staggered Realignment	Median Percentage Support for the Democratic Party		
	Stage 1: Presidential Vote	Stage 2: Party Identification	Stage 3: House Seats
The Break Year	1968	1984	1994
Before	53.8	57.5	59.5 259 seats
After	49.9	52.7	47.2 205.5 seats
Change	–3.9	–4.8	–12.3 53.5 seats

Note: The "Break Year" is the first election of the competitive staggered realignment era. For the two-party presidential vote percentage the "before" period includes 1932 to 1964 (N=9). The "after" period includes 1968 to 2012 (N=12). Party identification is macropartisanship (Democratic Party identifiers as a percentage of major party identifiers, including "independent leaners") among reported voters in presidential election years. The data are originally from ANES and have been corrected to the actual division of the presidential vote (see Campbell 2010; corrections to the 2012 ANES data were made by the author). "Before" elections for party identification include presidential elections from 1952 to 1980 (N=8). 1952 was the first year ANES collected party identification data. "After" elections are presidential elections from 1984 to 2012 (N=8). The "Before" period in House elections includes all national elections from 1932 to 1992 (N=31). "After" elections are those from 1994 to 2014 (N=11). For comparability purposes, third-party and independent seats were split evenly between the major parties.

tifications was evident. In the eight presidential elections from 1952 to 1980, about 58% of those identifying with a major political party were Democrats. The party identification gap favored Democrats by about 15 percentage points. In the eight elections since then (1984–2012), fewer than 53% of major party identifiers were Democrats. Although Democrats continued to outnumber Republicans, they had lost almost two-thirds of their prior lead.[65]

The third indication of the realignment's impact was the change in each party's share of House seats. Requiring institutional changes, the building of a viable southern Republican Party, this took even longer to develop. In the 31 national elections from 1932 to 1992, Democrats typically won nearly 60% of the seats. Their share of seats in the 11 elections from 1994 to 2014 dropped by about 12 percentage points. In House elections, Democrats had dominated. The parties are now nearly even, with the Republicans holding a slight edge. Though the three shifts occurred at different times, each occurred and each had essentially the same effect—to transform the party system from one in which Democrats dominated to one in which the parties were more competitively balanced.

A realignment with such major repercussions is in the most important respect "national," but it is often referred to (and seemingly minimized) as a "southern" or regional realignment. This designation leaves the false impression that the realignment was confined to white southern conservative voters. It was not. Like the New Deal realignment, the staggered realignment produced greater change in some places and among different demographic groups than in other places and groups. It also shifted some groups and regions toward the Democrats, though more overall toward the Republicans.

The effects of the realignment across different regions of the nation show up starkly in the extent to which the different regions sent Democrats to represent them in the House before and after the realignment.[66] The mean percentage of Democratic House members from six regions of the nation are presented in table 6.2 for the pre-realignment period (1932–1964) and the post-realignment period (1994–2012). As commonly acknowledged, the realignment turned the formerly solid Democratic South into a Republican-friendly region. Republicans since the breakthrough election of 1994 have won 60% of southern House seats. In the last few elections, more than 70% of the southern House delegation were Republicans. The realignment shift to Republicans in the border states was nearly as great. The movement of voters in northeastern states ran counter to the pro-Republican movement across the South, but was also a clear break from the region's past partisanship. Realignment effects in New England favoring Democrats were about as pronounced as realignment effects in the South favoring Republicans.[67] The realignment

TABLE 6.2. REGIONAL SHIFTS IN THE STAGGERED NATIONAL REALIGNMENT, 1932–2012

| Region | Mean Democratic Percentage of House Seats | | |
| | Time Period | | Change |
	1932–1964	1994–2012	
New England	42	82	+40
Middle Atlantic	47	58	+11
South	95	40	−45
Border	83	44	−39
Midwest	41	45	+4
West	56	51	−5

Source: Calculated by the author from Rusk (2001) and election reports compiled by the Office of the Clerk of the U.S. House of Representatives (various dates).

transformed New England from a bastion of staid Republicanism to one dominated by liberal Democrats.

The main point is that although some groups and regions moved toward the Republicans and others toward the Democrats, the overall sorting was not so much about regions or groups (religious, ethnic, racial, economic, or otherwise) as it was about ideology.[68] Political perspectives that had been out of sync with partisan affiliations for historical reasons were brought into line with the parties. This happened in all parts and segments of the nation, though the change was greater in some areas than in others. The parties became both more competitively balanced and more ideologically polarized.

The consequences of the staggered realignment for the polarization of the parties are far-reaching, extending beyond the period of the realignment itself. Most directly, the realignment better sorted the electorate into more ideologically homogeneous parties. In doing so, the ideologically distinct parties became more clearly the home of like-minded citizens and leaders for generations to follow. Liberals would feel at home with fellow liberals in the Democratic Party and would not find the conservative Republican Party to be so hospitable to them. Likewise, conservatives would feel comfortable in the more conservative Republican Party and alienated in the more liberal

Democratic Party. Internal party conflicts still existed and still could become quite heated, but they were conflicts among the generally like-minded. Once the parties became more clearly ideologically distinct from one another, further party polarization took on its own momentum. It became self-perpetuating. As we saw in table 1.3 in the first chapter, only a third of the electorate was ideologically aligned with a party in 1972. Forty years later, more than half of the electorate was ideologically aligned with a party.

In further polarizing the parties, the realignment also may have contributed to the greater polarization of the public. The staggered realignment simplified American politics by collapsing issues, particularly racial issues, into a single left-right dimension. Each of the parties now represented and articulated a definite ideological perspective. It is difficult to imagine that the ideological clarity provided by the two parties did not cause portions of the public to join in on either side. As the public polarized in the 1960s, the parties responded in the 1980s, and this fueled further polarization of the public in the years since.

LEADING AND FOLLOWING POLITICAL CHANGE

American party politics experienced tremendous change from the days of the New Deal party system with its ideologically diverse parties of the 1930s and even into the 1980s to the current party system with its highly polarized parties. This chapter has charted the course of that change, but a major question about it remains: who was responsible for this partisan change—the party elites or the public? Was the realignment and the increased polarization of the parties a top-down process in which political leaders recast the parties, or was it a bottom-up process in which the parties responded to what the public demanded of them?

Conventional wisdom contends that this political change resulted from political leaders and activists staking out opposing sides for the Democrats and Republicans, and rank-and-file partisans later followed their lead.[69] As Matthew Levendusky succinctly described this contention: "political change begins with elites and then spreads to the masses."[70] The rationale for political change supposedly being a top-down phenomenon is that elites are more politically sophisticated than average citizens and therefore adapt more quickly to changing political circumstances. They lead through both governing and campaigning and this slowly seeps out to citizens who follow.

Though this sounds plausible, the sequence of events in the staggered realignment tells a very different story. The partisan and ideological change in American politics from the late 1950s to the present was initiated primarily through a bottom-up process. The public changed first and political elites (sometimes known as "leaders") followed a good deal later. First, it was the voters in that fateful 1958 midterm election and in the early 1960s who elected liberal Democrats and began the dominoes tipping. Political change occurred not because political leaders changed their policy views, but because the electorate changed their elected political leaders. President Johnson and congressional Democrats were able to pass landmark civil rights legislation not because they suddenly saw the light, but because voters elected a large majority of liberal Democrats to Congress. Second, it was the public who grew increasingly polarized in the late 1960s and early 1970s while political leaders remained fairly constant in their political perspectives.

How is a bottom-up polarization process possible if leaders are so much more politically sophisticated and ideological than the mass public? There are two reasons why the polarization of elites lagged behind the polarization (general and party) of the public. First, though party leaders are more politically astute than most citizens, those leaders who matter most are those who have been elected. They have records and commitments and, most importantly, the means of self-preservation. They have a vested interest in political stability, not change. Stability keeps them in office. Particularly during the realignment transition, incumbents became quite adept at using the advantages of their incumbency to hold back the polarizing tides of their constituencies. There is no shortage of research on the growth of congressional incumbency advantages during this period.[71] From gerrymandering to credit-claiming to campaign spending advantages, elected leaders used their advantages to hold at bay the forces of political change in the electorate.

The second reason why the polarization of political leaders lagged well behind that of the public was the absence of a viable Republican Party in the South. Conservative white southerners could and did defect from the Democrats to vote for Republican presidential candidates from Eisenhower to Reagan, but congressional southern Democratic incumbents survived for decades, often with little or no Republican opposition.

The political history of the 1970s and 1980s offers a test of the bottom-up (polarization of the public first) and the top-down (polarization of elites first) theories of polarization's development. Two facts about the politics of this period are quite clear. First, it was a period of partisan dealignment. A large segment of the public turned away from the parties. This was evident in weaker party identifications, higher presidential vote defection rates, and increased split-ticket voting. Second, though there were signs of increased party polarization in Congress in the late 1970s and early 1980s, it substantially accelerated in the late 1980s.[72] The bottom-up sequence of polarization explains the mass partisan dealignment and why it was followed by elite polarization that then led to a restoration of partisanship. A polarized public felt poorly represented by weakly polarized parties in the 1970s and the parties' leaders responded later in the 1980s. The top-down sequence of polarization development would leave the partisan dealignment and the later congressional polarization unexplained. At least in this instance, political change took place first in the public. Change in the nation's political leadership followed later.

CHAPTER 7

ONE-SIDED PARTY POLARIZATION?

You can compromise between good, better, and best,
and you can compromise between bad and worse and terrible.
But you can't compromise between good and evil.

—Rep. Gary Ackerman (D-NY)[1]

By one reckoning, the parties in government are more polarized than they have been at any point since at least the 1870s.[2] The staggered realignment stretching from the late 1950s to the early 1990s sorted Americans ideologically into more distinctly left and right political parties and the parties responded by better representing the views of an increasingly ideological electorate. More well-defined political parties became more effective advocates for non-centrist political perspectives and this fueled further polarization in the electorate and between the parties.

REPUBLICANS GONE WILD?

Some contend that party polarization has grown particularly severe in recent years as political leaders and activists sought ideological purity within their parties, particularly within the Republican Party. The ultra-polarization of American politics, as the claim goes, has been largely a one-sided or asymmetric affair. Republicans became a far-right ideological party while Democrats remained a fairly moderate and pragmatic center-left party. This claim of one-sided party polarization was made most strongly by Thomas Mann and Norman Ornstein in their provocatively titled *It's Even Worse Than It Looks*.[3] Mann boldly claimed that "Republicans have become a radical insurgency—ideologically extreme, contemptuous of the inherited policy regime, scornful of compromise, unpersuaded by conventional understanding of facts, evidence, and science, and dismissive of the legitimacy of their political opposition."[4] The two parties became increasingly polarized through the sorting of the realignment, but the Republican Party's movement to the ultra-conservative right raised party polarization to new levels. The bitter and uncompromising divisions between the parties have taken a terrible toll on the functioning of the government and on achieving the compromises necessary to formulate sensible public policies. The result of Republican extremism and intransigence, according to this view, has been a seriously dysfunctional politics.[5]

Two related claims are embedded in the contention that party polarization has been largely asymmetrical. The first is a descriptive claim that the Republican Party has become more ideologically extreme than the Democratic Party. While the realignment caused both parties to be more ideologically distinct, Republicans are seen as having moved further to the right than the Democrats moved to the left. The far-right Tea Party wing of the Republican Party is seen as being especially intransigent and willing to take drastic measures, such as shutting down the government, to get what it wants rather than compromising with the Democrats. Mann and Ornstein contend that "the center of gravity within the Republican Party has shifted sharply to the right."[6] Democrats, in contrast, have "hewed to the center-left, with an emphasis on the center."[7]

A second contention concerns the reasons for the suspected asymmetry. This explanatory claim is that uncompromising and petulant right-wing zealots pulled the Republican Party to the far right. The roster of zealots includes extremely conservative Republican congressional leaders enforcing no-holds-barred party discipline on Republican legislators, bombastic and irresponsible media (Internet, talk radio, and Fox News) putting pressure on conservatives to be intransigent while belittling moderate-conservatives, wealthy ultra-right campaign contributors financing fringe candidates, and Tea Party activists insisting on ideological purity. The implication of this explanation is clear. If right-wing zealots diverted the Republican Party from a center-right position apart from the preferences of most of the party's rank-and-file and a sizeable portion of the American public, then the ultra-conservative Republican Party is unrepresentative of a large majority of Americans. By this reading, the Republican Party has been captured or misled by extreme conservatives who are out of touch with mainstream American politics and, through their obstruction, they have created a dysfunctional political process prone to gridlock, unproductive partisan bickering, and incivility.

The central question of this chapter is whether the two related claims of this perspective on party polarization are accurate. Is party polarization asymmetrical? Has the Republican Party moved to the far right and out of the American political mainstream? If so, why? Is it the result of the party being captured by right-wing ideological zealots? What does the evidence say?

PART OF THE STORY

There is a kernel of truth in support of the asymmetry claim, but it is far from the full story of party differences in polarization. First, there is evidence that the Republican Party has grown a good deal more conservative since the 1980s.[8] The Republican Party is now considerably more conservative than the Democratic Party is liberal, at least as gauged by Poole and Rosenthal's mean DW-NOMINATE scores of congressional roll-call voting. Poole and Rosenthal's scale is centered at zero with conservative roll-call voting producing more positive scores (generally below +1.0) and liberal roll-call voting indicated by negative scores (generally bounded by –1.0).[9] In 1981, the mean scores of each party in the House and the Senate were about equidistant from the center (negative .29 and .28 for the Democrats and positive .26 and .27 for the Republicans in the House and Senate, respectively). By 2013, the Democrats had moved about a tenth of a point in the liberal direction in both chambers, while the Republicans had moved nearly three times as much to the right in the Senate (to .55) and four and a half times as far to the right in the House (to .72).

From a different perspective, and again relying on Poole and Rosenthal's measures, the change in congressional Republicans is evident in the near extinction of its moderate wing. In 1981, more than half of Republican House members and nearly half of Republican senators were moderates (within .25 of the center of the DW-NOMINATE scale). By 2013, the percentage of congressional Republican moderates had declined to less than 1% in the House and 4% in the Senate. In contrast, using the same scale and standards, 13% of House Democrats and 9% of Senate Democrats were moderates in 2013. The ranks of moderates declined in both parties, but far more so among Republicans.

The increased conservatism of Republicans and the decrease in the number of Republican moderates, at least according to the DW-NOMINATE scores, is all the more impressive because the number of congressional Republicans increased at the same time. We would expect that Republicans would win first in the most conservative districts and states in the country and, as their numbers grew, they would be adding representatives from somewhat less conservative areas. If this were true, the average ideological voting record of Republicans should have become more moderate as Republican numbers grew. Instead, it grew more conservative, at least as Poole and Rosenthal's numbers have it.

Second, it is no secret that a good many conservative activists, campaign contributors, and media commentators have urged, contributed, and worked to have the Republican Party stake out and stand by more conservative policy positions.[10] It would be quite surprising if they had not had some influence. Even when they have not won nomination contests, the right wing of the Republican Party has had considerable influence on the party. Republican leaders with more moderate inclinations have had good reason to edge a bit more to the right than they otherwise might have in order to avoid a challenge from those on the far right. Professional politicians, as a group of survivors, tend to have pretty good anticipated reactions.

REASONS TO DOUBT

Despite the evidence suggesting greater Republican extremism, the asymmetry claim is difficult to believe. Why would one party allow itself to go off the deep end? Wouldn't competitive electoral pressures pull a party back from the political disaster of being seen as a party of extremists? And if it did not, wouldn't that party have met political disaster?

Asymmetrical polarization seems to fly in the face of a good deal of symmetry in the pressures on both parties. The Republican Party has a very conservative wing urging and perhaps even driving it ever further to the right, but the Democratic Party also must contend with a left wing pulling it to the far left. Neither party has a monopoly on or, for that matter, a shortage of extremists. One could easily assemble a tally sheet of the polar opposite forces in both parties—Fox News on the right and MSNBC on the left, the Tea Party on the right and the Occupy Wall Street movement and its sympathizers on the left, the Koch brothers on the right and George Soros on the left. The list could go on and on. Why would we expect conservative activists to have been more successful pulling the Republican Party rightward than liberal activists would have been pulling the Democratic Party leftward?

Then there are the issues. On a broad set of issues, ranging from national healthcare and environmental issues to gay marriage and the legalization of marijuana, the nation seems to have moved to the left. This has occurred despite supposed steadfast radical Republican obstruction. But these are impressions and, as noted in chapter 4, the ideological meaning of many issues may change in its historical context. More definitive evidence needs to be brought to the question.

CIRCUMSTANTIAL EVIDENCE

An important piece of circumstantial evidence sheds light on the asymmetry of party polarization contention. One change in American politics over the last half century that is beyond dispute is the change in the competitive balance between the Democratic and Republican parties. From the 1930s to the late 1960s (or the 1990s in congressional voting), the Democratic Party electorally dominated the Republican Party. This is no longer the case. As shown earlier (recall table 6.1), Democrats and Republicans have become more competitively balanced in presidential voting, in partisanship, and in congressional election outcomes. The arithmetic of the gravitation to partisan parity required a move at the expense of the Democrats and in favor of the Republicans. The evidence of this is as clear as it can be and is quite squarely at odds with the idea that Republicans have become markedly less representative of American voters.

If, as has been argued, the Republicans have been led out of the political mainstream to the far right wilderness of American politics, they should have suffered politically as a result. Political extremism should exact a price at the polls. If a party is out of step with a large majority of Americans, those voters should look elsewhere for representation. They certainly have had that opportunity. Even in a highly polarized public, and there is good evidence that the American public is highly polarized and has grown more so in recent decades, a party should lose ground to its very competitive opposition if it is seen by voters as being too extreme to represent the voters' less extreme political views.

If Republicans had become extremely conservative and Democrats remained relatively centrist, Republicans should have lost political ground to the Democrats. But they didn't. They not only did not lose ground to the Democrats, as the asymmetry claim would have predicted; they actually *gained* a good deal of ground on the Democrats over this time. A party that has moved to the fringe, out of the mainstream of American politics, should not gain political support. Yet Republicans did just that, and unmistakably so in presidential voting, in party identification, *and* in congressional elections.

The claim that Republicans have moved out of the mainstream is contradicted by their political success. In terms of party identification and electoral victories from state legislative races to the presidency, the Republican Party was once a distant second to the Democratic Party. Now they are near parity. Republicans are highly competitive with Democrats. So how is it possible for Republicans to have moved out of the mainstream but to have improved their electoral standing?

This is the ultimate reality check on the asymmetry thesis. Something is amiss with the claim that Republicans moved too far to the right for the electorate. Either Americans are more conservative than Mann and Ornstein believe, Republicans have not gone quite as far to the right as supposed, Democrats have gone even further to the left than believed, or some mix of the three.[11] The Republican Party cannot simply have become an unrepresentatively extremist conservative party while at the same time attracting more political support. So what happened? How can an extreme rightward shift of Republicans be reconciled with their improved electoral standing?

THE REST OF THE STORY

The reconciliation requires four additional pieces of evidence. Collectively, they indicate that the asymmetry in party polarization is more apparent than real. Increased party polarization *appeared* to be substantially the result of undemocratic forces pulling the Republican Party to the far right because of four missing pieces of the party polarization puzzle. These four missing pieces are: (1) the electorate's more conservative tilt in recent decades, (2) the parties' changing ideological compositions, (3) the staggered sequence of the Democratic Party's steady drift to the left followed later by the Republican Party's sharper turn to the right, and (4) problems with the issue-based measures (roll-call based, in this case) of ideological perspectives over time. Once these four elements are added to the initial evidence of one-sided Republican polarization, the findings of the direct evidence and the circumstantial evidence mesh. They indicate that *the polarization of the parties is essentially symmetrical, not asymmetrical.* We now turn to the four missing pieces of evidence that complete the party polarization story.

The Center Moved

The first reason why the Republican Party moved further to the right and why it appeared they strayed from the median voter more than the Democrats is that the ideological position of the median voter moved a bit to the right. As reported in chapter 3 (recall figure 3.4), the electorate over the last four decades grew more polarized, but that change was not perfectly symmetric. The increase in conservative ranks outpaced that of liberals. The differences are not breathtaking—macropolitical changes seldom are—but they reflect some real change in the political landscape. Liberal numbers edged up a couple of percentage points while conservative numbers increased by about four percentage points. A center-right majority had required the addition of nearly 40% of the votes of moderates to those already on the right. After the shift, a center-right majority required adding just more than a third of the moderates to the larger conservative base.

With a center-right electorate moving a bit further in the conservative direction in recent decades, both parties had electoral incentives to move a bit to the right as well. Republicans responded to the electorate's movement. Moreover, as their electorally competitive record suggests, they did not over-respond to the public's shift. The situation with the Democratic Party was quite different. Rather than moving a bit more to the right as the public had, congressional Democrats adopted *more* liberal policy positions. In the early and mid-1970s, according to Poole and Rosenthal's scale of roll-call voting, both House and Senate Democrats were fairly liberal (DW-NOMINATE means of around −.3). By 2013, they had become somewhat more so (means of about −.4). These were not the big changes in the conservative direction observed among Republicans, but the Republicans' changes were in the direction expected in response to the public becoming a bit more conservative. The Democrats' changes were in the direction *opposite* to that expected of a politically responsive party.

With the center of the electorate becoming a bit more conservative, the movement of Republicans further to the right and the seemingly more restrained movement of Democrats to the left is more equal than it first appears. The greater conservatism of Republicans contributed to party polarization, but also simply reflected a slightly more conservative electorate. The Democrats contributed as much to the polarization of the parties *by their failure to move a bit to the right* along with the electorate as well as by Democrats becoming more liberal. Put differently, by assuming that the center of the electorate remained unchanged over this period, when it had actually become a bit more conservative, the extent of the Republican Party's shift to the right is exaggerated and the Democratic Party's movement to the left is understated.

1960s

	D_1	M_1		R_1	

Liberal *Center* *Conservative*

2010s

	D_2		M_2		R_2

Liberal *Center* *Conservative*

Key:
M is the position of the median voter
D is the position of the Democratic Party
R is the position of the Republican Party

Figure 7.1. A moving center and increased party polarization, 1960s and 2010s.

Note: Analysis later in this chapter determines that both the *earlier* (1960s) party polarization and the *change* in party polarization were asymmetric. The Democrats in the 1960s (D_1) were closer to the median voter (M_1) than the Republicans (R_1) were: $|D_1 - M_1| < |R_1 - M_1|$. With roughly symmetric party polarization in the more recent period: $|D_2 - M_2| \approx |R_2 - M_2|$, the *change* in party polarization was asymmetric with greater Democratic change: $(|D_2 - M_2| - |D_1 - M_1|) > (|R_2 - M_2| - |R_1 - M_1|)$.

Figure 7.1 displays the spatial differences between the parties and the median voter across time. The relevant comparisons for evaluating the symmetry or asymmetry of party polarization is comparing the positions of the Democratic Party (D) and the Republican Party (R) to that of the median voter (M) at a particular time (subscript 1 for the 1960s, 2 for the 2010s). One-sided polarization involves the differences between the median voter and each of the parties in the 2010s (M_2 to R_2 and M_2 to D_2), not the changes in the parties' positions (D_1 to D_2 and R_1 to R_2).[12] By not taking into account any earlier asymmetry and the shift of the median voter (M_1 to M_2), the Republicans' change from R_1 to R_2 would look like one-sided polarization when it was not.[13]

Intraparty Political Change

A second key to the asymmetry puzzle involves the effects of the staggered realignment on the internal politics of both parties. As a result of the increased polarization of the public and the realignment

TABLE 7.1. PRESIDENTIAL VOTE SHARES FROM EACH PARTY'S IDEOLOGICAL BASE, 1976–2012

Presidential Election	Percentage of a Party's Two-Party Presidential Vote	
	Liberal Component of the Democratic Vote	Conservative Component of the Republican Vote
1976	29	44
1980	26	39
1984	28	46
1988	32	50
1992	33	50
1996	30	59
2000	34	48
2004	37	56
2008	37	58
2012	43	60

Source: Calculated by the author from the National Exit Polls (Roper 2013). The percentages are of the two-party vote.

of the parties, both parties drew more of their votes from their ideological wings. The portion of each party's presidential vote drawn from its ideological base is presented in table 7.1 for elections from 1976 to 2012. For the Republican Party, this is the percentage of its presidential vote obtained from self-described conservatives. For the Democrats, it is the portion of its vote from self-reported liberals. The calculations were made from National Exit Poll data.[14] The reliance of a party on votes from its ideological base should make a difference in the party's electoral and governing decisions. If all of a party's votes come from moderates and the party is able to win office, the party should be particularly anxious to keep those moderate voters happy and on board for the next election. The same would be true of ideological voters if they were the source of a party's support.[15]

Both of the parties receive a considerable amount of support from their ideological bases and both have grown a good deal more dependent on this support. In the mid-1970s and early 1980s, about

30% of Democratic presidential votes came from liberals. By 2012, more than 40% of the Democratic vote came from liberals. On the Republican side, about 40% to 45% of their support came from conservatives in the mid-1970s and early 1980s. By 2012, this had increased to 60%. The contribution to the presidential vote from the respective ideological bases increased by roughly fifteen percentage points within both parties. By the same token, this means that both of the parties were that much less beholden to voters outside of their ideological bases. This is a huge change.

The realignment's sorting of liberals and conservatives into their friendlier parties has made an enormous difference to internal party politics. Though liberals continue to be a minority within the Democratic Party, they are now a very large minority and one that must be reckoned with. Within the Republican Party, conservatives in the mid-1970s were quite strong (recall that then ex-Governor Reagan nearly took the 1976 nomination away from President Ford), but are now a sizeable *majority* of Republican voters. Liberals have a great deal to say about what Democrats do, but conservatives have even more to say about what the Republicans do. And we should note that the numbers reflecting the expansion of both parties' ideological base are the numbers of presidential election voters. This is a very broad and diverse population. It is not the more rarified ideological midterm or primary electorates, party activists, or the politically engaged.

The changing ideological composition of the parties explains what some see as the inordinate influence of ideological zealots, particularly within the Republican Party. Congressional leaders, media-spouters, campaign funding fat cats, and ideological activists in other capacities are, pardon the expression, middle-men for the ideological wings of the parties.

They appear to be leading or misleading their parties because many partisans want to follow. The influence of these ideological activists is not so much in their skills at oration, organization, or parliamentary politics as it is in their representation of large and growing numbers of each party's rank-and-file. In the past, the influence of liberals and conservatives had been dispersed between the parties—to the advantage of moderates. The staggered realignment concentrated the influence of each ideological base for both parties. Since the ideological base is largest within the Republican Party, that is where the difference is most visible.

Staggered Party Polarization

A limited time frame in examining the development of party polarization is a third reason why it appeared to have been one-sided. A major contributor to the polarization of the parties was their realignment and, as we reviewed it in the last chapter, that process was staggered. It developed over several decades. The initial political change precipitating the realignment in the 1960s favored the Democrats. Republican gains in presidential voting, in party identification, and congressional election outcomes came about slowly as Republicans gradually made inroads in the South. A consequence of this staggered process is that congressional Democrats moved out of the center and to more liberal positions *before* the Republicans moved out of the center and to their more conservative positions.[16] If the focus is only on the more recent changes of the parties, the earlier Democratic Party shifts are missed and the party polarization looks to be a Republican-only phenomenon.

Poole and Rosenthal's data again provide evidence. They use their DW-NOMINATE scores of roll-call voting to identify moderates among House and Senate members over time. As noted earlier, they identify moderates as those who score just off the political center of their scale ($-.25$ to $+.25$). From the beginning of the New Deal party system in the 1930s (and even before) to the mid- to late 1950s, moderates were a larger contingent of the Democratic Party than of the Republican Party in both the House and the Senate. In the 83rd Congress (elected in 1952), for example, 61% of House Democrats but only 45% of House Republicans were moderates. This changed in the late 1950s. With an influx of liberal Democrats and Republicans not yet picking up conservative southern seats, the Republican Party became the more moderate congressional party. By the 96th Congress (elected in 1978), the ranks of moderates among House Republicans had increased to 55%, while the moderate wing of the Democratic caucus was reduced to only 36% of its membership. In the late 1980s and into the 1990s, the later stages of the staggered realignment, the numbers of moderates continued to decline among Democrats, though not as fast or as much as they did among Republicans, especially in the House. By 2013, Poole and Rosenthal's head count of moderates in the House found only 23 among 199 Democrats (12%) and only one moderate (Jones of North Carolina) out of 243 Republicans (less than 1%).[17]

While the asymmetry claim understandably focuses on the virtual extinction of moderate Republicans, the ranks of moderate Democrats have also been depleted. A majority of congressional Democrats had been moderates in the 1950s. Their numbers are now less than a quarter of that, by Poole and Rosenthal's count. If we only focus on what has happened since the late 1970s, party polarization looks asymmetric. However, if we broaden the time horizon to include developments since the 1950s, then a more complete picture emerges. The dwindling of moderate ranks started earlier for Democrats and later for Republicans. This reflects the staggered realignment process. It has the appearance of having gone further for Republicans than it has for Democrats for reasons already discussed (and other reasons soon to be discussed). In a highly polarized and ideologically aligned center-right nation, the more liberal party must reach out to the center to remain competitive and the more conservative party faces stronger internal pressures to represent its larger ideological base.

Measuring Ideology with Issues

The fourth and final element in resolving the asymmetry puzzle concerns a conflict between different measures of party polarization in Congress. Poole and Rosenthal's DW-NOMINATE scores produced by their highly sophisticated roll-call scaling methods indicate that Republicans moved much more in the conservative direction since the early 1960s than Democrats moved in the liberal direction. In the early 1960s in the House, according to the measure, Democrats were about as liberal as Republicans were conservative. By 2013, though both parties had become less centrist, Republicans were far more conservative than Democrats were liberal.

The two most prominent organizations monitoring ideological roll-call voting paint a different picture. The ratings of the Americans for Democratic Action (ADA), a champion of liberalism since the 1940s (as noted in chapter 1), indicate that Democrats moved further left than the Republicans moved right.[18] As the ADA saw it, House

Democrats from 1960 to 1966 voted the liberal position on key votes about 62% of the time. From 2002 to 2008, their support for liberal positions increased to 88% of the time, an increase of 26 percentage points.[19] On the Republican side of the aisle, change was much smaller. House Republicans from 1960 to 1966 voted for the liberal position 18% of the time. Their support declined by only six percentage points in the more recent period (2002–2008). By these ADA numbers, there has been over four times more change among House Democrats than among House Republicans. Comparisons of ADA ratings between the Senate parties produce substantively similar results.[20]

Congressional roll-call ratings from the American Conservative Union (ACU), an organization dedicated to the advancement of conservatism (as noted in chapter 1), also see Democrats as having moved farther left than Republicans moved right. Founded in 1964, the ACU did not begin issuing congressional roll-call ratings until 1971. By their numbers, average House Democrats in the early 1970s (1971–73) voted for the conservative position about 35% of the time. In 2012 and 2013, they typically supported the conservative position only 11% of the time, a 24 percentage point drop.[21] Support for conservative policies among House Republicans increased in this same period from 68% in the early 1970s to 80% in 2012 and 2013, a 12 percentage point increase. According to the ACU's ratings, liberalism among House Democrats increased about twice as much as conservatism increased among House Republicans.[22]

Have congressional Republicans veered more to the right as Poole and Rosenthal's scaling indicates, or did congressional Democrats move further to the left as the ADA and ACU scores report, or does the truth lie somewhere in between? Which of the ratings should we rely on? Each of them faces the inherent difficulties of inferring ideological perspectives from issue positions, in this case positions expressed in roll-call votes. These problems as they related to estimating the ideological perspectives of citizens from issue items on surveys were discussed in some detail in chapters 3 and 4. The problems of inferring ideologies from issue positions are no less for representatives in Congress than they are for average citizens. In trying to extract ideological perspectives over time from issues preferences (whether measured by survey responses or roll-call votes), there are evolving interpretations of ideologies, changes in the issues and in the proposed policies, changes in preferences, changes in participants, changes in the political and policy context in which the decisions are made or preferences expressed. There are lots of "moving parts." Any inference of ideological perspectives from issue positions requires some heavy assumptions, particularly when done over time. Still, as with the ideological views of the public, issue evidence is valuable and each of the ratings has strengths and weaknesses.

The ADA and ACU ratings have considerable merits. First, they are explicitly intended to rate support for liberal or conservative policy positions by the two groups dedicated to advancing these political perspectives. Individually, either rating might be criticized as biased, but this should not be a problem when the two are combined. Both groups also compose their ratings from what they regard to have been the most important roll calls of the year. As percentages of support on these votes, their ratings are simple, transparent, and easily interpreted. These ratings, however, also have their shortcomings. Each considers only a small number of all congressional roll calls (each as few as 10 and no more than 25 per year). Their dependence on a small number of votes introduces some additional instability and unreliability to the ADA and ACU ratings.[23] Various ulterior strategic motives (aimed at particular representatives) may also affect which roll calls are picked for each year's index.

Poole and Rosenthal's DW-NOMINATE scales also have much to commend them and have won widespread acceptance by legislative scholars. Rather than imposing an idea of which votes best reflect liberal or conservative orientations, their approach is inductive. Their scaling method identifies underlying dimensions that best fit the pattern of votes and the main dimension is interpreted as the ideological spectrum. A second strength is that the scale is based on a comprehensive consideration of all of the roll-call votes cast by representatives in both sessions of a Congress. In recent years in the House, this amounts to anywhere from about 700 to more than 1,400 roll calls in a two-year period. On the downside, the scale is not explicitly about ideology and does not distinguish between critical roll–call votes and those that are not.[24] Also, compared to the simplicity of the ADA and ACU ratings, Poole and Rosenthal's methodologically sophisticated ratings are quite complicated and, as a result, less transparent.

Despite the many differences between the simple ideological ratings of the ADA and the ACU and the complex scaling of roll-call
votes by Poole and Rosenthal, they are very highly correlated with
each other *within* a congressional term.[25] The ratings from the 112th
Congress, elected in November of 2010 and serving in 2011 and 2012,
illustrate their strong correspondence. The ADA's and the ACU's
combined 2011 and 2012 ratings (the mean of the two years) can be
compared to the biannual DW-NOMINATE scores. The ADA and
ACU ratings are very highly correlated with each other ($r = -.96$) and
just as highly correlated to the DW-NOMINATE scores, both separately ($r = -.95$ for ADA and $r = .97$ for ACU) and in combination
($r = .97$). For all practical purposes, for comparing the roll-call voting of representatives within a single Congress, the three indices are
interchangeable.[26]

The ratings are at odds over which party moved further from the
ideological center not because of differences *within* a congressional
term, but because of differences over how they treat ideological
change *across time.* The case of former Senator Richard Lugar, Republican of Indiana, illustrates the difference. Senator Lugar served six
terms from 1977 to 2013. He took office in 1976 after defeating the
Democratic incumbent and retired after being defeated by a Tea Party
backed challenger in the 2012 Republican primary. Hare, McCarty,
Poole, and Rothenthal observe that Lugar's DW-NOMINATE scores
"did not change very much over time," becoming just about 5% less
conservative over his 30-plus year career.[27]

Both the liberal ADA and the conservative ACU see considerably
more movement toward the center in Senator Lugar's record. According to ADA scores, Lugar voted for the liberal position only
about 11% of the time between 1977 and 2005. In the last seven years
of his career (2006–2012), however, he voted with the liberals 26%
of the time. The same movement is evident in the senator's ACU
ratings. From 1977 to 2005, he voted with conservatives on 81% of
the key votes. From 2006 to 2012, his support for conservative positions dropped to 66%. By both ADA and ACU measures, Senator
Lugar moved 15 percentage points toward the center, not five percentage points.

The differences between the DW-NOMINATE scores on the one
hand and the ADA and ACU scores on the other are a consequence

of whether ideological measures are left intact to reflect evolving expressions of ideologies over time or whether they are adjusted to simulate constancy across years with different issues. The ADA and ACU ratings take an entirely contemporary perspective of ideological votes. The roll-call voting of representatives is rated as more or less in line with liberal or conservative perspectives based on what those ideologies mean at the time in the context of current politics and conditions. There is no effort, apart from the natural continuity of common-use language, to define liberal or conservative voting consistently from one year to the next. Standards are free to float with the context and meaning of the times. DW-NOMINATE, on the other hand, takes a longer-term and more context-free perspective on ideological votes.[28] It makes an effort to maintain ideological standards fairly constant through time. The measure attempts to make what it means to be or to vote as a liberal or conservative roughly the same from one year to the next.

Which approach to measuring ideological views is most appropriate? The prevailing view within political science is that they should be context-independent or nearly constant across time.[29] The contention is that comparisons across time can only be validly made if what it means to be a liberal or a conservative is the same at different times. If what it means to be a liberal or conservative is in flux, then what would it mean to say that conservatives' ranks increased or decreased? Has the composition of the electorate changed or has the meaning of the terms changed (e.g., unchanged liberals now called conservatives)? It would be comparing apples at one time to oranges (now called apples) at another.

Although this seems eminently sensible on its face, there is also a strong case that changing contexts should be taken into account when determining ideological orientations from roll-call votes. Someone who firmly holds an ideological perspective may vote in different ways at different times because of changing circumstances and changing political and social climates. The expression of an ideological orientation may change even when the orientation itself is constant because the contexts in which ideological views are applied may have changed.

The same-sex marriage issue offers a good example. Most die-hard liberals would not even have raised the issue of legalizing same-sex marriage in the 1990s, but by the 2010s a majority of Americans favored it, including about a third of Republicans. Was President Obama any more liberal when his position on same-sex marriage, like a good deal of the public's, evolved from opposition to support over this time? Probably not. His ideological orientation had not changed. The political and social context of the issue had changed. Support for same-sex marriage had become less controversial. In 1990, a political leader who advocated making gay marriage legal would have been seen as a radical. Not so by 2010. What it meant to be a liberal or a conservative had not changed, but how either was expressed changed because the context had changed.

There would seem to be little question that ideologies evolve over time and that they are expressed in different ways in different contexts. They are context-sensitive, not context-independent. The public and political leaders should be evaluated within their own times, and there is no more certain way of ensuring the application of contemporary standards than using measures that were produced at the time. Unless there are very strong reasons to set them aside, deference should be paid to those contemporary evaluations, whether they are individuals declaring their ideology (or their partisanship) or the ADA or ACU declaring a representative to have voted more or less along the liberal or the conservative line.[30]

Ironically, though often cited as the reason for adjusting ratings for comparisons across years, consistency also argues for the use of the contemporary (ADA and ACU) scales rather than the over-time adjusted (DW-NOMINATE) scales for tracking and comparing the polarization of party leaders. If the public's political views (ideology, issues, and votes) reflect contemporary standards at different times, then consistency requires that the views of political leaders should be measured by the same contemporary standards. To do otherwise (to use non-contemporary standards for elites and contemporary standards for the public) would really be comparing apples with oranges.

SYMMETRICAL PARTY POLARIZATION

When all of the pieces of the party polarization puzzle are gathered and assembled, it is clear that the current polarization of the parties is not one-sided. The parties have become more polarized from one another as each of their ideological bases expanded following the realignment. They better reflected an increasingly polarized public. The public moved a bit further to the right and, in stages, political leaders followed. Democrats drifted to the left and Republicans later moved further to the right, in part to reflect its more conservative base and in part to reflect a public that had become a bit more conservative.

Drawing on both the circumstantial evidence of the national competitiveness of the congressional parties (Democratic dominance from the 1930s to the 1990s and electoral parity since) and the contemporary measures of the ideological orientations of the congressional parties, a general picture of what happened comes together. Though neither congressional party had been highly ideological from the 1930s to the 1960s, with their combined southern and non-southern wings, Democrats were more heterogeneous. Because of this, they were more centrist than Republicans. There was asymmetry in the extent of party polarization then and it benefitted Democrats electorally. Democrats controlled the U.S. House of Representatives for 58 of the 62 years from 1932 to 1994 and the U.S. Senate for all but ten of those years.

By the time the realignment deepened into congressional elections in 1994 and the increased polarization of the parties was well under way, Democrats had moved a good deal to the left and the Republicans had begun their move more to the right (by ADA and ACU accounts).

Though the *change was asymmetrical*, it produced *a more symmetrical party system*. Democrats moved more, but they were more centrist to begin with. In the post-realignment period both parties were well removed from the political center (and that center had itself moved a bit to the right), but they were closer to being equidistant from the political center of the electorate than they had been. As a result, Democrats were no longer electorally dominant. The parties were now quite evenly and intensely competitive in both presidential and congressional elections.

Beyond being consistent with the contemporary ideological scales and changes in the parties' electoral standings, the greater ideological *change* of congressional Democrats also makes sense in terms of the changing coalitions of the parties. The subtraction of southern conservatives from an otherwise fairly liberal Democratic Party made a bigger difference to the ideological balance within the Democratic Party than the addition of those southern conservatives made to an otherwise already fairly conservative Republican Party. The former moved the Democrats to the left. The latter mostly reinforced the Republicans on the right. This was partially offset, but only partially, by the subtraction of the smaller group of non-southern moderates and liberals from the Republicans and their addition to Democratic ranks. As the net gains for Republicans in Congress and in the electorate indicate, Republican gains substantially exceeded those made by Democrats in the realignment.

As to the original claim of an out-of-step, insurgent Republican Party, it is inconsistent with the ADA and ACU ratings and, more importantly, with changes in each party's record of electoral success. The idea that the Republican Party grew from its minority status to being at parity with the Democrats while the Democrats maintained a mildly liberal position and Republicans veered off to the far right just does not add up.[31] It may be true that the centrist median voter is not the be-all and end-all that he or she is cracked up to be, a point explored in the next chapter, but parties still do not put themselves in better positions electorally by running too far away from the political center.

The original asymmetry claim had it backwards. The pre-realignment parties were asymmetrically polarized, with the Democrats being more centrist by virtue of the mix of southern conservatives with non-southern liberals. As a result, Democrats were the majority party. In the post-realignment, parties are more greatly polarized, but also more symmetrically polarized. As a result of the new symmetry, the parties are near parity.

None of this is to deny that there are plenty of uncompromising, even belligerent, conservative purists in the Republican Party. There are, both among leaders and followers. However, Republicans are not unique in this regard. Both highly polarized parties have their wild-eyed ideological extremists. There are many Democrats as well as Republicans who are outside the political mainstream, as wide as that mainstream has become. Whether Democrats or Republicans have the more embarrassing extremists in their ranks may be impossible to determine. For the time being, as far as electoral evidence indicates, it appears that the public sees this contest as a draw.

THE POLITICS OF FRUSTRATION

The question of whether the polarization of the parties is asymmetrical or symmetrical has been answered—but there remains a loose end. Speculation that party polarization was asymmetric grew out of a sense that Tea Party conservatives in the Republican Party were practicing a particularly antagonistic and uncompromising brand of politics. Were they?

The charge that the Republicans' ideological base has been less reasonable than Democrats' base is difficult to prove. The more extreme elements of either party are generally not inclined toward compromise and the base of the out-party should be the most intransigent. Moreover, there are usually two sides to every story. Compromise requires a good-faith effort from both sides. Liberal Democrats have not been simply innocent bystanders in this street-fighting.

Even so, the Republicans' Tea Party conservative base seems to be more demanding and obstinate than the Democrats' liberal base. Tea Party conservatives are generally held responsible for taking the nation to the edge of "the fiscal cliff" in 2011 over opposition to raising the debt ceiling and for shutting down the government for 16 days in 2013 in their efforts to repeal the Affordable Care Act (Obamacare). As American policy conflict goes, these brinkmanship tactics are beyond normal bounds and beyond the behavior of liberal Democrats when a Republican occupied the White House. If asymmetric polarization does not explain this intransigence, then what does?

I suspect the answer is frustration. Very conservative Republicans may have good reason to feel quite frustrated, much more so than very liberal Democrats. This frustration grew out of a trail of conservative Republican disappointments since President Reagan left office in 1989. Since Reagan's days, an idyllic Camelot for conservatives, the right has felt neglected. The liberal presidencies of Bill Clinton and Barack Obama account for much of this frustration. The aggressive overreaching of presidential powers, particularly in the Obama years, may have amplified this alienation.[32] The natural tensions engendered by party polarization, however, are not the only reason for conservatives "behaving badly."

A great deal of the anger of Tea Party conservatives is directed at the Republican establishment. Many conservatives in the party's base feel poorly represented—at times even betrayed—by their own party's leadership. As many in the base see it, Republican presidents, presidential candidates, and congressional leaders have often been more concerned about striking deals with liberal Democrats than standing up for conservative principles. It began with President George H. W. Bush reneging on his "Read my lips, no new taxes" pledge. The moderate-conservative and ultimately failed presidential candidacies of Bob Dole in 1996, John McCain in 2008, and Mitt Romney in 2012 did nothing to endear the GOP's establishment to the base. Conservatives also felt that they could not count on their own party's congressional leadership to advance conservative positions. Internal party battles between Tea Party conservatives and Republican leadership escalated in frequency and bitterness. Tea Party attacks on party leaders, including the threat to hold back floor votes on party leadership positions, resulted in House Speaker John Boehner's resignation in 2015 and the ensuing turmoil over the party's congressional leadership.

The frustration of conservative Republicans with their party's establishment is not confined to the maneuverings of disgruntled firebrand representatives. Conservative frustration is found in the public as well. An unusual number of conservative Republican Party identifiers hold unfavorable views of their own party. A Pew study in mid-2015 found that 27% of Republicans held unfavorable views of the Republican Party. Only 11% of Democrats had unfavorable impressions of their party.[33] This difference between the parties may be electorally costly for Republicans, since turnout often suffers among partisans who feel alienated from their own party (more on this in the next chapter).

Despite outnumbering liberals by a wide margin, their importance to the Republican Party, and some big electoral victories (most notably the 2010 and 2014 midterm elections), conservatives have not had much policy success to cheer about in a long time. Arguably, their last major policy victory was the passage of the Bush Tax Cuts of 2001. Since then, liberals have enjoyed numerous victories, from the $800 billion stimulus bill in 2009 and the Affordable Care Act of 2010 to the Supreme Court's rulings on that act as well as its gay marriage ruling. A Pew Research Center study in 2015 reported that liberal Democrats were about evenly split over whether their side had been winning more than losing. The right was not so divided. Conservative Republicans were nearly seven times more likely to see themselves as usually on the losing side in political disputes.[34]

An exhaustive assessment of whether liberals or conservatives have met with greater policy success in recent decades might reach a different conclusion. Objectively, perhaps conservatives might not have been treated so badly. Perhaps their expectations are unrealistic. That is open to question. The point here is simply that there are very plausible reasons for conservatives to believe that they have not had their views well represented in the process and for them to be infuriated by this. It is understandable that this frustration and anger might boil over. Whether of the left or right, and whether advisable or not, Americans who feel unrepresented often act out. It is a signal that, for them, the system is dysfunctional. Sometimes they hold protest marches on Washington or occupy Wall Street. Sometimes they pour tea into a harbor. Sometimes they shut down the government.

CHAPTER 8

WHY ARE THE PARTIES POLARIZED AT ALL?

It can safely be said that the only extreme that is attractive to the
large majority of American voters is the extreme center.

—Richard M. Scammon and Ben J. Wattenberg,
The Real Majority[1]

It is the most fundamental tenet of American two-party politics:
elections are won by parties and candidates that win the support of
the political center, the median voter. It is elementary democracy. In
a two-way race, 50% plus one wins. The median voter is that revered
"plus one."

Drawn from this basic understanding is the cardinal rule of campaigning: capture the center. Since the votes of swing voters in the
political center decide elections, the thinking is that political campaigns and the appeals of the parties and candidates should focus
laser-like on attracting the votes of centrists. And attracting the votes of
centrists means that the parties and their candidates should advocate

centrist views and back them up with centrist policies. From formal theories of two-party politics to prominent political observers to on-the-ground political strategists, centrism is a core practical political principle.[2]

THE LURE OF THE CENTER?

The formal statement behind the centrist creed is the median voter theorem. The claim that competition between two parties leads to their positioning at the median was developed by Harold Hotelling, refined by Arthur Smithies, and extended and immortalized by Anthony Downs in *An Economic Theory of Democracy*.[3] The well-known logic is best reviewed in figure 8.1 drawn from Downs.[4] This should be familiar since it was used to explore possible asymmetric polarization in the previous chapter. As in that discussion, the figure represents a single dimension (the liberal-conservative ideological spectrum) on which voters make their choice, the positions of two political parties or candidates (D and R), and the preferred position of the median voter (M), whose position perfectly divides the rest of the electorate (half being more liberal and half more conservative).

As configured with the parties equidistant from the median voter's position, the parties are in an electoral standoff. Each draws the votes of those voters whose positions are more extreme than the party's position as well as the votes of voters holding more moderate positions between the party's position and that of the median voter. Both the parties have an incentive to adjust their position more toward the centrist median voter's position. If Democrats, for instance, staked out a slightly less liberal position, they would keep the voters already inclined toward them and would also be more attractive to the median voter and even some very mildly right of center voters. The same reasoning applies on the Republican side. Each party's move toward the center gains it more votes, costs the other party votes, and should provoke a countermove toward the center by the other party. The parties should eventually converge on the position of the median voter. Electoral self-interest should propel each party inexorably to the center. Until a party reaches the position of the median voter, there are votes to be gained by moving to the center and votes to be lost to the opposition by not moving to the center. Ulti-

D	M	R
Liberal	*Center*	*Conservative*

Key:
M is the position of the median voter
D is the position of the Democratic Party
R is the position of the Republican Party

Figure 8.1. Spatial competition, the median voter, and the logic of party convergence.

mately, perfect competition should produce parties with identically centrist positions.

Long before it was formally codified as a theorem, the efficacy of the centrist strategy was understood by political advisors and commentators. It is the conventional wisdom. If the infamous thief Willie Sutton robbed banks because, as he quipped, "that's where the money is," political strategists guide candidates to the center because that's where the votes are.[5] It is elementary. If elections are won in the political center, then campaigns should be single-minded in appealing to voters in the center.

Nowhere has the case for centrism been made with greater force than by the highly esteemed psephologists Richard Scammon and Ben Wattenberg in *The Real Majority*.[6] Their study of the American electorate in the late 1960s and early 1970s was a plea to the Democratic Party to avoid being captured by its passionately immoderate left wing. As the epigraph for this chapter attests, their advocacy of centrism was plain and unequivocal. Put most simply: "the winning coalition in America is the one that holds the center on the attitudinal battlefield."[7] The drive to the center is at once democracy at work, representing the public's views as well as possible, and smart, self-interested practical politics.

Twenty years earlier, the renowned author and political commentator Walter Lippmann offered a similar assessment. "Success in operating free institutions through governments by parties," according to Lippmann, "is the force which draws the two parties closer and closer together as they face the voters—until when election day arrives, it often seems as if on measures and principles the choice is between tweedledum and tweedledee."[8]

Dedication to the centrist appeal is not limited to distinguished political sages. It permeates the thinking of most political practitioners. This was exposed in an embarrassing slip of candor during the 2012 presidential campaign. In late March 2012, as Republican Mitt Romney sat on the verge of clinching his party's nomination after a protracted contest with multiple opponents running to his right, his senior campaign advisor Eric Fehrnstrom was asked whether candidate Romney had been forced to take positions that were too conservative for the general electorate in order to mollify the powerful right wing of his party that had controlled the nomination. Fehrnstrom indicated that Romney's apparent shift to the right for the nomination would not present a problem in the general election. The candidate could easily shift back to more centrist positions. As Fehrnstrom put it: "you hit a reset button for the fall campaign. Everything changes. It's almost like an Etch A Sketch. You can kind of shake it up, and we start all over again."[9]

The remark created an uproar because it suggested that the candidate's issue positions were simply matters of political expediency and not sincerely held beliefs. What went largely unnoticed was that both the question and the answer and most everyone else commenting on them later accepted as a political fact of life that general election appeals should move to the political center in order to be viable. It was assumed by everyone. It was a no-brainer.

With the belief so ingrained in the thinking of everyone from political sages to on-the-ground political tacticians that elections are won in the center and that campaigns should formulate and adjust their appeals to win over crucial centrist swing voters, one would think that the political parties would converge on the center, that they would not be polarized at all. If the central goal of parties is to win elections, and you can't do much unless you do, and elections are won by winning the vote of the median voter, and that vote is won by presenting that voter with a set of policies that he or she finds most agreeable, then the political gravitational pull of the center on competitive parties should be overwhelming. They should not only not be polarized. Democrats and Republicans should both occupy the center.

But they don't. Not even close.

NON-CENTRIST PARTY POLITICS

Despite the enshrined wisdom that electoral success requires centrist positioning on the issues, study after study has shown that parties have not positioned themselves in the political center defined by the median voter. Many of these studies have been noted in our discussions of the increased polarization of the parties in chapter 1 as well as in the last two chapters. All of the congressional roll-call measures of the parties' decision-making in government, for instance, indicate that the parties defied the centrist strategy, long before their increased party polarization of recent decades. Similarly, several major studies of the policy positions of presidents indicate that they quite often do not represent the preferences of the median voter.[10]

A number of other studies of the party and candidate positions reach the same conclusion. It is not that the parties are deceptively non-centrist once in office; they are not especially centrist in seeking office. For instance, in his impressive study of the issue positions of presidential candidates in the 1960s and 1970s, Benjamin Page concluded that there were significant, though not "immense," party differences on the issues and Page's study was conducted before the increase in party polarization.[11] In a methodologically sophisticated and ambitious study of the issue positions of congressional candidates from the 1870s to the 1990s, Stephen Anolabehere, James Snyder, and Charles Stewart found a remarkably consistent pattern of ideological differences between Democratic and Republican candidates for the U.S. House.[12] Both parties in elections routinely diverge a good deal from the median position of their constituencies, so much so that they are blamed for making later compromise within government significantly more difficult.[13] Based on this evidence, the claim that the parties' electoral self-interests drive them to converge in the political center fails as an empirical prediction. Parties and candidates certainly do not ignore the median voter's views, but they do not seem to be especially driven to adopt those views either.[14]

In different ways with different data and different methodologies over different periods of time, a variety of studies arrive at the same destination: the American parties and their candidates do not converge on the political center. Even before the relatively recent period of increased party polarization, the parties were marked more by their differences than by their similarities. The divergence is large enough and consistent enough that most voters are aware of it.[15] If parties and candidates are attempting to converge on the median voter in order to win elections, as the sages of centrism advise them to do, they are doing a very poor job of it.

If centrist politics are such smart politics, as in winning politics, why haven't the parties converged on the center? Why have the parties been unable or unwilling to converge on the political center? Why are the parties polarized *at all*?

REASONS FOR NON-CENTRIST PARTIES

At the most basic level, parties differ from the base and from each other because there would be little reason for them to exist if they were identical. A party's distinctiveness from the opposition is its raison d'être. If both parties converged on the position of the median voter, why would leaders or voters become Democrats or Republicans? There might be some personal reasons among voters or organizational power reasons among leaders to affiliate with the parties, but perfect convergence on the center would undermine the central representational motivations for loyalty to either party. This existential reason for non-centrism, however, might only be cause for seeing daylight between the parties' positions, the lack of perfect convergence.[16] It does not explain the larger differences that routinely have been found.

There are a number of reasons beyond the existential reason why the parties have not converged near the political center, why they are routinely polarized to some substantial degree. The first two are practical complications with securing a centrist position. These are reasons why parties would be unable to execute a centrist strategy. Beyond practical limits or obstacles to centrism, there are three other reasons why parties would not want to adopt a purely or even substantially centrist strategy—even if they were able to do so. In seeking electoral victories, parties and candidates have important concerns beyond pleasing the political center of the nation. As seemingly compelling as the logic of centrism is, views beyond those in the national political center are also important to winning elections.

Two Obstacles

The first reason that parties do not abide by the strategic mandate of centrism is that intraparty politics are messy. No one is in charge. Even in the heyday of party bosses, the bosses were usually plural. Parties are not monolithic, single rational actors. They are groups of individuals who bring different resources to the party and seek different benefits from it. Activists and the candidates all have their own personal ideas about where the party should be headed. Even if the most powerful people in the party bought the centrist strategy hook, line, and sinker, they would face substantial internal obstacles to moving the party to a set of centrist issue positions. Huge, loosely structured, complex organizations that depend heavily on the good will of many of its "members" are not easily led anywhere.

A second obstacle to the convergence of the parties on the political center is that the political center is not obvious. This problem goes well beyond the simple fact that parties lack full information. As the consideration of the ADA-ACU roll-call scales compared to the DW-NOMINATE roll-call scale in the last chapter illustrates, determining where the center lies is not an easy matter even retrospectively and with hard votes. Moreover, are we interested in the median position of all eligible voters, plausible voters, likely voters, or actual voters? Are we interested in the views of everyone or only of those who care most about the issue?

Beyond these variables, the determination of centrist positions in the heat of real-time politics is unavoidably subjective and carries with it some routine biases. There is a strong tendency for people to think that their positions are more popular or centrist than they actually are. Selective perceptions and plain old wishful thinking are two reasons for this misperception. It is also the case that most people talk with people who have views similar to their own and this is particularly true of people who have strong non-centrist views.[17] As a result, even if a party were in control of people who wanted to place the party at the political center of the spectrum, they would have a skewed idea of what that actually meant in real terms. Their idea of what was politically centrist would most likely not match up with everyone else's.

Multiple Political Centers

A third reason why the parties do not converge on a single national political center is that political competition in American politics involves competition in multiple constituencies. Each contest in each constituency has its own political center and each of these may differ a good deal from the political center of the nation. The multiple constituencies in which parties compete present conflicting political centers that can not be simultaneously occupied.

The most often noted of these is the conflict between each party's nomination constituency and its general election constituency.[18] In order to win a party's nomination, candidates must attract votes that come largely from their party's dominant side of the political spectrum. Democratic hopefuls must take more liberal positions to attract the votes of Democratic primary voters and Republican hopefuls must take more conservative positions to satisfy their generally more conservative partisans. Whether nomination contests draw more ideological voters to the polls or simply reflect the ideological tilt of the party, the median of each party's nomination constituency is a good deal removed from the larger and more moderate general electorate.[19] Candidates routinely try to ease a bit more to the middle after their nominations and before the general electorate notices, but this can only be done successfully at the margins.[20] The memories and skepticism of voters, the attention of the media to flip-flops, and the negative campaigning of an alert opposition, all enhanced by modern video recording, place severe constraints on the effectiveness of Mr. Fehrnstrom's magical political Etch A Sketch to wipe away a candidate's ideologically appealing position in a nomination campaign and replace it with a believably centrist position for the general election's campaign.

In addition to the conflicting pulls of nomination and general election constituencies, there are the conflicting pressures of different geographic constituencies. In House elections, the parties must respond to 435 different median voters, one for every congressional district.[21] In Senate and presidential elections (because of the electoral vote system), there are 50 state median voters (plus one in DC for presidential elections). The median voter in each of these different constituencies may differ a good deal from the median voter of the overall national electorate. It could be said, for instance, that the median voters of very liberal Vermont and of very conservative Utah are themselves highly polarized from one another.

Beyond the competing demands created by different nomination and election constituencies, candidates and parties also must respond to the informal constituencies who voluntarily provide the resources necessary to mount effective modern campaigns. This is the "invisible primary" of presidential nomination campaigns writ large.[22] In addition to responding to the median voters of both nomination and general election contests, candidates and their parties must attract the support of the resource providers—the activists who supply much of the labor for campaigns, the contributors who finance campaign operations, and the media who make choices about the extent and tone of campaign coverage.

Because of these multiple constituencies, every candidate is faced with winning the support of several median voters (resource, nomination, and election electorates) that differ from each other and differ from one candidate to the next, and none of these median voters is the median voter of the national electorate. These many competing demands undoubtedly lead the parties to depart significantly from the nation's political center. To adapt Lincoln's famous observation borrowed from poet John Lydgate, a party cannot please all of these median voters at any one time.

Performance Counts

A fourth reason parties are not driven to the political center is that ideological values are not the only consideration affecting election outcomes. A party's performance in office also matters. Liberals, moderates, and conservatives all care about a range of public conditions, from public safety and national security to a clean environment and economic prosperity. Voters who evaluate the record of a party positively on these consensus or "valence" issues may support the party even if they are not so positive about its ideological perspective. Conversely, voters who regard a party as failing on these issues may vote against it even if they are ideologically compatible. In evaluating what the parties are likely to do if elected, voters look both to the parties' ideological values and the issue positions based on those values as well as to the parties' records of past performance in office. Retrospective evaluations of the parties' records have a strong impact in presidential voting.[23]

In a sense, the parties' relative performance in office is a second dimension on which the parties compete.[24] The competition of the parties is not unidimensional on the ideological spectrum as the median voter theorem assumes. The parties must compete over the voters' perceptions of the parties' ideological inclinations, but they also compete over the voters' views of the parties' past performance on the array of valence issues. This second dimension of performance relieves some of the pressure on a party to move more closely to the center than the opposing party. Election results do not rest simply on which party has the optimal ideological position.

The elections of two modern presidents suggest how important performance considerations are and how they may trump concerns about catering to the ideological center. The two presidents are Ronald Reagan and Barack Obama. President Reagan is often considered to have been the most conservative president since the 1920s. President Obama may be the most liberal president in this same period. While some might quibble with these assessments, neither of these presidents could remotely be labeled as a centrist. Yet both were elected and reelected. In Obama's case, he was elected and reelected over seemingly more moderate opponents.

How were these decidedly immoderate presidents elected? One plausible answer is that they were elected because of the poor performance of their predecessors in the opposite party. Republicans did not need to be more centrist in 1980, because Democratic President Jimmy Carter had failed on performance grounds. Similarly, in 2008, the Democrats could elect a non-centrist because Republicans under President George W. Bush had left the country mired in two wars and with an economy in collapse. In dissatisfaction if not despair, voters turned to the out-party candidate, centrist or not.

Compounding the competing effects of performance is that moderates are more likely to emphasize performance considerations in their voting decisions and non-centrists are more likely to emphasize values considerations in theirs. All voters are looking for a basis to make their decisions, some important difference between the parties or candidates. Centrists are likely to be torn between the parties when it comes to their ideological values—that is what makes them centrists. So they are more likely to be more performance-minded in deciding how to vote. Non-centrists, on the other hand, are more likely to have strong ideologically based value preferences for one party over the other. As a consequence, the parties have an even greater incentive to pay attention to the non-centrist values of those in their bases than to the centrist values of those occupying the middle of the ideological spectrum.[25]

THE POWER OF THE BASE

Beyond the impediments of parties having to deal with conflicting internal demands and the difficulties associated with accurately locating the ideological middle of the public, beyond the distractions of being pulled to multiple centers of different constituencies and contending with concerns about performance as well as values, there is a more elementary reason why the parties do not converge on the political center: contrary to the median voter theorem and the conventional wisdom of centrism that has developed around it, *it is not in the electoral self-interests of the parties to converge at the center of the ideological spectrum*. Single-minded centrism is not politically smart.

It is true that elections in a two-party system are won by the party securing the vote of the median voter. That is majority rule (and would be true even if the electorate's views were bimodal). This, however, does *not* mean that the median voter is the only one who counts, the only voter with power, the only voter who the parties must respond to in order to win elections. Even if parties were single rational actors, even if they competed only in one national constituency and if voters cast their ballots purely based on which party held ideological views closest to their own, the optimal electoral strategy of the parties would not call for them to converge on the political center. Parties should not ignore centrist voters, but they should not cater to them either. To some extent, the parties should be polarized. The reason for this is that *neither party can afford to take the votes of its political base of non-centrists for granted*. Non-centrists, through their turnout, have considerable leverage over the parties and they compete with the swing votes of centrists for influence over the parties' positions.

Two Puzzles, One Solution

Why can't parties depend on the votes of their non-centrist base which would allow them to focus single-mindedly on winning over centrist voters? This non-convergence puzzle is entwined with the second major puzzle left by Anthony Downs's *An Economic Theory of Democracy*. That is the turnout puzzle: since the probability of anyone's vote deciding the election's outcome is essentially zero, why does anyone bother to vote? Whether you vote or not, the election will turn out the same way and the policies of the government will affect you in the same way. If you vote, you get X. If you don't vote, you still get X, only you had to go through all of the trouble of voting (getting registered to vote, informing yourself about the candidates and their positions, deciding who to vote for, and then taking the time to go to the polls on election day, waiting in line, and voting). It is a classic collective-action problem. Voting seems to entail bearing costs without gaining any additional benefits. It appears to make no sense to vote. Yet tens of millions of Americans do vote. Moreover, as study after study has shown, the most educated and best informed among us are most likely to vote, to behave in this seemingly irrational way.[26] Why?

The answer is that though people understand that they are not dictators, that they will not individually decide election results, they do have a chance of making some difference by acting in concert with other like-minded voters.[27] The more people favoring a party who turn out to vote for it, the better that party's chance of winning. A voter cannot determine the election's outcome any more than a single soldier can determine a war's outcome or a single contribution to a charity can help cure a disease, but each can do what he or she can to help the common cause. Helping at the margins is the most anyone can do.[28] The question is whether even this small contribution to a common cause is worth the effort.

Whether a potential voter should bother to vote depends on the perceived costs and the perceived benefits of voting. Voting is not an expensive undertaking, but neither is it cost-free. Aside from the official hurdles of registering and getting to a polling place on election day or securing an early voting ballot, voters must obtain and digest information about the candidates and parties and decide their vote. Then there are the opportunity costs. Would a potential voter rather be engaged in doing or thinking about something other than the election? These costs are not high, many seem to have plenty of time on their hands (judging by how many partake of what passes for entertainment), and official requirements for voting are low and have been reduced even more in recent decades. Even so, they are high enough that many think they are not worth bearing. Potential voters must have strong enough vote preferences to offset their perceived costs, otherwise they will steer clear of the election.[29] Voters with strong vote preferences will generally bear the costs of voting, those with weak vote preferences may not.

Preference Strength

What affects the strength of a potential voter's vote preference? Boiling down the numerous reasons for liking or disliking a party to a single ideological dimension, the strength of a potential voter's preference depends on two considerations: (1) the perceived difference between the two parties and (2) the proximity of the closer or more favored party.[30] This second consideration is sometimes referred to as the expressive reason to vote or abstain from voting, though it would seem that expression probably does not have a great deal to do with it. After all, at risk of understatement, there are many more effective ways of expressing an opinion than the solitary act of casting a secret ballot in the privacy of a voting booth.

The two considerations affecting preference strength are illustrated in figure 8.2, in this case with a non-centrist conservative potential voter. In condition 1, there is a big difference between the two parties and the closer of the two parties and the potential voter hold very similar views. Since the potential voter sees a big difference between the parties and sees one that he or she agrees with, the potential voter's preference is likely to be strong enough to make voting worthwhile. In condition 2, the more conservative party has moved much closer to the political center. In this situation, the difference between the parties is relatively small and the potential voter and the less objectionable party are far apart in their views. Under these circumstances, with two fairly similar parties and neither one representing the potential voter's views very well, it may be difficult for the potential voter to muster up enough enthusiasm to bother voting for a party he or she feels only lukewarm about.[31]

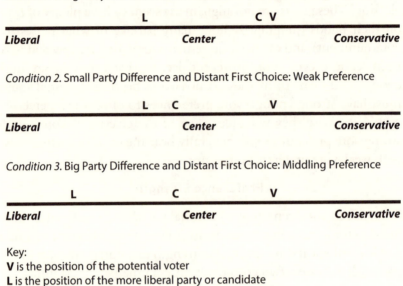

Condition 1. Big Party Difference and Proximate First Choice: Strong Preference

Condition 2. Small Party Difference and Distant First Choice: Weak Preference

Condition 3. Big Party Difference and Distant First Choice: Middling Preference

Key:
V is the position of the potential voter
L is the position of the more liberal party or candidate
C is the position of the more conservative party or candidate

Figure 8.2. Party differences, first choice proximity, and strength of vote preference.

Responses to the 2004 ANES illustrate the association. Respondents were asked to rate their feelings about the presidential candidates on a "thermometer scale" from zero (most negative) to 100 (most positive). Only 62% of those who were relatively cool (59 degrees or lower) toward their preferred candidate reported voting. Reported turnout increased to 68% for those indicating a rating in the 60s and to 74% for those rating their candidate in the 70s. Those hotly enthusiastic about their candidate, rating their choice anywhere from 80 to 100 degrees, reported a turnout rate of 86%. The strength of the vote preference is not just about party differences; which party is relatively closer than the other to the potential voter, the absolute proximity of a party to the potential voter matters as well. Both affect the willingness of potential voters to turn out.[32]

There are two reasons why proximity matters. The first is that voters want to feel sure that they are doing the right thing. They want to be proud of their vote, not uneasy or even ashamed of it. They would like to feel comfortable that they are placing trust in a party or candidate worthy of that trust and would like to avoid feeling complicit in the election of someone who they might later consider embarrassing. Potential voters are often reluctant to vote for a party they think would not represent their views, even if that party is less abhorrent than its opposition. The importance of the proximity of the closer party to the potential voter is illustrated by a comparison of conditions 1 and 3 in figure 8.2. In this pair of conditions, the potential voter's views are the same and the extent of differences between the parties is the same. The difference between the two conditions is that the potential voter and the closer of the two parties (the more conservative party, in this case) hold quite similar views in condition 1 and very different views in condition 3. Though the potential voter has reason to vote because of the party differences in both conditions, condition 1 holds the additional incentive of voting for a party that the potential voter feels comfortable about. In condition 3, the potential voter is being asked to hold his or her nose and vote for a party he or she does not really like. This is not a pleasant task and it is a natural inclination to avoid unpleasant tasks if they can be avoided.[33]

A second reason why distance from the more preferred party matters to the preference strength of a potential voter is that this distance affects perceptions of the importance of the difference between the parties. This is a psychological application of the Euclidean linear perspective. The idea of linear perspective is that heights or distances appear greater when close and smaller when viewed from a longer distance. The idea has been stated in different ways in a variety of disciplines. The common example involves the perceived distance between the rails of a railroad track. At close range, they appear wide apart and parallel. When viewed from a great distance off on the horizon, they appear to converge to a point. A town 50 miles away from your home seems a long way away. A 50-mile distance between objects on the moon appears to be a speck. So, too, in politics. Differences appear smaller at a distance. A centrist might see a difference between the parties as being of great consequence, while someone at the outer edge of the political spectrum may regard the same difference as inconsequential, mere trivial tweaks of the established mainstream. As a result, when some non-centrists are asked to choose between a left of center Democrat and a right of center Republican, they may see the difference, but conclude that both are so establishment-oriented that there is not enough of a difference to care about, not a big enough difference to bother voting.

If the turnout of non-centrists depends on parties responding to them enough that they feel comfortable about voting for a party and perceive the differences between the parties as significant enough to warrant their attention, then the parties have good reason *not* to be obsessed with pleasing the centrist voter. This does not mean that the median voter is not decisive. The majoritarian principle ensures that he or she is. What it means is that there is not a single fixed-in-place median voter in any election. The ideological position of the median voter moves with the turnout of each party's base. If Democrats can roust more liberals to vote and Republicans are unsuccessful in convincing Tea Party conservatives that a Republican vote will sufficiently advance the conservative agenda, then the median voter is found a shade more to the left. In effect, for every non-centrist voter a party turns out in an election, the median voter moves one vote closer to the party's side of the ideological spectrum. For every potential vote of a party's base that sits out of an election, the median voter moves one vote further away. The median voter matters. It is just not set in stone where that median voter is located. The turnout of non-centrists has a great deal to say about where that median is, and parties cannot afford to ignore this.

Non-Centrist Turnout

There are, then, good reasons why non-centrists might not turn out to vote if their favored party moved too much to the center. And this variable turnout of non-centrists would provide the parties with good reason not to converge on the political center. The question we now turn to is whether there is evidence that non-centrist turnout varies from election to election and whether the turnout of non-centrists is associated with the parties' electoral fortunes. Is partisan polarization in the electoral interests of the parties?

The possibility of an abstention effect on positioning was initially raised by Smithies.[34] Downs repeated the possibility, noting that the convergence of the parties on the center may result in "political extremists becoming disgusted at the identity of the parties, and refusing to vote for either if they become too much alike."[35] Subsequent studies, however, produced mixed results about the rational abstention of neglected or alienated non-centrists. Some of the early studies conducted in single elections considered the effects of alienation or distance from a first-choice candidate to be minimal or significant, but not large.[36] However, since these studies only involved single elections, they could not evaluate the electoral consequences of turnout rates of a party's non-centrist base changing across multiple elections. Evaluating alienation effects as well as indifference effects (the difference between the candidates) in elections from 1960 to 1980, John Zipp found that potential voters were significantly less likely to vote the further their views were from those of their preferred candidate.[37] Adams, Dow, and Merrill similarly found that "citizens' tendencies to abstain are significantly related to their perceived policy distances from the candidates."[38] Leighley and Nagler reconfirm these findings.[39] My research on the theory of surge and decline on congressional election outcomes and on the effects of presidential campaigns and swing voters on presidential election outcomes found that the turnout of a party's base has been critical to its electoral success.[40]

Too Important to Neglect

The empirical evidence regarding whether the parties could take their ideological bases for granted is limited and complicated by the fact that they have never really taken their base for granted, as their consistent non-centrist positions attest.[41] Still, there are three pieces of evidence suggesting that the parties cannot afford to neglect their ideological bases.

First, as observed in the previous chapter (recall table 7.2), the parties receive a substantial proportion of their votes from their ideological bases. In elections from 1976 to 2012, exit poll data indicate that Democratic presidential candidates on average drew one-third of their votes from liberal Democratic Party identifiers and Republican presidential candidates on average drew about half of their votes from conservative Republican Party identifiers. Votes from their ideological bases are not sufficient for either party to win elections, but they are a necessary component to any majority coalition. Neither party can win without the strong support of its ideological base, and it is hard to imagine that they would ever risk that by moving too far away from the views of their bases.

TABLE 8.1. TURNOUT, SIZE, AND LOYALTY OF THE PARTIES' IDEOLOGICAL BASES, 1972–2012

Presidential Election	Liberal Democrats			Conservative Republicans		
	Size	Turnout	Democratic Vote %	Size	Turnout	Republican Vote %
1972	16.1	72.1	86.2	17.5	78.1	95.8
1976	12.9	70.4	88.7	13.2	76.9	94.5
1980	11.9	69.2	87.5	15.1	75.0	95.3
1984	12.5	67.1	89.3	18.3	74.7	96.5
1988	12.1	60.8	93.1	19.3	73.0	94.5
1992	12.8	77.2	98.2	18.2	82.3	94.2
1996	13.7	62.0	98.5	21.0	76.3	91.5
2000	13.3	71.9	92.3	19.3	76.8	96.1
2004	14.4	75.3	97.6	22.9	74.5	94.9
2008	17.0	76.7	94.3	22.3	82.7	94.6
2012	18.8	70.8	97.4	25.6	74.1	95.9
Mean	14.1	70.3	93.0	19.3	77.6	94.9
Std. Deviation	2.2	5.4	4.6	3.5	3.3	1.4
Mean of Party Centrists	34.6	51.5	79.2	17.8	53.0	83.5

Note: The data are corrected data from the ANES (Campbell, 2010). Size, turnout, and the vote choice percentages have been reweighted to the actual turnout rates of the voting eligible population and to the actual division of the official presidential vote results. The vote choice percentages are of the two-party vote. The size is the percentage of the entire electorate, non-voters and independents included.

The second piece of evidence that the parties have good reason to appeal to non-centrists involves the level of turnout of those in the parties' ideological bases. Table 8.1 reports the turnout rates, the vote divisions, and size of each party's non-centrist bases in the 11 presidential elections from 1972 to 2012. The mean size, turnout, and loyalty rates for partisans outside each party's base are also provided for comparison purposes. This breakdown of the vote applies Robert Axelrod's analysis of group voting in the parties' coalitions to the ideological and party identification components of the vote.[42] The party's non-centrist bases are self-reported liberals identifying with the Democratic Party and self-reported conservatives identifying with the Republican Party. Those "leaning" toward either party are counted as identifying with that party. The size of each party's base is its percentage of the entire electorate, including non-voters and independents. The vote divisions are of the national two-party presidential vote. The data are originally from the ANES and have been corrected to reflect the actual turnout rates in these elections as well as the actual vote choice percentages. Reported turnout rates are routinely much higher than actual turnouts and there are also differences between the official vote division for the presidential candidates and those reported in the surveys. Since these errors are known and may also lead to erroneous conclusions about both turnout and vote choice levels and changes, the data have been reweighted to bring them into line with the actual turnout rates and vote choice divisions.[43]

Turnout levels among those in both parties' bases are quite high, though well short of perfect, and variable from one election to the next. Turnout among liberal Democrats averaged 70%, about 20 points higher than among non-liberal Democrats. In some elections turnout among liberal Democrats exceeded 75% and in others was barely 60%. Turnout among non-liberal Democrats topped out at 57%. Among conservative Republicans, turnout averaged 78%, nearly 25 points higher than among non-conservative Republicans. Conservative Republican turnout varied from a high of 83% to a low of 74%. The highest turnout rate achieved by non-conservative Republicans was 61%. In short, the base shows up. Sometimes more strongly than other times, but always much more strongly than more moderate partisans.[44]

The very high turnout rates of non-centrists may give some the impression that the parties can take votes from the base for granted, but just the opposite is the case. The high level of support from the base reflects the fact that the parties do not take these votes for granted, and with good reason. With two-party loyal vote rates of around 90% and higher rates in recent decades when party polarization increased, any increase (or decline) in turnout (or the size of the base) translates quite directly into a gain (or loss) in votes—and maybe not just in the current election. Votes from the base are not a sure thing. Those in the base tend to be particularly attentive to politics and often quite demanding, in some cases unrealistically so. The last thing a party would want to risk is losing support among so many prospective voters who are strongly disposed to vote for the party's candidates, who have been with the party from election to election, and who turn out to vote at such high rates.

To be sure, as high as the turnouts of the ideological bases are, there are not enough votes in either party's base alone to win elections. The strong support of its base is necessary for a party's victory, but it is not sufficient for its victory. Parties must broaden their appeal to win votes in the center as well. The dilemma is that appeals to the center may cost votes in the base and appeals to the base may cost votes in the center. The net impact of a campaign appeal is the critical consideration in determining a party's strategy, but the pertinent point here is that unabashed centrism does not make good political sense. A party's movement toward the center to appeal to centrist votes is not cost-free. Moreover, with the difference in both loyalty and turnout rates between a party's centrists and non-centrists, upsetting non-centrists can be a good deal more costly in votes than upsetting centrists, particularly with the growing numbers in each party's base.

The third piece of evidence is that turnout rates within each party's ideological base vary by their perceptions of their party's ideological position. Liberal Democrats and conservative Republicans are more likely to vote if they believe their parties share their ideological perspectives. Figure 8.3 presents the mean turnout rates in presidential elections from 1972 to 2012 of conservative Republicans and liberal Democrats by their perceptions of their own party's ideological orientation. The data are originally from the ANES. Respondents were asked to place the political parties on the same seven-point scale from extremely conservative to extremely liberal that respondents placed themselves. As in table 8.1, the data have been reweighted to the actual turnout and presidential vote distributions. Party identification designations include as party identifiers those who indicate they "lean" toward a party.

Turnout rates are a good deal higher among those in a party's ideological base who believe their party shares their ideological commitments.[45] This is true of both liberal Democrats and conservative Republicans. Conservative Republicans and liberal Democrats who

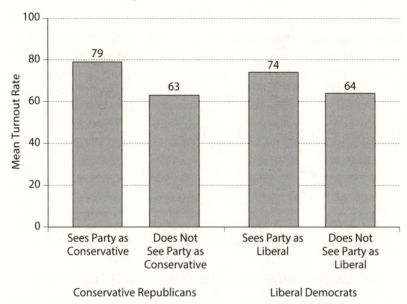

Figure 8.3. Turnout of the ideological bases by their perceptions of their party's ideology, 1972–2012.

Note: The data are from the ANES cumulative election file and the 2012 ANES study. The means are of the 11 presidential election year surveys from 1972 to 2012. The data have been reweighted to the actual turnout and presidential vote choice distribution levels. Leaning independents are counted as partisans. The mean percentage of conservative Republicans seeing their party as conservative was 82.7. The mean percentage of liberal Democrats seeing their party as liberal was 72.4.

feel their parties represent their ideological perspectives are quite likely to vote and, as observed in table 8.1, their votes go almost exclusively to their party's candidate. For conservative Republicans who see the Republican Party as conservative, the average turnout rate is 79%. For liberal Democrats who see the Democratic Party as liberal, turnout is nearly as high (74%). In contrast, turnout suffers among those in the parties' bases who do not think they are being ideologically represented. Turnout drops to 64% among liberal Democrats who regard their party as moderate or conservative and to 63% among conservative Republicans who see their party as being moderate or liberal.

What this suggests is that in moving toward more centrist positions (shaking the political Etch A Sketch?) parties risk alienating some in their ideological base. Since non-centrists are also among the more politically attentive in the electorate, their party's quiet move to the center may not go unnoticed. Conservative Republicans or liberal Democrats who feel taken for granted and poorly represented by their parties may not bother to vote for "the lesser of two evils." On the other hand, there are votes in the center as well and a party may increase its share of these by moderating its positions. The differential in turnout rates between non-centrists who believe that their party shares their views and others who don't indicates there is an offsetting price to be paid for moderation and, ironically, every vote lost by a disgruntled non-centrist in the base staying home means that the prized median voter sought by moderation is one vote further away. By the same token, every vote from the base roused to the polls moves the median voter one vote closer to the party.

POLARIZATION: THE ELECTORAL CONNECTION

Many factors pull the parties away from the median voter. Most reasons for party polarization could be characterized as negative reasons, obstacles to the parties converging on the center or performance considerations that compete with the centrist strategy. The pull of the base, however, is a positive and compelling reason for party polarization. Ultimately, the parties are polarized because it makes electoral sense for them to be polarized. Neither party can win elections without strong support from their bases, and they are unlikely to receive sufficiently strong support from their bases unless potential non-centrist voters believe that their views are being well represented. In elections from 1976 to 2012, according to exit poll data, Democratic presidential candidates typically could count on about a third of the votes needed for a popular vote majority from liberals. Conservatives typically accounted for just over half the votes needed for a Republican majority.[46] The numbers are far too high (and growing) for the parties to neglect. Neither party can reach the median voter unless it has satisfied its ideological base.

The electoral incentive for polarized parties, however, is only half the picture. The vote contributions of liberals to the Democrats and conservatives to Republicans are necessary for their election, but fall well short of being sufficient for either party's election. Parties depend on a good share of votes from their base and not just in one election, but in one election after another. But even though they depend on this loyal and high turnout constituency and cannot win without them, they also cannot win with only the votes of their bases. Just as a winning electoral strategy cannot be all about the political center, it cannot be all about the ideological bases either.

Some level of polarization is, thus, a consequence of the tug of war between centrists and non-centrists fighting for the representation of their views. As the median voter theorem contends, elections are won by winning the vote of the median voter, but exactly where the median voter is positioned depends not just on the views of centrists but on the views and turnout decisions of non-centrists as well. Everyone matters, not just the exalted median voter. From this standpoint, as unpleasant and contentious as it often becomes, party polarization of some degree is a natural characteristic of competitive democratic party politics.

The level of party polarization should reflect the extent of public polarization. It is representative politics. When Americans are more moderate and agreeable with one another, centrists have more leverage over the parties and the parties should gravitate toward the center. By the same token, when Americans are politically divided as they commonly are, and especially when they are sharply divided and more adamant about their views as they have become in recent decades, the non-centrists have the upper hand and the parties should gravitate away from the center in seeking votes. Like everyone else in a democracy, the median voter may not be entirely happy about this but must understand that among the many millions of Americans with conflicting views, as Mick Jagger and Keith Richards put it, "you can't always get what you want."

CHAPTER 9

POLARIZATION AND DEMOCRACY

At the root of all politics is the universal language of conflict.

—E. E. Schattschneider, *The Semisovereign People*[1]

The polarization of American politics has been greatly misunderstood. Among the many false contentions are that Americans are not highly polarized, that they are not more polarized than in the past, and that they are operationally more liberal than conservative despite reporting themselves to be quite the opposite. There are as many or more misconceptions about the polarization of party elites. These include the belief that increased party polarization is primarily the result of more effective partisan gerrymandering, increased income inequality, ideologically extreme party activists and conniving rich campaign contributors, a bellicose partisan media, or polarizing presidents. Even the general staggered realignment of the parties, the basic reason for increased party polarization, is often mischaracterized as a more limited southern or regional realignment. The sequence by which polarizing views were spread through the political system was also mistaken as an elite driven top-down dynamic rather than a public driven bottom-up process. The greater polarization of the parties has also been inaccurately portrayed as a one-sided affair, with Republicans veering to the extreme right while Democrats remained in the mainstream, just left of center. Finally, the age-old misunderstanding of party polarization is that it should not exist at all, that the electoral interests of the parties and the self-interests of both centrist and non-centrist voters dictate that the parties converge on the political center.

The reality of American politics is quite different. The evidence indicates that Americans are highly polarized, that they have been so since the late 1960s, and that they have become significantly more so in recent decades. Americans have become *less* centrist. There are more liberals and even more conservatives. The increased polarization of the parties in government lagged behind the greater polarization of the public. The increased polarization of the parties was fundamentally the result of a staggered realignment of the parties and a more polarized electorate—not gerrymandering, income inequality, ideological activists, the partisan media, or polarizing presidents. Changes in the polarization of the parties in government were greater and earlier among Democrats than among Republicans, because the greater heterogeneity of pre-realignment Democrats (southern conservatives and non-southern liberals) had left that party's coalition unusually close to the political center. With the realignment and the competitive balance it created between the parties, party polarization is now quite symmetrical. Finally, with a better understanding of what affects turnout decisions, it is clear that parties cannot focus their campaigns on the political center to the exclusion of non-centrists. The turnout of non-centrists is important and must be won. The crucial median voter of the electorate in any election is not a fixed point. The position of the electorate's median voter moves with the size and turnout of each party's non-centrist base.

The preceding chapters covered a great deal of ground, but three important and especially difficult questions remain about polarization in American politics. Although the answers here are speculative, the questions are too important not to raise. These big questions concern the *causes, consequences, and possible cures* of polarization. First, what are the underlying causes of the public's polarization?[2] Is polarization of the public a natural outgrowth of democratic politics? What are we polarized about? Second, what are the consequences of polarization for the political system? What difference does polarization make? Is the high level of polarization responsible for gridlock and a dysfunctional government? Is there an upside or any benefits from Americans being polarized? Third, is the polarization of American politics something we should attempt to rectify or "cure"? Is polarization inevitable, a normal state of politics in a democracy with everyone having different values and perceptions, or is it an aberration, a pathological condition that something can be done about? If so, what is to be done?

CAUSES

Developing Political Differences

What causes the polarizing political differences among Americans? This is a question that can be addressed at varying depths. At a deep level, individual opinions and perspectives may differ because they are formed by people who have different personalities and different life experiences and information.[3] These personality differences themselves may be shaped by past experiences and social, psychological, and biological factors. In a highly ambitious and provocative series of studies, John Alford, John Hibbing, Kevin Smith, and their collaborators present fascinating research that fundamental biologically based—perhaps genetically based—personality traits may predispose individuals toward liberal or conservative political perspectives.[4] It is not that reason and experience cannot bring people together, but that people are inclined to see things quite a bit differently.

How we travel from generations of crying infants (or even squirming fetuses) to the same generations decades later of bickering liberal, moderate, and conservative adults is well beyond the scope of this study. There are, however, at least four things we might safely suppose about this development.[5] The first of these suppositions is that, though the fallibility of human reasoning may contribute to differences of opinion, as Madison suggests in *Federalist No. 10* (quoted as chapter 2's epigraph), it is not the only or most important source of political discord. The variety of perspectives, values, priorities, information, and other elements that people bring to forming their political opinions ensure great differences.

The second supposition is that the deep reasons for different *political* orientations undoubtedly are not narrowly political. Whatever and however liberal and conservative perspectives are formed are quite likely embedded in much broader outlooks on life, human nature, and how the world works. Since the political world is not the focal point of most people's lives, how people come to see politics has a great deal to do with how they see the world in general. Personalities differ in many ways. There are optimists and pessimists, idealists and realists, self-centered and outward-looking, trusting and suspicious, envious and ambitious, change-inclined and stability-inclined, forward-looking and traditionalists, risk-averse and risk-acceptant, individualists and group-oriented, reverential to authority and challenging to authority. And the dimensions go on. This array of personality traits when combined with observations about how people think and behave as well as pressures to conform socially contribute greatly to the formation of political orientations. Political perspectives are not an island.

The third supposition about the causes of political orientations and polarization is that there are a great many routes that people travel from political innocence to the political perspectives of adulthood. There is not one path to becoming a liberal, another to becoming a conservative, and a third path somewhere in between to becoming a moderate. People with very different predispositions, coming from very different conditions and subject to very different social influences (parental, peer, educational, religious, and other affiliations) with very different experiences may end up having the same general outlook on politics and government. We tend to focus on common threads that seem to link conservatives to other conservatives and are different from those characteristics that seem to be held in common by liberals. And while many of those distinguishing traits, experiences, and perspectives are significant, they are also routinely violated. Many travel quite different roads to arrive at the same overall perspective.

The final supposition springs from the previous observation about multiple paths to political orientations and returns to a point raised in chapter 3. Like species of plants and animals, the political perspectives of liberals, conservatives, and moderates contain within themselves many different variations.[6] Some common values and beliefs join conservatives together with other conservatives and liberals with other liberals, but there are differences beneath each umbrella as well.[7] This is not unique to ideologies. There are internal differences within parties, religions, interest groups, social movements, and every other general class of categorization. A rose may be a rose, but all roses are not identical.

This internal diversity within ideologies has a consequence for the question of what causes polarization. Just as liberals may differ with other liberals and conservatives with other conservatives, the most important reason that they are polarized or at odds with the other ideology may also differ in various ways. Still, though there are probably multiple reasons why Americans are politically divided from each other, one overarching common denominator must structure the simple "us vs. them" polarization of an ideological spectrum.[8]

The Subject of Polarization

What is the great divider? What are Americans fundamentally polarized about? What brings together a variety of differing viewpoints on one side of the ideological spectrum and at the same time divides it from an equally diverse set of perspectives at the other end of the spectrum? The short answer is government.[9] The common thread that ties liberals together is a general predisposition to use government to solve problems. Conservatives are generally predisposed *not* to use government to solve problems. The use of governmental powers to address problems is often the first resort for liberals and the last resort for conservatives. Liberals are eager to call on the government and conservatives are reluctant to call for government intervention.

Some evidence of this underlying basis of ideological perspectives in views about the scope of government was presented earlier in chapter 3 (recall table 3.1). Those data showed that over the 13 presidential and midterm national elections from 1982 to 2012, liberals were more than twice as likely as conservatives to favor the government providing many more services, even if it meant an increase in government spending, and conservatives were nearly three times as likely as liberals to favor the government reducing services and spending.

Liberals and conservatives appear to be fundamentally divided over the extent, limits, and uses of governmental powers. Conservatives value individualism and seek to restrain the government's powers, except in cases in which government provides security and order so that individual liberties can be safely exercised. Liberals are more inclined toward using the government's powers for collective benefits, as in Hillary Clinton's *It Takes a Village*.[10] Conservatives take a stricter view of what government can do to advance a less expansive view of the public interest. Liberals take a more relaxed view of what government should do to advance a more expansive view of the public interest. When government involvement is thought to be warranted, liberals are inclined to use it more aggressively, imposing more requirements and more specifically targeting its application. Conservatives, on the other hand, are disposed to apply governmental powers more generally and less intrusively.[11]

The foundation of polarization in attitudes about the use of government is real, but more nuanced than often supposed. It is not simply about being pro- or anti-government. Liberalism and conservatism are mainstream ideologies, not all-or-nothing dogmas. Neither liberalism nor conservatism extends to the outer limits. Liberalism does not call for limitless government (totalitarianism) and conservatism does not call for the elimination of government (anarchism). They mark the opposing poles of mainstream political views. It is also not simply about trusting the government. Both liberals and conservatives can be cynical about how well the government presently works, often for very different reasons.[12] As previously noted, there are also many (generally minor) variations of conservative and liberal views about government. Just as they evolve over time and in different historical contexts, they take on different hues in different regions and social groups. What is central to polarization and these ideological orientations is that liberals are more likely than conservatives within a given context to see problems as the public's problems and to favor the use of the government's powers as a way of solving these problems. Conservatives are more skeptical about using government to solve problems.

Attitudes about the proper role of government may be developed in many different ways, but however they are developed, their centrality to politics and polarization seems to be inevitable. Political polarization is about government because politics and policies are about government. Virtually every policy issue entails questions about whether, how much, and in what ways the government's powers should be used. If an overarching view of the proper role of government did not guide positions on these various issues in the first place, it seems likely that such a general view of government's responsibilities and possibilities would tend to emerge over time from experience with these issues and policies. It is unavoidable.

Polarized politics is normal. Views about what government should do and how it should do it gravitates naturally toward being polarized.[13] First, politics tends to focus on what divides people rather than on what unites them. Issues that unite people can be settled one way or the other quickly and without fanfare. What remains are divisive issues. Second, government itself provides focus to political conflicts, a common thread that links one issue to another. Rather than the web of disparate and cross-cutting conflicts envisioned by Madisonian pluralism, conflicts are aligned by underlying predispositions about the use of governmental powers. Third, as Maurice Duverger argued in explaining tendencies toward two-party systems under majority rule, opponents have reason to coalesce in their opposition so that they do not splinter their votes, especially those fearing defeat.[14] This reasoning applies as well to ideological views. There is a good deal of pressure on everyone to choose sides. The natural division along a single polarized dimension is embedded in the age-old polarizing question: "are you with us or against us?"

CONSEQUENCES

Pluralism Displaced

A highly polarized public mixed with a pair of highly polarized parties have substantial consequences for the political system. The nature of these consequences may be anticipated by the pluralist politics that polarized politics displaced. Pluralist politics are very much the antithesis of polarized politics. Whether these consequences are regarded as good or bad depends ultimately on one's values. Pluralism had its share of both admirers and detractors. Polarization may receive the same split verdict (though there is always a tendency to focus on political problems rather than any merits). But whatever values one brings to the table, the strengths or weaknesses found in pluralist politics will likely be found in their opposite in polarized politics.

The idea of pluralism can be traced back at least as far as James Madison's *Federalist No. 10*. Madison argued that the possibility of tyranny from a majority faction would be greatly reduced in an extended republic of diverse and competing minority factions. Pluralism was elaborated and refined to characterize mid-twentieth-century American politics by David Truman, Robert Dahl, Nelson Polsby, and a host of others.[15] Pluralist politics is the competition over issues among many different interests in which opponents on one issue may be allies on other issues. Divisions are cross-cutting, not overlapping. Those on the winning side on one issue may well find themselves on the losing side of the next—no permanent winners, no permanent losers. Majorities are only assembled by piecing together coalitions of political minorities brought together by bargaining and compromises. No one gets everything they want, but most get something. The resulting moderated policies are in the public's interest or, at least, not greatly harmful to it.

Polarized politics is different in virtually every respect. It entails one overriding political division or an equivalent set of overlapping cleavages. Since the sides are set in ideological stone (at least at any one time), there are clear winners and losers across a range of issues. Ideological bonds displace incentives to bargain and compromise. Arrogance can take hold on one side and frustration on the other, but there is also greater clarity and accountability in polarized politics.

The general difference between pluralism and polarization is that pluralism diffuses conflict and polarization concentrates it. As a caveat, it is important to keep in mind that American politics 50 years ago was not purely pluralistic and that American politics now is not purely polarized. As chapter 1 observed, these are matters of degree. The era of pluralist politics involved a good deal of polarization (recall chapter 5), and current American politics, though highly polarized, is not at the outer bimodal limits of polarization. In addition, the transition from the heyday of pluralism in the 1940s and 1950s to the current high levels of polarization in the 2010s was anything but smooth. Still, even with these caveats in mind, the increase and high levels of polarization in the public and between the parties, and the greater intensity of conflict associated with them, may have had important consequences.

The Polarized Public

The consequences to the political system of a highly polarized public are complex. With increasing public polarization in recent decades, in general, turnout has increased, partisanship has strengthened, and split-ticket voting has declined (as discussed in chapter 5). However, these changes reflected the resolution of the mismatch between a relatively less polarized party system and a more polarized public, rather than the growth of polarization per se. Recall that turnout and partisanship were at relatively high levels and ticket-splitting was infrequent in the 1950s, a less polarized period for both the public and the parties.

The effect of polarization on the public may best be understood by revisiting the suspected effects of pluralism on the public. More than 60 years ago, Bernard Berelson wrote a highly influential evaluation of public opinion's role in American pluralist politics.[16] For the most part, according to Berelson, Americans failed to live up to the standards envisioned for them in democratic theories. Americans were typically uninterested in and uninformed about politics. This was the downside of pluralist or pre-polarized politics, perhaps the downside of democratic politics at any time. The upside was that most Americans had some interest and information, just not as much as democratic theories unrealistically demanded, and that a sufficiently large segment of the public was interested and informed enough to satisfy more realistic standards of democratic governance. Additionally, what many might regard as the shortcomings of much of the public were interpreted positively by Berelson.[17] That segment of the public that was uninvolved, uninterested, uninformed, and uncommitted about politics unwittingly contributed to the functioning and stability of the political system. Their lack of demands and tacit support for the political system allowed the system to foster compromises and to deal more effectively with those who were more demanding. Berelson and other pluralists of that era were satisfied with an American public that entertained divisions enough to support incremental changes, but was not so divided as to be destabilizing or "destructive of the society as a whole."[18]

The pluralist vision of centrist public opinion and democratic governance was widely, if not universally, accepted at mid-century. It was summarized almost poetically by Clinton Rossiter in 1960 in the opening of *Parties and Politics in America*: "NO America without democracy, no democracy without politics, no politics without parties, no parties without compromise and moderation."[19] Conflict in the pluralist system took place near the center, cross-cutting on many levels. It was, therefore, restrained and manageable. Pluralist politics led to moderate policies changing at the margins over time.

The now highly polarized public is quite different from the centrist public evaluated by Berelson and Rossiter.[20] More Americans now have strong opinions about the course of government and are a good deal more divided in those opinions. On the positive side, the greater attentiveness of the public and their more definite views can be read as evidence of a more engaged democratic process. With an increased recognition of and identification with a political ideology, it may be surmised that more Americans care more deeply about the direction of their politics and government.[21] It is not merely an amorphous sense of civic duty that gets many Americans to the polls. Many Americans are politically engaged because they think more is at stake. They identify with a political party and its candidates, not because their parents and grandparents had, but because they find one party well represents (if perhaps imperfectly) their views about government much better than the opposing party. Fewer Americans are discouraged by alienation or indifference to the choices offered them. In these respects, it might be considered closer to an idealized representative democracy than the more muddled politics of pluralism.

On the negative side of the ledger, as Berelson and others feared, strongly held and divergent opinions may be less easily compromised and conflict can easily become inflamed. Polarized politics may become uncivil politics in which each side demonizes the other. Tolerance of opposing views can be strained and may often come up short. Polarized political views may also lead to a more isolating politics, in which political differences go unaired because of discomfort about potential conflict. Those at each end of the spectrum enter ideological cocoons in which the like-minded tell each other how wise they are and how dumb or venal those who disagree with them are.[22]

Continually reinforced and deeply held polarized convictions can become quite inflexible and unreceptive to compromise.[23] Governing under polarized politics can be especially challenging. As former congressman Gary Ackerman suggests in the epigraph for chapter 7, "you can't compromise between good and evil."[24] Sounding a similar warning more than 60 years earlier, Walter Lippmann wrote that a nation "divided irreconcilably on 'principle', each party believing it is pure white and the other pitch black, cannot govern itself."[25] Highly polarized public opinion, so the argument goes, produces conflict that is too intense and too disruptive for the political system to manage effectively, leaving large segments of the public both active and frustrated. This is not a politically healthy mix.

Although the high level of polarization in the public places a good deal of strain on the government, the warnings may be a bit hyperventilated. First, the American public is not entirely bereft of moderates. As high as our levels of polarization are in the public, according to the calculations in chapter 3, about 44% of the public in 2012 were moderates or were unaware of their ideological perspectives. National elections cannot be won without getting a good deal of support from the center. Centrist voters do not hold all the cards (as observed in chapter 8), but they hold many of them. Centrists still wield enough power to buffer the conflict that might otherwise rage between liberals and conservatives.

Second, though highly polarized, the American public's decisions are not just about ideological values. The performance of those in government matters a great deal. President Obama's election in 2008 is Exhibit A. A conservative-leaning electorate elected then Senator Obama over his Republican opponent Senator McCain even though McCain's record in the Senate was moderately conservative and Obama's was quite liberal and, as the exit polls attest, voters accurately perceived these differences.[26] The Wall Street financial crisis, an economy sinking into recession, and two protracted wars in Afghanistan and Iraq led some conservatives (about 20% by the exit polls) to cross party lines to vote for Obama and led many other disappointed conservatives to simply sit out the election. The point is that virtually everyone in the public, from extreme liberals to extreme conservatives, cares about basic national conditions, from public health and safety to the economy and national security. These performance considerations, like the political weight of moderates, can buffer politics from the otherwise intense ideological conflict of a highly polarized public. In short, the highly polarized public makes governing more challenging, but not impossible.

Polarized Government

As with its consequences for the public, polarization's consequences for governing may be best understood by its contrast with how government functioned and public policy was developed in more politically pluralistic times. Policy-making in the pluralist era dealt with many small conflicts across the range of separate policy areas. In Congress, this was reflected in a strong and decentralized committee system.[27] Interest groups were also relatively strong and internally diverse political parties relatively weak in shaping public policy.[28] Political parties were so diverse that they avoided issues that might have inflamed internal divisions and were, as a consequence, less programmatic. American party politics often was characterized as four-party rather that two-party politics, with each party divided into either presidential and congressional wings or between its ideological base and its more moderate wing.[29] With many elected party representatives having some ideological empathy with those in the other party, bipartisanship and compromise was frequent and conflict muted. In such decentralized politics, policy change was incremental. Policy-making was a process of "muddling through."[30] Admirers of pluralist government extolled its management of political conflict, its moderation, and its stability. By their estimation, the pluralist system worked.

Pluralist politics, however, also had its critics. It was seen by some as failing to represent the concerns of many Americans and discouraging broad-based participation.[31] From this standpoint, pluralism was a clubby system biased in favor of organized wealthy interests and the status quo.[32] The most aggressive challenge to pluralist politics was that it did not provide the necessary conditions for "responsible party government."[33] These critics found the political parties in pluralist politics to be too fragmented, uncohesive, and non-issue-oriented to offer voters clear and meaningful choices. In addition, these ideologically heterogeneous parties were thought too weak to govern effectively. From this perspective, the combination of parties not strong enough to govern and not ideologically identifiable enough to be answerable for governing amounted to a government that could not be held accountable by the public. "Muddling through" pluralist government was a poor substitute for a robust, even if more combative, representative democracy.

The polarized politics of American government in recent decades is everything that its pluralist politics of the mid-twentieth century was not. Pluralist government facilitated compromise, sometimes at the expense of representing and raising clearly contrasting views. Polarized government vigorously represents those sharply contrasting views, sometimes at the expense of policy gridlock.[34] From the pluralist perspective, polarized politics is hyperbolic and dysfunctional politics. Conflict is not managed into compromised and broadly acceptable public policies.[35] From the polarized or responsible party government perspective, pluralism is an attempt to evade the representation of strongly opposing views. From this perspective, any delay and even occasional gridlock in the legislative process is the price exacted by democracy when the nation is itself politically divided.[36] One side of the debate emphasizes the government's inefficiency in reaching policy agreements, while the other emphasizes the representation of a decidedly divided public.

Fighting through Polarization

Although conflicting values underlie much of the debate over the consequences of polarized government (or, for that matter, pluralist government), two important points are beyond dispute. First, it is an inescapable fact that the political conflict of polarization inside as well as outside the government is at a high level and is greater than in recent decades. As Schattschneider reminds us in this chapter's epigraph, conflict is omnipresent in politics—but it has reached uncommon heights. Whereas shared party loyalties bridged differences between liberals and conservatives when parties were more ideologically heterogeneous, loyalties to more ideologically homogeneous parties now inflame differences between liberals and conservatives. Polarized government is more contentious, more difficult, often mired in gridlock, and prone to testing constitutional limits on institutional powers.

Second, despite the greater conflict and obstacles to compromise and policy adoption, many policies emerge from the process. Polarized government is not absolutely gridlocked. In the decade from 2001 to 2011, despite its high level of party polarization, Congress enacted more than 2,000 public laws. Although fewer than the legislative output of the 1960s (about 3,700 laws), the 1970s (about 3,100 laws), or the 1980s (about 2,900 laws), this is still a great deal of legislation.[37] Some might say too little, some too much; but either way it is a good deal of legislating.[38]

More tellingly, polarization has apparently not prevented the enactment of *important* laws. For his path-breaking study *Divided We Govern*, David Mayhew conducted a systematic and exhaustive search of the "important laws" enacted since 1947.[39] The updated count indicates that 392 important laws were enacted from 1947 to 2012. A small subset of these (a total of 39) were classified by Mayhew as historically important. These include enactments such as the ratification of the NATO Treaty in 1949 and the passage of the Medical Care for the Aged Act (Medicare) in 1965. Table 9.1 presents the numbers of important and historically important laws enacted in each decade since the 1950s. What is most interesting in this list is that, despite all of the gnashing of teeth and hand wringing about the debilitating effects of polarization, more important legislation was enacted in the highly polarized first decade of the 2000s than in the average of the preceding five decades. To top that off, *more historically important* legislation was enacted in the highly polarized first decade of the 2000s than in any of the five preceding decades, including the Great Society decade of the 1960s.

This is not to claim that the high level of polarized politics, in the public as well as between the parties, has not had substantial consequences. It has. Much as Berelson had anticipated, polarization has stressed the system. There is much more conflict to contend with and more resistance to achieving a compromise. Polarized constituents put pressure on party leaders not to "sell out" by compromising with the opposition. Party leaders are loath to be seen as equivocating in dealing with the other side of the aisle and are concerned about being challenged in primaries by an intransigent base in their party. There is more than the usual amount of posturing to embarrass the oppo-

TABLE 9.1. ENACTMENT OF IMPORTANT LAWS BY DECADE, 1951–2011

Decade	Mayhew's Designation of Enactments	
	Important Laws	Historically Important Laws
1951–1960	37	1
1961–1970	88	9
1971–1980	74	1
1981–1990	46	4
1991–2000	50	6
2001–2010	68	12

Source: Calculated by the author from Mayhew (2005, 2015).

sition and to throw "red meat" to the ideological bases. There can be long delays as the small plots of common ground are found and recalcitrant policy-makers are coaxed onboard. Some issues may be entirely untouchable because both sides are so entrenched.[40] The process is more painful, unpleasant, and at times even nasty and uncivil. The compromised policies that are eventually arrived at may or may not be as sound as those arrived at in a less vituperative process. However, despite all of this, a good deal of public policy is made.

With the forces of polarization stacked against it, how does the policy-making process move forward? Why hasn't polarized-induced gridlock caused the policy-making to come to a standstill? As polarized as the American public and its political leaders have become, there is still a wide range of important issues on which there is a consensus about the policy goals. These are the valence issues. Liberal Democrats and conservative Republicans and everyone in between (and maybe even further out of the fringes at either end of the spectrum) want peace and prosperity, clean air and water, affordable energy, an educated, employed, and healthy citizenry, care for those who truly are unable to care for themselves, safe neighborhoods, fair and low taxes, efficient government, a government that pays its debts, and so forth. These are what used to be called the "motherhood and apple pie" issues. Who could be against them?

These valence issues are matters that need to be tended to and parties in government are judged to a significant degree by their performance on these issues. The parties come to these issues with different understandings about what these goals entail as well as how best to achieve them. Regardless of these differences, they will be judged by the public by their contribution to securing these goals. As polarized as Americans are, they are at the same time quite pragmatic. Results count, and this puts tremendous pressure on the parties (pragmatic about elections as they are) to work together as best they can for the general welfare as the public sees it.[41]

Beyond the general pressure on the parties to be seen as working together for the public's common interests, policy-making does not grind to a halt in the face of polarizing conflict because of the pressure of events. If something must be done, political leaders will often (though not always) get around to doing it. Crises spur action and provide opportunities for action. Polarization remains a major obstacle to policy change, but not an insurmountable one.[42] When political leaders from different perspectives feel the heat, as the saying goes, they often see the light or what advocates for a policy interpret as "the light."

Political leaders can and do fight through polarization to reach policy agreements, but they are not always successful in this and sometimes the battle may seem so futile that it is not even seriously engaged. This has always been the case. Even in the heyday of pluralism, major issues were often shunted aside as too hot to handle to get through the process (e.g., civil rights before the late 1950s, abortion, gay rights). The American political system was not designed to produce laws efficiently. It was designed to require an extraordinary majority to work its will through a system of diffused powers across separated institutions, from the House through to the Supreme Court. The system was designed in this way so that the power of the government would not be exercised without the consent of the people, and this consent was not simply a narrow and fleeting majority.

Policy-making in the American political system has never been easy, nor was it supposed to be, but the critics of polarization are probably quite right in their claims that governing has become much more difficult with highly polarized parties. More issues are now seriously raised with an effectively expanded spectrum of ideas, but more of these are now stuck in legislative limbo between the two highly polarized parties.[43] Conflict has increased, often to frustrating levels, and is too often accompanied by incivility.

Where the critics are wrong is in concluding that this is dysfunctional government, the result of the irresponsible conduct of renegade ideologues. There are undoubtedly some of these in the process, but the fundamental reason for polarized government and impassioned impasses over policies is that the parties in government represent *a highly polarized public*. When the will of the people is divided, as it is, similar divisions should be expected among responsible democratic leaders. Sometimes a non-decision is effectively a decision.[44] In this sense, inaction in many areas of policy-making actually indicates that the government is fairly well aligned with the polarized public it was elected to represent.[45]

Although gridlock is generally the focus of concerns about polarization in government, a more serious danger to the political process may be efforts to avoid legislative impasses by bypassing constitutional processes. When polarized politics creates logjams in establishing policies, frustrated presidents may look to create policy unilaterally by extra-constitutional and perhaps even unconstitutional means. This presents a threat to the political system itself. Issuing executive orders and pushing regulatory limits are not proper substitutes for constitutionally enacting legislation. Executive agreements are not proper substitutes for constitutionally ratified treaties. As tempting as it might be to a frustrated president locked in standstill negotiations, end runs around constitutionally proscribed processes (even when armed with a bundle of legal opinions) are not the proper answers to policy gridlock. There is no easy remedy to this. The potential usurpation of powers is a problem in any constitutional system. The only answer to it is resistance, both to the temptation to bypass constitutional limits and in any attempted usurpation. The competitive balance between the parties should help in this regard. A precedent set for one party's president could easily cut the other way when the White House changes hands.

WHAT IS THE PROBLEM?

The increase of polarization in the public and then between the parties has been disruptive. American politics is not what it once was. Some change has been for the better. Because politics is now more highly polarized, more Americans have reason to think that the stakes in elections are high enough to bother voting, that one of the parties basically shares its worldview and is worth strongly identifying with, and that the parties are distinct enough that they can hold the government somewhat accountable by voting for or against a party and its candidates. But there is also a downside.

Because of the high level of polarization, more Americans are dissatisfied with and frustrated by their government and partisan bickering. Given the aversion of many Americans to political conflict, it is hardly surprising that the public's approval rating of Congress, where that conflict is most openly on display, languishes in the teens.[46] Party polarization in government is frequently indicted as the source of dysfunctional politics—intense conflict, incivility, hyperpartisanship, cynical posturing on issues, issue avoidance, and policy gridlock. This downside is often exaggerated. Policy-makers are often able to fight through the impediments posed by polarization, but sometimes they cannot.

Unavoidable Conflict

The crux of the complaints against the high level of polarization is that it engenders extreme and uncivil levels of conflict in society and in the government. The conflict associated with polarization is of two sorts. The first arises directly from the polarized views of liberals and conservatives in the public as well as among political leaders. Political disagreements between liberals and conservatives—whether across the dinner table, at a pub, or on the floor of the Senate—are to be expected given the extent and fundamental nature of their differences. Many citizens and political leaders care deeply about the political system and their views about what is best for it. They have strong views and the clash of these views yields intense conflict. This is further intensified by the ideologically homogeneous parties being as competitive as they have been since the completion of the staggered realignment in the 1990s.

Liberals and conservatives may be so far apart on some issues that even good-faith attempts to find mutually acceptable compromises may fail. Some disagreements are so great that they cannot be reconciled even when argued in a reasoned and respectful way. Enlightened leadership can emphasize and frame issues in ways more likely to unite than divide, but enlightened leadership is often difficult to come by and contentious opinions, once adamantly held, are not readily set aside.[47] When common ground cannot be found between the parties, when differences are irreconcilable, an impasse is an understandable outcome of the democratic process. With the growth of polarization, the frequency of these non-starter issues also grows. Although the lack of movement on an issue is sometimes construed as dysfunctional government, when the public is sharply divided on an issue, it is understandable, perhaps even laudable, that a functioning democratic system would respect the public's indecision.

The political conflict springing directly from the honest opposition of liberals and conservatives to each other's views may be lamentable (in that everyone does not come together), but necessary and functional in a democratic political system. If disagreements are not aired in a democratic system, then that system is not working properly. The airing and confrontation of different views is vital to democracy. The civil but strenuous advocacy of sincerely held different views about what the government should do and how it should go about doing it is the price of democracy. If political conflict springing from polarized views confronting each other is considered a problem, then it is a problem not so much with polarization as it is with the contentious politics intrinsic to our Madisonian system of dispersed governmental powers and, more fundamentally, with the principles of free thought, free speech, freedom of association—even with democracy itself.[48]

Unnecessary Conflict

It is unreasonable to fault those who stand up for what they believe, bargain in good faith with those they disagree with, and are still unable to reach a position that both sides can accept. Those are just the breaks of democratic politics and an open society. But too often, one or both sides are not committed as much as they should be to trying to compromise to find a common ground. Too often political

differences become overheated and dysfunctional. This conflict associated with polarization is unnecessary to the representation of divergent views.

Dysfunctional political conflict, though linked to polarization, is
not strictly speaking a product of polarization. The real problem is
not in many people holding divergent views about politics, but in
how people hold these views and *how* they think and act toward those
who disagree with them. Some people can hold opposing political
views and discuss their differences calmly, rationally, respectfully, and
with a common understanding of and respect for the facts. It used to
be said that the U.S. Senate was "the world's most exclusive club," that
senators could engage in intense debate over a bill for hours and
then enjoy a few friendly drinks together after the vote. The conflict
was not personal. It was about the issues. Unfortunately, conflict is
not always handled in this mature way. Other people can hold the
same opposing political views and a screaming fight breaks out. They
approach conflict, when they must, as amateurs or purists.[49] Differences are taken personally and exchanges are emotionally charged,
often disrespectful, intolerant, and uninformed by the facts. This
adds an uncomfortable layer of unnecessary and dysfunctional conflict to politics. Productive discussions and the possibility of compromise are the last things on the minds of those engaged in this sort of
politics.

Four aspects of the amateur's view of politics, in particular, frus-
trate good-faith attempts to fight through polarization. First, among
more politically engaged Americans, many overestimate the popularity of their views. People talk to and listen to the like-minded and
so presume most people think like they do. This is too often true of
even sophisticated political observers.[50] This misimpression presents
a serious barrier to bridging political differences. If you think your
views are shared by most people, then you will see no necessity for
compromising. Second, many are too certain that their views are absolutely right and no one can tell them any different. This breeds a
rigidity and intransigence, an obstacle to bringing people with even
slightly different views together. Third, it is easy for many liberals
and conservatives to be intolerant of and disrespectful to those with
opposing views. Liberals and conservatives often uncharitably attri-
bute dishonorable motives to each other. Demonizing the other side

is a lazy way to reinforce one's own views without having to consider seriously alternative views. The fourth problematic aspect of the amateur perspective is its disparagement of compromise itself. For many, "compromise" is a euphemism for selling out. The hero of political amateurism is the posturing show-horse standing up for principle at all cost and against the odds, not the boring workhorse of effective compromise. You will not find Henry Clay's profile carved into Mount Rushmore.

Any remedy to the perceived problems of polarization must start with the realization that these amateurish dispositions coupled with highly competitive politics, and not polarization itself, are the source of dysfunctional conflict in government and society. The spectrum of concern is not the left-right spectrum of liberalism and conservatism, but the professional-purist (or amateur) spectrum of how conflicting political views are approached. At one end of this spectrum are mature debaters and at the other are infantile fanatics throwing tantrums. To put it most bluntly, the pathologies often ascribed to polarization are not so much the result of too many people being liberals and conservatives, but of too many of these polarized people being a bit too pig-headed, narrow-minded, unrealistic, disrespectful, and ill-informed.

CURES?

What is to be done? What, if anything, can be done to dampen the political animosities associated with polarization and to revive a spirit of working together civilly for the common good across party and ideological lines? What can be done to convince liberals and conservatives to be a bit more flexible, open-minded, realistic, and tolerant in their views, to make good-faith efforts to reach mutually satisfactory compromises in the public interest when possible? There are no easy solutions to avoiding the rancor of polarization, but two different approaches for making changes at the margin are plausible.

Reforming Government

With attitudes toward government at the center of American ideological views, it should not be surprising that some turn first to changes in government to address the excessive conflict associated with polarization. Pietro Nivola and William Galston as well as Thomas Mann and Norman Ornstein suggest a long agenda of electoral and governmental reforms aimed at curing or counteracting the mischiefs of polarization.[51] These range from those designed to increase voter turnout to those that would circumvent obstructionist congressional minorities (e.g., filibuster reform in the Senate). But there are several problems with this approach.

First, many of these reforms are directed at the wrong target. The problems associated with polarization are not the result of government structures and rules (cloture rules on filibusters, etc.) and party polarization in government. The government is highly polarized because the public is highly polarized. Efforts to make those in government behave as though they were not polarized run headlong into electoral incentives to represent a highly polarized public. That is a losing and anti-democratic battle. Since polarization in government springs from the polarization of the people, prescriptions for solving the problem should be directed to toning down the excesses of the public's polarization.

Second, the proposed reforms are not designed to attack the real problem: the amateurish my-way-or-the-highway, take-no-prisoners hostile dispositions that have made conciliation and cooperation across the polarized divide so difficult. Take the often suggested reform of placing more restrictions on the use of the filibuster in the Senate or even its elimination. By current Senate rules, cloture requires 60 votes. This requirement allows a minority of 41 senators to block legislation, thereby adding to gridlock, but also provides the majority with an incentive to reach out to some members of the minority in order to find some compromise they can live with.[52] If the filibuster were eliminated, more bills might win passage and government would more efficiently churn out laws, but this would not happen because polarized differences had been bridged. To the contrary, a high-handed majority could pass what it pleased without the necessity of compromise. The long-term repercussions would be quite predictably an escalation in conflict.[53] The old advice to those who believe that they have been treated badly was not to get mad, but to get even. In polarized politics, they usually do both. The bottom line is that political and governmental reforms of structures and rules are not the answer to the problems associated with polarization.

A New Civics

To smooth the edges of their sharply polarized differences, Americans need to be convinced that they should not allow differences over their political views to degenerate into bombast and rancorous conflict. Without some commonly understood rules or norms of behavior, conflict degenerates into a brawl. Polarized Americans need to learn more restrained and respectful ways of engaging in political disagreements. They need a bit more humility in their own views, understanding that they may not be 100% right all of the time and that well-intentioned, informed, and intelligent people may disagree with them. They should try to understand how the other side sees things.[54] They need a more accurate understanding that their views (and the views of many they associate with) may not be representative of the broader public. Finally, they need to understand that compromise is a necessity in a popular government that is trying to represent millions of people with almost as many different views about public policies. There are good deals and bad deals, depending on one's views and political circumstances, but the very idea of political compromise is embedded in democracy. In short, to the extent that polarized politics creates unnecessarily bitter conflict, it might be reduced by Americans adopting a more restrained and reasoned disposition toward politics—a new approach and commitment to civics.

Getting people to handle political disagreements in even a slightly more mature way will not be easy. It may not even be possible. The most plausible vehicles for any success in this are the nation's mediating institutions—particularly those in journalism and education. American politics could benefit greatly from more constructive mediating institutions that have credibility across the spectrum of mainstream political views and a renewed commitment to conveying and exhibiting proper perspectives on how to deal with political differences. In their present conditions, these mediating institutions have too often served as instruments and reinforcers of polarization and amateurish political dispositions. Old professional norms of balance, diverse views, and a sincere attempt at objectivity have given way too often and too completely to ideological advocacy—often thinly veiled, sometimes blatant "in-your-face politics," as Diana Mutz puts it.[55] If the broad credibility of these mediating institutions can be restored, and if they can also provide a broadly accepted understanding of the facts in political disputes, they may be able to elevate and temper political disagreements.[56]

Even if our mediating institutions were somehow remade to be more unifying than divisive, and even if Americans were then persuaded to take restrained attitudes toward political disagreements, polarization inevitably entails a great deal of conflict. Politics, even if practiced with civility, can be rough and many Americans are quite sensitive to conflict.[57] Many avoid politics because they are uncomfortable or squeamish about the conflict it involves. This condition adds another item to the new civics agenda: Americans need to develop thicker skins when it comes to politics. They need to lighten up. Americans should not take offense so easily to political views with which they differ. Differences should not be made personal, but they also should not be taken too easily as personal. Political issues are too important not to be discussed openly, frankly, frequently, and widely. The price of having strong opinions is the willingness on occasion to defend them—this just comes with the territory. Perhaps the best way to develop a thicker political skin is for people to talk about politics more openly, to get used to hearing different opinions. Civil political discussions should not be off-limits. They should be welcomed. They can be fascinating, enlightening, and even entertaining. It is peculiar that a nation that takes pride in celebrating diversity in most every respect should be so squeamish when encountering diversity in political opinions. Making Americans more receptive to discussing their political differences may be the biggest challenge to reducing dysfunctional political conflict.[58]

The Benefits of Exhaustion

Changing political institutions or how people think about politics are Herculean tasks. They are unlikely to be undertaken and, if undertaken, are even less likely to be successful. There are too many reasons why Americans are fundamentally divided, why they are likely to remain that way, and why these divisions will continue to be reflected in our national political institutions, from our political parties and the media to the government. In short, there is little reason to suspect that Americans any time soon will resolve the large political differences that now divide them. Those differences seem more likely to widen further than to diminish. There is also little reason to expect that Americans will grow significantly more respectful, tolerant, realistic, and civil in dealing with their differences.

There are, however, also reasons to think that there are limits to the dysfunctional consequences often associated with polarization. Two have already been noted. Despite declining numbers, a large minority of Americans still count themselves as moderates. They cannot be ignored. Moreover, many liberals and conservatives are not zealots. There is still an audience for moderation and compromise. Second, as divided as Americans are, there is still an across-the-board concern about performance in delivering on the consensus or valence issues—a strong economy, a nation securely at peace, and other aspects of what used to be called the American way of life. Both of these factors provide limits to the harmful effects generally linked to polarization.

A third factor may also limit or even lead to the retrenchment of polarized conflict: the exhausting effects of stressful polarized conflict. Although seldom even asked anymore on surveys, politics is well down the list of priorities for most people.[59] Americans have a long list of personal concerns to attend to before they even think about politics. These range from their personal finances and their jobs to their relationships, families, and friends. Even in highly polarized times, the moderate to low priority given to political differences is reflected in modest turnout rates and the fact that only about a quarter of respondents in ANES polls report being interested in politics "most of the time" (and these reports are likely exaggerated). We also know many Americans are averse to conflict. These two characteristics quite probably place limits on the extent and duration of severe polarization, much as Berelson suggested for pluralism.[60]

A review of American history leads to the same conclusion: Americans do not have the stomach for intense and protracted political conflict. Throughout American history there have been cycles of surges in political interest followed by periods in which political interest wanes. The intense politics of the Founding was followed by "The Era of Good Feeling." In the twentieth century, the intense politics of the Progressive Era and World War I gave way in the 1920s to what

President Harding called a "return to normalcy." The intensity of politics in the Great Depression and World War II was followed in the late 1940s by a period of consolidation lasting into the mid-1960s.

All of this is to suggest that intense political disagreements are exhausting and perhaps unsustainable. This may be an organic regulator or limiter of the dysfunctional consequences of extreme polarization. Until this polarization fatigue sets in, though it rings with futility, there unfortunately may be no better advice than that given by the British government during World War II to the British public: "Keep Calm and Carry On." This admonition is no cure for the mischiefs of polarization; but at least, if followed, it is not likely to make bad matters worse and that may be the best we can do.

AFTERWORD

Since *Polarized* first appeared, additional evidence of polarization in American politics has accumulated. New polling data on ideological divisions in the public provide more evidence of the state and development of polarization in the American public and between the parties. Beyond polls aimed directly at polarization are the events and results of the brutal presidential election of 2016. The nomination contests, the election campaigns, and the aftermath of this unprecedented election shed more light on the polarization of the public and the parties and the implications of both for American democracy. First, to the polls.

THE POLLS

As one new poll after another attests, the public and its parties are highly polarized and Americans know it. Polls in late 2016 and early 2017 reported that 77% thought Americans were divided over important values and 86% believed the nation was now more politically divided than in the past.[1] Partisan animosities reflecting these differences have grown increasingly bitter. Over 40% of Democrats and Republicans say the other party is a "threat to the nation's wellbeing."[2] Posed with a choice between describing the nation as a tight-knit family in challenging times or a dysfunctional family on the verge of breaking apart, roughly three-quarters of Americans found the dysfunctional family analogy more fitting.[3] Could so many Americans be wrong? Possibly, but they aren't.

A Highly Polarized Public

Americans are more polarized than at any time in at least the last seventy years, probably much longer. Self-reports of ideological perspectives provide direct evidence of the public's polarization. Six new poll readings of ideology can be added to the 120 annual poll observations examined in chapter 3.[4] Based on these updated data, 42% of Americans in 2016 were moderates or unable to report an ideology, 36% were conservatives, and 22% were liberals. With these new data and the comparison time frame extended to 2016 (instead of 2012), conservative and liberal ranks have each increased by about 4 percentage points since 1972 while moderates (plus "don't knows") dropped 8 points.

Two important findings emerge from this update. First, amending chapter 3, the increase of liberals nearly equals that of conservatives. Conservatives continue to outnumber liberals by a wide margin (about 13 points), but both conservative and liberal orientations have grown by about the same amount since the early 1970s. Conservatives experienced greater growth in the earlier years, but this has been offset by the greater growth of liberals in recent years.[5]

Second, and most importantly to questions of the level and change in polarization, the American public has become a bit more polarized.[6] In 1972, ideologicals (conservatives plus liberals) and non-ideologicals (moderates plus "don't knows") were near parity. As of 2012 (figure 3.4), ideologicals outnumbered centrists by 12 percentage points. In 2016, the polarization gap was nearly 16 points. Americans are far more likely to be either conservative or liberal (58%) than moderate or non-ideological (42%).[7]

Highly Polarized Parties

New survey data also provide evidence of the extent of polarization between the parties in the electorate. Based on 2016 ANES data, the ideological alignment of the parties continues to progress. More of the public now have ideological views and more who have ideological views now identify with the party sharing those views. Of reported voters who were liberals, 89% identified as Democrats. Among conservative reported voters, 84% were Republicans. Overall, including independents, moderates, and those not reporting an ideological view, a majority of reported voters in 2016 were ideologically aligned partisans (55.6%). Most of the rest were either non-ideologicals or independents (39% combined). The ideologically misaligned (liberal Republicans and conservative Democrats) were on the road to political extinction (5.5%). Setting these numbers in context (see table 1.3), ideological ranks have continued to grow and the correspondence of ideological views and party identifications has continued to tighten.

The ideologically heterogenous parties celebrated by pluralists for fostering bipartisanship and derided by responsible party advocates for obscuring accountability are long gone. With a more polarized public and realigned parties, Democrats and the Republicans have become more ideologically distinct from one another. They have also become more ideologically homogenous internally. The Democrats' base is clearly liberal and the Republicans' base is even more clearly conservative.[8] However, as the 2016 nomination contests, the presidential campaign, and the policy disputes in the first year of Trump's presidency demonstrate, ideological homogeneity should not be mistaken for ideological unity. Battles between strains and degrees of an ideology can be fierce. Polarization has not simply sorted out existing views in conflict. It has expanded that conflict.

THE ELECTION

The effects of polarization ran throughout the turbulent presidential election of 2016. The rancor of the election had a great deal to do with how the campaigns were conducted (particularly, but not solely, Mr. Trump's campaign), but the harshness of the election was not merely about nasty barbs and deplorable insults. Underlying polarization substantially affected both parties' presidential nomination contests as well as the raucous general election campaign. Real politics was going on amid this "food fight" of an election.

Polarization and the Nomination

The anti-establishment uprisings in the nominations of both parties are rooted in polarization. On the Democratic side, an energized and increasingly liberal base enthusiastically supported Senator Bernie

Sanders, a self-described democratic socialist. Sanders mounted an unlikely but impressively strong challenge to the presumptive nominee Hillary Clinton. Having been a fixture on the national political stage for a quarter century, Clinton was as establishment as it gets. The choice was between Clinton's pragmatic but staid liberalism and Sanders's boldly inspiring but less politically viable liberalism. Despite the groundswell of support for Bernie, with a strong assist from her party's establishment "superdelegates," Clinton survived Sanders's challenge.

Polarization played a far different role in the Republican nomination. Many frustrated conservative Republicans (chapter 7) were not looking so much for the most pure, extreme, or dependable conservative candidate as they were for one who could finally win for them, who would end their frustrating years of neglect by the government and their own party's establishment. They found this candidate, they believed, in the ultimate non-politician: the bellicose and erratic billionaire real-estate tycoon and celebrity Donald Trump.

Trump emerged from a crowded field to capture the Republican nomination. An unlikely populist-conservative, promising to "make America great again" in a conservative mold, he was the un-Obama, the un-Clinton, and, for many, the unimaginable. Politically incorrect to the nth degree, he made liberals cringe. The problem for Republicans was that he made many conservative Republicans cringe as well. Unlike any nominee in history, his own party's leadership– from past presidential nominees to congressional leaders and major rivals for the nomination–stood at arm's length (or as far as possible) from Trump and many refused to give his candidacy even a perfunctory endorsement. They regarded him as boorish, crude, ignorant, unprincipled, garish, childish, superficial, narcissistic–you get the picture. "Never Trump" spread as a movement among ordinary conservative Republicans, not only among party elites. More than a third of Republican-party identifiers who were polled just weeks before the election reported having unfavorable views of their party's nominee.[9] This division within the conservative-dominated Republican Party presented the crucial question of the general election campaign: Could a party so deeply divided over its nominee possibly win the election?

Candidates, Conditions, and Polarization

Polarization, both its high level in the public and its reflection in the parties, had a great deal to do with the general election's outcome, but its impact is best understood in conjunction with two other factors. The first of these is the relative evaluations of the candidates. A majority of Americans held unfavorable views of both Hillary Clinton and Donald Trump, but more thought poorly of Trump. He was a greater liability to his party than Clinton was to hers. In the first half of 2016, unfavorable views of Trump averaged nearly ten points higher than those of Clinton (62% versus 53%).[10] Despite a disliked nominee of their own, Democrats had the good fortune of running against an even more widely disliked Republican.

The other important factor in 2016 was the public's negative perception of the state of the nation, especially the economy. Through the first half of 2016, a large majority thought the nation was moving in the wrong direction (63%) and even more saw national economic conditions as only fair or poor (72%).[11] These negative impressions were supported by an average economic growth rate of barely two percent since the Great Recession ended in 2009. A dissatisfied public was inclined toward change. As the out-party, this favored Republicans and presented Democrats with a major obstacle to a third consecutive term.[12]

Reactions to the candidates and national conditions posed different problems for Democrats and Republicans. While some liberals wondered whether Clinton was liberal enough to vote for and some may have been dispirited by national conditions and a weak economy, most united quickly behind Clinton's candidacy. Polarization as well as the alternative being Donald Trump made this an easy call. Despite factors that might have depressed turnout and loyalty, liberal turnout was unchanged and split strongly in favor of Clinton. In the end, between Clinton and Trump, about 90% of liberal votes went to Clinton.[13]

On the Republican side, party unity came neither so quickly nor so easily. Republicans were sharply divided between Trump enthusiasts and those who considered him unacceptable on every dimension of leadership–from knowledge of policy and consistency of principles to temperament, character, and judgment. Many anti-Trump Republicans seriously contemplated sitting out the election, an easy "out" in states whose electoral votes were not seriously in doubt.

In the closing weeks of the campaign, however, with what they saw as a Clinton victory looming darkly over the horizon, many disgruntled conservative hold-outs came back to the Republican column. As they rationalized or reconsidered their choice, unfavorable opinions about Trump among Republicans declined (about 7 points).[14] Even so, about a fifth of Trump's voters admitted that they still held an unfavorable view of him. More than a quarter of Trump's voters said their candidate lacked the temperament to be president.[15] For many, "Never Trump" had become "Reluctantly Trump." They held their noses and cast their votes. Between Trump and Clinton, about 85% of conservative votes went to Trump.[16] Along with sour views of national conditions, polarization had offset or overridden the grave reservations many conservatives had about a Trump vote.

Widespread and intense polarized views, across the public and between the parties, shaped the 2016 election. On one side of the spectrum, polarization compelled liberals to overlook Clinton's scandals and deficiencies as a candidate as well as a sputtering economy and unstable international conditions. On the other side, dissatisfaction with national conditions and polarization compelled conservatives to vote for a candidate many thought lacked the rudimentary leadership qualities needed in a president. Non-ideological centrists again were caught in the middle–by ideology, by the candidates' considerable shortcomings, and by generally dreary views of national conditions. Their vote split favored Clinton over Trump (52% to 40%, with 8% going to minor party candidates), close to its two-party division in 2012. The three components of the vote (polarization, the candidates, and national conditions) left voters closely enough divided to make an electoral vote majority for Trump possible.[17]

Comey and the Russians (not a rock band)

Although the above explanation of the election is supported by the evidence and fits established theory, two other controversial explanations have gained some currency. They trace Trump's surprising victory to Russia's meddling in the election (by hacking Democratic emails and releasing them through Wikileaks) and FBI Director

Comey's late October letter, re-opening the investigation into Clinton's mishandling of confidential national security emails. Some, including Clinton herself, contend Wikileaks and Comey's letter caused the collapse of Clinton's lead over Trump in the closing weeks of the campaign.[18]

The evidence says otherwise. Contrary to the speculation, neither Wikileaks nor Comey's letter had anything to do with the shriveling of Clinton's lead. If either had been responsible, they would also have caused more voters to view Clinton negatively–but opinions about her did *not* grow more negative. Unfavorable opinions of Clinton were remarkably steady. From August to late September, Hillary Clinton's unfavorables in Gallup polls averaged 55%. Her unfavorables in the Gallup poll completed on the day Comey released his letter (October 28) stood at 55%. In the exit polls, after Wikileaks and after Comey's letter, her unfavorables were *unchanged* at 55%. Opinions about Hillary Clinton, a figure in the political spotlight for a quarter century, had long been highly and solidly polarized. Nothing Wikileaks revealed or Comey said was going to change minds about her at that late stage of the game.[19]

The race tightened in the last weeks of the campaign because Trump's unfavorables declined (by about 5 points). They declined as some conservatives and moderates with qualms about Trump came to the unpleasant realization that voting for Trump was the only possible way they could help prevent Clinton's election.[20] Some dealt with the dissonance of voting for a candidate they disliked by rationalizing, reassessing, or otherwise softening their views of Trump, trying to convince themselves that maybe "the lesser to two evils" was not really so awful after all. In voting, as in everything else, people tend to postpone unpleasant decisions as long as they can and make them as painless to themselves as they can.

The decay of Clinton's October poll lead was not about Russian and Wikileaks meddling in the election and not about Comey's letter. It was about polarization, in conjunction with dissatisfaction about national conditions, belatedly overriding the serious concerns many voters had about Donald Trump as a potential president. Trump's candidacy put polarization to the test. His election testified to how powerful polarization has become. The highly polarized views of Americans and the highly polarized positions of the parties were critical to how voters perceived and responded to the candidates' shortcomings and the nation's problems.

Like the staggered realignment and the polarization of the parties, the 2016 election reflected the public's will, whether that will was wise or not. Despite the perennial concerns about media biases, campaign spending influence, and poorly informed and manipulable voters as well as the unusual concerns about the October surprises of Wikileaks and Comey's letter, the election turned on the voters' reasonable and supportable impressions of the major party candidates and national conditions judged from their ideological perspectives. The election's results reflected the public's difficult and strenuously contested choice (albeit filtered through the parties' byzantine nomination systems and the electoral vote system), not the easy manipulation of external forces or passing news stories.

THE NEW NORMAL

Americans and their major political parties are highly polarized and, in the short time since *Polarized* reached print, they have become a bit more so. Growth in the public's polarization should eventually level off when additions to the ranks of liberals and conservatives must be found among the less politically conscious members of the public. Further polarization between the parties may also slow down with fewer ideologically misaligned available to realign their ideological or party identifications. But for now, there are no signs of polarization either in the public or between the parties slowing, much less reversing. In fact, if current trends continue, the polarization gap between ideologicals and centrists in the public as well as the percentage of ideologically aligned partisans will edge up another point or two by 2020.

Polarization in American politics is unlikely to recede as long as its principal cause remains. Beyond the standard political differences based on varied backgrounds, experiences, and values, polarization depends on the public being divided over whether the government has been successful in advancing the common core of the nation's public interest–primarily peace and prosperity. Consensus over the efficacy (or inefficacy) of government in promoting the public interest would greatly reduce polarization. However, since experts are often divided on the question of whether government action on any matter is effective, ineffective, or even counter-productive, it is not surprising that ordinary citizens reach different conclusions as well. And since concerns about government action focus on those matters in contention, not areas in which everyone accepts or rejects government's role, different conclusions are understandably quite common.

From this perspective, the polarizing ideological battle between liberalism and conservatism is an elevation of a very practical battle over what works.[21] If most see more government leading to greater peace and prosperity, polarization breaks down with a movement to the left and a weakening of the right. Conversely, if most see less government as the answer, the left shrivels and the right ascends. In either case, big parts of the dominant ideology become widely accepted, ingrained in a new and expanded center of a less polarized system. I suspect that this is what happened in the 1930s and 1940s. Widely credited with steering the nation through the dark days of the Great Depression and World War II, FDR's New Deal liberalism was ascendant. Its success with the public led to its absorption into the relatively placid center that carried through the 1950s and early 1960s.

For Americans to reach a relatively unpolarized consensus about whether government advances the public interest, they must be convinced by a compellingly clear answer to the question of whether the broadly increased use of government to promote the public interest works. Anything less than a compellingly clear answer to this question allows denial or minor ideological adjustments (see the same-sex marriage issue) and the preservation of existing polarized views. Reversing polarization requires a public-wide jolt rendering a clear and broadly held verdict in favor of or against the greater use of government to advance the common good. This is likely to happen only as the result of government's success or failure in dealing with a national catastrophe. As Madison in the tenth *Federalist* wrote with respect to destroying liberty in order to prevent the mischiefs of faction, the cure in this case is worse than the disease. If it would take a response to a national catastrophe to reverse polarization, we are probably better off being highly polarized. Polarization is with us and is likely to be with us for the foreseeable future–and, given the likely alternative, that might not be such a bad thing.

APPENDIX A

FIVE IDEOLOGICAL SERIES

The analysis of the ideological polarization of the public uses self-reported ideology data from five sources. The sources, their time spans in this study, the number of annual or annualized observations available (N), and the question wordings and possible responses are presented below.

1. American National Election Study (ANES), 1972–2012 (N=19). The question: "We hear a lot of talk these days about liberals and conservatives. Here is a 7-point scale on which the political views that people might hold are arranged from extremely liberal to extremely conservative. Where would you place yourself on this scale, or haven't you thought much about this?" This provides for a seven-point scale.
2. CBS/New York Times, 1976–2015 (original individual polls N=304, annual N=40). The question: "How would you describe your views on most political matters? Generally, do you think of yourself as liberal, moderate, or conservative?" This provides for a three-point scale.
3. Gallup, 1992–2014 (N=23). The question: "How would you describe your political views—very conservative, conservative, moderate, liberal, or very liberal?" This provides for a five-point scale.
4. General Social Survey (NORC), 1974–2014 (N=28). The question: "We hear a lot of talk these days about liberals and conservatives. I'm going to show you a seven-point scale on which the

political views that people might hold are arranged from extremely liberal—point 1—to extremely conservative—point 7. Where would you place yourself on this scale?" This provides for a seven-point scale.

5. The National Exit Polls, 1976–2012 (N=10). The question: "On most political matters, do you consider yourself to be liberal, moderate, or conservative?" This provides for a three-point scale.

APPENDIX B

REGRESSION ANALYSES OF
IDEOLOGICAL ORIENTATIONS

TABLE B.1. TREND IN SELF-REPORTED IDEOLOGICALS (LIBERALS PLUS CONSERVATIVES)

Dependent Variable: Ideologicals (Conservatives plus Liberals as Percentage of Total)

Regression	ANES 1972–2012	GSS 1974–2014	CBS/NYT 1976–2015	Gallup 1992–2014	Exit Polls 1976–2012	Pooled 1972–2015
Year	.30** (.05)	.06* (.02)	.12** (.03)	.37** (.04)	.27** (.07)	.17** (.02)
Constant	−540.12	−64.35	−185.42	−678.37	−479.64	−281.19
N	19	28	40	23	10	120
Adjusted R^2	.63	.17	.29	.82	.59	.76
Std. Error of Est.	2.64	1.51	2.10	1.18	2.60	2.25
Durbin-Watson	2.64	2.12	1.47	1.83	2.08	1.75
Expected 1972	43	57	50	—	46	49
Expected 1992	49	59	53	54	52	52
Expected 2012	55	60	55	61	57	56

** $p<.01$, one-tailed. * $p<.05$, one-tailed. Standard errors are in parentheses. In surveys in which the degree of an ideological orientation is ascertained, conservatives include those who are slightly conservative, conservative, and extremely conservative. Liberals also include the three degrees of that perspective. Expected percentages in 1972, 1992, and 2012 were calculated using coefficients to four decimal places. The Pooled equation included dummy variables for the polling organization with the Exit Polls serving as the baseline excluded category. The coefficients for the other polling organizations were ANES ($b = -2.97$, se $= .88$), GSS ($b = 7.16$, se $= .83$), CBS-NYT ($b = 1.19$, se $= .80$), and Gallup ($b = 4.52$, se $= .87$). An expected value in 1972 is not calculated for Gallup since its series did not begin until 20 years later. For comparability, reported poll percentages have been adjusted to total to exactly 100%.

TABLE B.2. TREND IN SELF-REPORTED CONSERVATIVES

Regression	ANES 1972–2012	GSS 1974–2014	CBS/NYT 1976–2015	Gallup 1992–2014	Exit Polls 1976–2012	Pooled 1972–2015
			Dependent Variable: Conservatives (as Percentage of Total)			
Year	.21**	.08*	.06**	.08*	.11	.10**
	(.04)	(.03)	(.02)	(.04)	(.06)	(.02)
Constant	−381.95	−118.93	−91.04	−120.21	−180.05	−161.81
N	19	28	40	23	10	120
Adjusted R²	.58	.13	.18	.14	.21	.70
Std. Error of Est.	2.05	2.13	1.46	1.16	2.09	1.81
Durbin-Watson	1.92	1.60	1.86	1.41	3.01	1.81
Expected 1972	26	31	31	—	30	31
Expected 1992	30	32	33	37	32	33
Expected 2012	34	34	34	39	34	35

Note: See note to appendix table B.1. The coefficients for the polling organizations other than the Exit Poll baseline were ANES (b = −1.85, se = .71), GSS (b = .64, se = .64), CBS-NYT (b = .70, se = .67), and Gallup (b = 5.22, se = .70).

TABLE B.3. TREND IN SELF-REPORTED LIBERALS

Dependent Variable: Liberals (as Percentage of Total)

Regression	ANES 1972–2012	GSS 1974–2014	CBS/NYT 1976–2015	Gallup 1992–2014	Exit Polls 1976–2012	Pooled 1972–2015
Year	.09*	−.04	.06**	.29**	.16**	.07**
	(.04)	(.03)	(.02)	(.03)	(.05)	(.02)
Constant	−158.17	54.59	−94.38	−558.16	−299.59	−119.38
N	19	28	40	23	10	120
Adjusted R²	.15	.00	.14	.84	.53	.71
Std. Error of Est.	2.20	1.77	1.54	.86	1.74	1.83
Durbin-Watson	1.94	1.42	1.04	1.33	1.46	1.30
Expected 1972	17	26	19	—	16	18
Expected 1992	19	26	20	17	20	20
Expected 2012	20	26	22	22	23	21

Note: See note to appendix table B.1. The coefficients for the polling organizations other than the Exit Poll baseline were ANES (b = −1.12, se = .72), GSS (b = 6.45, se = .68), CBS-NYT (b = .55, se = .65), and Gallup (b = −.70, se = .71).

NOTES

INTRODUCTION

1. Key (1966).
2. Ladd (1994).
3. Ranney and Kendall (1956, 471).
4. Campbell et al. (1960, 249).
5. Lewis-Beck et al. (2008, 279).
6. Hotelling (1929); Downs (1957).
7. See McClosky, Hoffman, and O'Hara (1960); Page (1978); Ansolabehere, Snyder, and Stewart (2001).

CHAPTER 1. KNOWNS AND UNKNOWNS

1. Maraniss (1999).
2. The distinction between first- and second-order polarization involves whether leaders or citizens are in some way grouped for the examination of polarization. First-order polarization concerns differences among ungrouped leaders or citizens. Second-order polarization concerns differences among groups of leaders or citizens. In this sense, the polarization between citizen-partisans could be examined or between income groups or demographic groupings of citizens or leaders.
3. Some contend that bimodality should be the standard establishing polarization. Besides being unrealistic (given the considerable errors in measuring opinions), bimodality is not necessarily indicative of the extent of political conflict structured along a single dimension. For example, great variance around the political center would reflect substantial polarization of opinions even if the distribution of opinions were unimodal.
4. Hetherington (2009, 447).
5. Converse (1966).
6. MacKuen, Erikson, and Stimson (1989).
7. Campbell (2006b).
8. Campbell (2010a); Norpoth (1987).
9. Amos (2012); Gibbons (2012).
10. McClosky, Hoffman, and O'Hara (1960).
11. Constantini (1963); Montjoy, Shaffer, and Weber (1981, 289).
12. Converse (1964).
13. The McClosky Difference between elite and mass polarization is a finding that applies both to first-order or general polarization as well as to second-order or party polarization.

14. Campbell et al. (1960); Hetherington (2009); Abramowitz (2010).

15. Key (1961, 263–87). Also, evidence of latent opinions not being necessarily moderate is suggested by the self-reported ideology data examined later in chapter 3. In those data, there was a significant decline in recent decades in the percentage of respondents reporting that they were unable to declare themselves as moderates, conservatives, or liberals. Notably, this decline was not accompanied by a commensurate rise in the number of moderates. To the contrary, the ranks of both conservatives and liberals increased. While some of these increases may be due to true change in orientations over time, it is probably the case that many respondents with latent ideological views became more aware of their views and the labels associated with them in recent years.

16. Stewart (1964).

17. When the true views of voters are highly polarized, random measurement error in the expression of those views on a seven-point scale should underestimate the variance or extent of polarization since the error component can only move the measurement toward the center position. A true view of 6 on a 0 to 6 scale, for example, might be reported as a 5 or a 4, but could not be reported as a nonexistent 7 or 8. This point will be extended in chapter 4 to identify a problem with relying on the variance of issue preferences to detect changes in polarization. This suggests that the leader-follower difference may be substantially a consequence of measurement error.

18. See Abramowitz and Saunders (2008).

19. It is important to recognize that the politically disengaged will not be polarized in any meaningful way; on the other hand, some number of these disengaged may have been turned off to politics because of prior experience. Because of this, we should not apply the political awareness or engagement standard too strictly.

20. Even with this unintentional filter, there will be some apoliticals in the mix who ideally should be weeded out or taken into account in establishing benchmarks for polarization. Without a filter for those who are politically aware or an adjustment to a benchmark of polarization, the electorate will appear to be a bit more moderate than it really is.

21. Binder (1996, 36). Also see Poole and Rosenthal (1991).

22. Binder (1996, 39).

23. Binder's later update through 2000 placed the percentage of centrists in the House and Senate at under 10%. See Binder (2005, 12).

24. Bond and Fleisher (2004), see also Poole and Rosenthal (1997).

25. The mean percentage of nonconformists in the Senate prior to the 1980s was 41% in the 1950s, 45% in the 1960s, and 43% in the 1970s.

26. Poole and Rosenthal (2007); Poole (2014).

27. Poole and Rosenthal (2007, 106). An earlier analysis by Jerrold Schneider (1979) had also concluded that congressional roll-call voting in the 1970s fell largely along a single liberal-conservative dimension.

28. Poole and Rosenthal (2007, 107).

29. Ibid., 108.

30. Poole (2014).

31. Fleisher and Bond (2000a).

32. Ornstein, Mann, Malbin, and Rugg (2013).

33. Mann and Wakeman (2013).

34. The American Conservative Union is the conservative counterpart to the ADA. It also rates members of Congress on an ideological scale. There ratings tend to be highly correlated (but inverse) with ADA scores. Unfortunately, the ACU scoring did not extend back into the 1960s. A comparison of their scores from the 1970s versus post-1990s scores, however, produces very similar results. Party differences increase from about a 40 percentage point gap to about 70 percentage points in the more recent era.

35. Groseclose, Levitt, and Snyder (1999, 42).

36. There is widespread consensus about the increased extent of party polarization among elites, especially those in Congress. Included in a very long list of those concurring are Poole and Rosenthal (2007); Theriault (2008); Stonecash, Brewer, and Mariani (2003); Hetherington (2009); Levendusky (2009); Abramowitz (2010), and many others too numerous to cite.

37. Committee on Political Parties (1950).

38. Burns (1963); Bond and Fleisher (1990).

39. See Manley (1973); Brady and Bullock (1980); and Shelley (1983).

40. Liptak (2014).

41. Carlson, Livermore, and Rockmore (2016).

42. Pew Research Center (2012, 1).

43. Iyengar, Sood, and Lelkes (2012, 421).

44. For the former reason see Abramowitz (2010) and for the latter see Fiorina (2006; 2009, 61).

45. The increased connection of ideology and party has been observed in a large number of studies. Among others, see Abramowitz and Saunders (1998, 2008); Abramowitz (2010); Baumer and Gold (2010); Bafumi and Shapiro (2009); Fiorina (2009, 61); Jacobson (2000); Hetherington (2009, 441–43); and Layman, Carsey, and Horowitz (2006, 94).

46. Abramowitz (2010, 59).

47. See Jacobson (2000); Abramowitz and Saunders (2008); Bafumi and Shapiro (2009); DiMaggio, Evans, and Bryson (1996); Layman and Carsey (2002).

48. Fleisher and Bond (2000b); Jacobson (2001, 2011).

49. The data were originally collected by Gallup. Gary Jacobson generously shared these quarterly approval data with me (correspondence on June 8, 2013).

50. Feldman and Zaino (2012).

51. Hetherington (2009, 429).

52. Fiorina (2006). Fiorina (2017, 25) now refers to moderates as "the modal category."

53. Bafumi and Shapiro (2009); Fiorina and Abrams (2008).

54. Theriault (2008).

55. Hare, McCarty, Poole, and Rosenthal (2012).

56. Mann and Ornstein (2012, 51–52).

57. Pomper (1967).

58. Scammon and Wattenberg (1970).

59. Page (1978); Campbell (1983); Ansolabehere, Snyder, and Stewart (2001).

60. Poole and Rosenthal (1997).

61. Fiorina and Abrams (2008, 567).

62. Evans (2003, 87); Fiorina (2008, 569–74); Hetherington (2009, 431).

63. Fiorina (2006, 76).

CHAPTER 2. HISTORY AND THEORIES

1. Hamilton, Madison, and Jay (1787).

2. Fiorina (2006); Hetherington (2009).

3. Poole and Rosenthal (1984); Nice (1984).

4. Binder (1996); Fleisher and Bond (2000a, 2004).

5. Hunter (1991).

6. DiMaggio et al. (1996); Evans (2003).

7. Pomper (1972); Abramowitz and Saunders (1998).

8. Fiorina (2006).

9. Fiorina with Abrams (2009, 8 and 14).

10. Fiorina (2002, 526; 2006, 61); Levendusky (2009).

11. Fiorina (2009).

12. Hetherington (2009, 443).

13. Abramowitz (2010; 2013).

14. Abramowitz (2013, 13).

15. Abramowitz and Saunders (1998); Abramowitz (2013, 37–45).

16. Abramowitz (2013, 48).

17. Fiorina (2009, 12).

18. Lipset (1960, 306).

19. McClosky et al. (1960).

20. The post–World War II period saw a general deflating of antagonisms among ideologies in the non-communist or free world. Lipset recounts a conference of intellectuals of different persuasions in 1955 in which "the traditional issues separating the left and the right had declined to comparative insignificance" (1960, 404).

21. Boorstin (1953).

22. Ibid., 19.

23. Hartz (1955).

24. Ibid., 19–20.

25. In even broader terms, the "end of ideology" or "decline-of-ideology" theme ranged throughout the study of non-communist political systems in the 1950s and 1960s. See the exchange between LaPalombara (1966) and Lipset (1966). As Lane (1962, 15) interpreted it, these treatises envisioned analysis replacing ideology as the political battleground over public policy. As a precursor to this intellectual exchange, Arthur Schlesinger, Jr. (1949) wrote of the importance of "the vital center," a brand of moderate New Deal liberalism, as he saw it, in fending off totalitarian pressures from both the left and the right. The placid politics of the post–World War II era were mistakenly extrapolated to envision a harmonious, nearly alienation-free utopia by Robert Lane (1965) in "The Politics of Consensus in an Age of Affluence."

26. Campbell et al. (1960); Converse (1964).

27. Lubell (1956, 4).

28. Lane (1962).

29. Lazarsfeld, Berelson, and Gaudet (1948); Lipset (1960).

30. See Field and Anderson (1969) and Pierce (1970). Conclusions about the general absence of ideological thinking in the American public in the 1950s were undoubtedly exaggerated due to their basis in questions that did not directly ask respondents about their ideological thinking. The evaluations were based on responses to questions about what people liked or disliked about the candidates and parties. Unless ideological reasons were near the top of a respondent's list of likes and dislikes, they might not be revealed.

31. Newhart (1975).

32. Boller (1984, 295).

33. This contrast was commonly noted by studies of that period. For examples, see Nie and Anderson (1974, 544) and Converse and Marcus (1979, 47).

34. RePass (1971); Pomper (1972); Kessel (1972); Carmines and Stimson (1980).

35. Nie, Verba, and Petrocik (1976); Nie and Anderson (1974).

36. Miller and Miller (1976); Lewis-Beck et al. (2008, 247–48).

37. Miller and Levitan (1976).

38. Scammon and Wattenberg (1971); White (2003).

39. Burnham (1970); Broder (1971); Norpoth and Rusk (1982).

40. Wattenberg (1981, 1994).

41. Miller et al. (1976, 753).

42. Fiorina, Abrams, and Pope (2008) later wrote that "either the American population is not more ideologically polarized today than a generation ago, or it was already polarized a generation ago but no one noticed" (556). As even the title of the 1972 NES post-election article makes clear, polarization over four decades ago was well recognized.

43. Hunter (1991); Greenberg (2004); White (2003); Abramowitz (2010).

44. Saad (2012).

45. Though worded differently, in a USA Today and Bipartisan Policy Center survey conducted in February 2013, more than three-quarters of the respondents agreed that Americans politics has become more divided in recent years. Only 4% said it had become less divided and 18% said conditions were about the same as in the past.

46. Carmines and Stimson (1989); Layman et al. (2006, 90).

47. Evans (2003); Fiorina (2008).

48. Abramowitz (2010, 38).

49. DiMaggio et al. (1996); Evans (2003); Fiorina (2002, 2006, 2009); Fiorina et al. (2008).

50. Fiorina (2009, 20).

51. DiMaggio et al. (1996); Evans (2003).

52. Evans (2003, 71).

53. Fiorina and Abrams (2008, 569).

54. Hetherington (2009, 431).

55. Hetherington (2009, 433) appropriately recognizes the lack of a benchmark problem in the DiMaggio et al. analysis. He also, in essence, takes note of the strawman problem of setting unrealistic standards for mass opinion polarization (essentially, the McClosky Difference issue). Unfortunately, the standard he devises using differences between southerners and non-southerners of civil rights issues in the early 1960s has several problems. It is an examination of second-order polarization between groups rather than general or first-order polarization in the general public. It also defines an outer extreme rather than a standard. It could be compared to using the views of a Grand Kleagle of the KKK as a standard for racism. Of course those views would be racist, but views that are not nearly so extreme might also be properly labeled racist.

56. Carmines and Stimson (1989); Levendusky (2009).

57. Fiorina (2008, 581).

58. Layman et al. (2006, 94–95).

59. Ansolabehere et al. (2001); Poole and Rosenthal (2007).

60. Fiorina (1999); Layman et al. (2006).

61. The circumstantial or indirect evidence examined in chapter 5 consists of whether suspected levels and changes in polarization are consistent with other generally acknowledged characteristics and changes in American public opinion and behavior.

CHAPTER 3. IDEOLOGY AND POLARIZATION

1. Lubell (1965). Originally published in 1951.

2. Cantril (1951, 575–76).

3. Free and Cantril (1967); Scammon and Wattenberg (1970).

4. Stimson (2004, 84–95); Ellis and Stimson (2012).

5. Ellis and Stimson (2012, 69–70) found earlier self-reported survey data, but respondents were not offered an explicit option of a moderate or non-ideological response. These data were, thus, not helpful in gauging polarization.

6. Over four decades, each of the organizations made many changes in how they conducted their surveys. These include changes in sample designs, contact methods, and survey protocols. For example, the ANES has begun combining respondents surveyed through the Internet with those surveyed in person by an interviewer (face-to-face). This particular change was associated with a sizeable drop in the numbers reporting that they had not thought much about their ideology. For consistency with previous ANES data, only face-to-face interviews in 2012 were used in this chapter's analysis. Apart from this exception, I relied on each survey organization's decisions regarding what they

considered to be their most accurate reading of public opinion. While it is true that these organizations change methods over time, they usually do so with accuracy in mind. Consistency in striving for accuracy is generally more important than being wedded to a particular contact method.

7. As a check on the robustness of these findings, the portions of the electorate not qualifying their ideological orientations as either "slightly" liberal or conservative were examined separately in the two series in which those designations were used (ANES and GSS). The estimated increase in ideologicals remained statistically significant (p<.01).

8. Campbell (2006, 158); McCarty, Poole, and Rosenthal (2006, 72).

9. Polarization grew annually by nearly two-tenths (b = .17) of a percentage point according to the trend regression of ideologicals from 1972 to 2015, as reported in appendix B. Restricting the trend regression to the period from 1972 to 1998 only slightly lowers the estimated growth rate of polarization (b = .13). In both cases, the trends were statistically significant (p<.01). Including an interaction trend term for post-2000 years made virtually no change in the percentage of explained variance.

10. DiMaggio et al. (1996); Evans (2003); Fiorina (2006).

11. Fiorina et al. (2008, 556).

12. The standard deviation under asymmetric perfect polarization (a 60-40 split of conservatives and liberals, close to the actual proportional split) is nearly identical to that under symmetric perfect polarization (standard deviations of .49 vs. .50).

13. Clausen (1968–69); Traugott and Katosh (1979); Cassel (2004).

14. Keith et al. (1992); Petrocik (2009).

15. Campbell (2010a).

16. The exit poll data in the 2012 election corroborate these numbers. Of the two-party vote, the exit poll reports that 89% of liberals said they voted for President Obama and 83% of conservatives said they voted for Governor Romney. See also Jacoby (2009) and Abramowitz and Saunders (2006).

17. Some of these apparent misidentifications may be the more skewed views of ideological purists (the far left taking exception to what they see as too conciliatory Democrats and the far right similarly taking exception to what they regard as wishy-washy Republicans), but most misidentifications appear to be outright misapplications of the ideological terms. In 12 ANES studies asking respondents to identify which of the major parties was more conservative, on average, only 14% said that the Democratic Party was the more conservative party.

18. Lane (1962); Conover and Feldman (1981).

19. Lindqvist and Östling (2010).

20. Even though a good deal of early voting research suggested a lack of widespread ideological sophistication in the electorate (Campbell et al. 1960), this may have been somewhat exaggerated because of the open-ended questions used and the ideologically placid politics of the 1950s. Gallup surveys from the 1930s and 1940s, for instance, indicate substantial ideological awareness. Fully 97% of those surveyed by Gallup in 1939 identified President Roosevelt as a liberal or radical. Only 1% thought of him as a conservative (Cantril 1951).

21. Like the spending and services question, the size of government question also involves a number of measurement issues that would attenuate its association with ideology. For instance, a conservative might object to "the less government, the better" if he or she believes that more government is needed to protect the right to life, to provide police and fire protections, or for national defense. A liberal might object to military spending. Responses may not match up perfectly to self-reported ideologies in part because the questions themselves are unavoidably imperfect. In either view, there may also be some who see the government as already having gone beyond their "ideal" point. Liberals do not necessarily favor an unlimited expansion of government and conservatives do not necessarily favor unlimited reductions.

22. Jacoby (2014).

23. Converse and Markus (1979, 42) found a good deal of continuity in the self-reported ideology measure in the 1972–1976 panel data, though they speculated that this might be the result of a large percentage of respondents opting for the "haven't thought much about it" filter. This invitation to opt out was not provided in many other ANES questions, including the party identification questions.

24. The vacillation of those on the cusp has no effect on the polarization estimates. In the aggregate the sometimes moderate and sometimes slightly ideological numbers are appropriately split quite evenly between the centrist and ideological groupings.

25. The ANES 1990–1992 panel data are from Wood and Oliver (2012, 640). Their interpretation of the measurement's "notoriously poor reliability" (p. 637) is rebutted in this examination of actual change and where it was coming from (a drift between a moderate and slightly ideological responses) as well as the analysis of ANES data during the 2012 election. The discussion in chapter 4 of the lower reliability of issue items provides further perspective on the relatively greater reliability of the ideology measure.

26. Campbell (2010a, 621, 628).

27. A similar situation involves tapping into influences on the vote choice. Voters are asked a battery of forced-choice scaled issue questions as well as a set of open-ended questions about their likes and dislikes about the candidates and parties. A simple summary of the count of the open-ended likes and dislikes questions routinely corresponds much more closely to the reported vote choice than a regression weighted fit of forced-choice issue questions (Kelley and Mirer 1974). With the open-ended questions, voters can address the issues and concerns that they find important and framed in their own way. The forced-choice questions reflect what the survey researcher suspects the voter is interested in and further imposes a set structure on the question and possible answers.

28. Wood and Oliver (2012, 637) present a list of five alleged problems with the self-report measure. Included in this kitchen-sink list are (1) that it ignores the multi-dimensionality of belief systems, (2) that it conflates moderates with don't knows, (3) that it assumes an equal interval among categories, (4) that it assumes that liberalism and conservatism are poles apart on the same dimension, and (5) that it is an unreliable measure. We already dispensed with the reliability charge. As to the other four claims, no one claims that ideology captures everything about a person's political thinking. If there is another dimension that is widespread and relevant, then go to it, but the vague assertion that other dimensions might exist does nothing to undermine the conventionally structured liberal-conservative dimension. The charge that moderates and don't knows are conflated is only an issue in ANES data because of its peculiar decision to invite non-responses. As we have already seen, this is not even a question with other major data sources. Moreover, while there are undoubtedly differences between those who claim to be moderate and those who say they haven't thought much about it, each has more in common with each other than with those claiming a liberal or conservative ideological perspective. It seems fair to count moderates and don't knows as non-ideological or less ideological. As to the equal-interval charge, this applies to all forced-choice survey questions (issue preferences as well as party identification). This only suggests a possible source of correctable measurement error. If they do not think the measure is equal interval, rescale it. This issue also constitutes less of a problem when the scale is collapsed from seven to three categories. Finally, the strong associations with criterion variables (issues and the vote) as well as the fact that jumping from liberal to conservative is an exceedingly rare event would seem to establish liberals and conservatives as being on the same dimension. This may sometimes appear not to be the case because of varying positivity biases among respondents (Knight 1984).

29. Campbell et al. (1960).

30. Converse (1964); Neuman (1986).

31. Converse (1964, 229).

32. Field and Anderson (1969); Achen (1975); Erikson (1979); Neuman (1986); Smith (1989).

33. Free and Cantril (1967).

34. Ellis and Stimson (2012).

35. Ibid., 27.

36. Defense was also included, but reverse coded so that the expected conservative response favored an increase rather than a decrease in spending.

37. Ellis and Stimson (2012, 113) use the GSS version of this question. The question wording differs a bit from the ANES measure. The GSS wording is: "We are faced with many problems in this country, none of which can be solved easily or inexpensively. I'm going to name some of these problems, and for each one I'd like you to tell me whether you think we're spending too much money on it, too little money, or about the right amount on ... (insert policy)?" In this case, the policy was "halting the rising crime rate." The GSS wording appears to elicit even more pro-spending responses than the ANES wording.

38. Ellis and Stimson (2012, 105).

39. Ellis and Stimson report responses of consistent liberals, consistent conservatives, conflicted conservatives (self-identified conservatives who are operationally liberal by their measure) on nine issues (2012, 105). They find the conflicted conservatives to have positions more akin to those of consistent liberals than consistent conservatives. They do not observe, however, that a majority of so-called conflicted conservatives agree with a majority of consistent conservatives on five of these nine issues and are evenly split on a sixth issue.

40. Ellis and Stimson (2012, 96, 173, and 106).

41. Ibid., 72.

42. This is a variation of the charge of some very conservative Republicans that less conservative or moderate Republicans are RINOs, "Republicans-in-name-only." See also Fiorina and Levendusky (2006, 105–6).

43. Ellis and Stimson make much of the non-political appeal of conservatism as a symbol. In support of this view, they report what they believed to be the first survey question about liberal versus conservative preferences, a Gallup survey conducted in May 1936. Even in the early days of the New Deal realignment, the conservative view was preferred to the liberal by a 53% to 47% margin (Ellis and Stimson 2012, 61). However, according to Cantril (1951, 576), Gallup had conducted a survey several months earlier in which the liberal view was preferred by a 58% to 41% margin. The results of a third Gallup survey, conducted in February 1937, also favored liberals, 52% to 48%. More to the point, we should take note that the New Deal realignment was not a purely ideological realignment or a ringing endorsement of liberal policies. A May 1936 Gallup survey indicated that 37% of Democrats nationally and 49% of southerners, who were overwhelmingly Democratic in that era, would have opted to join a conservative party rather than a liberal party (Cantril 1951, 576). A major component of the New Deal coalition was segregationist white southerners, and one of the major missteps of FDR's presidency was attempting to purge the Democratic Party of its conservative wing in the 1938 midterm elections (Dunn 2010). The appeal or lack thereof of the conservative and liberal labels would appear to be largely influenced by the public's appraisals of the political policies and leaders associated with those labels, rather than non-political influences.

44. See Jacoby (2014); Pew (2014); Maddox and Lilie (1984); Noel (2013); and Carmines et al. (2014).

45. Hibbing, Smith, and Alford (2014, 44–56).

46. The adaptability of ideological labels to different times and places should be regarded as a virtue of the measurement. Ideologies should be realistically adapted to

the political context in which they are held. One would hardly expect, for example, that the most liberal person in 1950 Mississippi would be a staunch civil libertarian, pro-redistribution, feminist by 2014 New York standards. The fact that they fell short of 2014 New York standards should not cause them to be considered any less of a liberal in their day and place.

47. The Pew Research Center's study of political polarization is another example of the hazards of researchers attributing ideological views to respondents. That study rated respondents as liberals or conservatives based on responses to a set of ten items (2014). Many of the options offered were not balanced and responses between the liberal and conservative positions were not invited. One "conservative position" option, for instance, remarkably began with "Poor people today have it easy ..." and another stated the "conservative" position on gay rights as the extreme position that "Homosexuality should be discouraged by society." The result of this was a very volatile index that reported liberals to have increased by 13 percentage points between 1994 and 2014 and conservatives to have declined by three percentage points in the same period after having first dropped by 12 points between 1994 and 2004.

48. Aside from the problem of defining "operational conservatism" as a very stingy orientation, the Ellis and Stimson index and the ten GSS questions it relies upon have a number of flaws. The first, as they recognize (pp. 28 and 104), is that the measure depends entirely upon spending questions that do not indicate where the funding comes from (e.g., higher taxes, higher deficits, inflation, or even cuts in other spending in programs not mentioned) or how it will be spent (e.g., in government programs, vouchers, government worker salaries). These are essentially "free lunch" questions in that there is no explicit price to be paid by anyone as the result of an increase in spending (and no one explicitly benefits in any way from a cut in spending). Though they observe that introducing a tax increase tradeoff in the question does not dampen enthusiasm much for increased spending on a program, respondents are not offered the option of paying for the increased spending by cutting government elsewhere. Second, there seems to be little reason not to balance the spending questions with questions about cutting or increasing taxes. Both are operational questions. The third problem is that these questions ask about "more or less" spending. Responses depend not only on a respondent's views about the activity of government (how the response is interpreted), but on the perceived level of spending by the administration (and even inflation levels). Thus, a liberal respondent may well say that the government is spending too much and still be truly a liberal if the respondent believes that the government itself is too liberal and spending far too much. Conversely, a conservative may say that the government is spending too little if the respondent believes that a conservative administration has gone beyond the spending cuts favored by the respondent. A response, in short, may reveal more about what he or she thinks about current spending (a relative evaluation) than his or her overall preference for spending on the program (an absolute evaluation). Fourth, the question and response wordings of the ten questions are often leading and tilted toward a pro-spending response. Many of the issues are framed in a very positive way which invites a pro-spending response (Rasinski 1989). Jacoby (2000) documents the framing effect of presenting spending issues as individual specific items (favorable to a liberal response) versus as in general items (favorable to a conservative response). For example, respondents are told in the question lead-in that none of the problems that they are asked about can be solved "easily or inexpensively." Four of the problems are described as "improving" a public problem. Whether or not a policy actually leads to an improvement of a problem is usually a matter for debate, but it is assumed to be the case in the wording of these questions. Finally, the decision-rule distinguishing liberals from conservatives based on the simple difference of whether they favored increased spending versus decreased spending in more of the ten policy areas is arbitrary and not necessarily politically neutral.

49. Jacoby (1991).

50. Poole and Rosenthal (2007) document the extent of Republican conservatism in Congress, while Mann and Ornstein (2012) document that it has often been uncompromising and stubborn in character.

51. Clinton, Jackman, and Rivers (2004).

52. This comports with William Jacoby's findings that there is "a largely consensual belief that modern government is responsible for supporting certain kinds of collective goods, ..." and that "non-welfare spending attitudes are largely insulated from traditional sources of public opinion such as partisanship and ideology ..." (Jacoby 2005, 169). Ellis and Stimson (2012, 27) also report a virtual consensus, in principles, for current or increased spending for some purposes. By including several near-consensus spending items in their index, it may be that the operational ideology measure may be better suited to distinguish ultra-conservatives from mainstream conservatives (and everyone else) rather than mainstream conservatives from mainstream liberals.

53. For discussions of party identifications being independent of their use see Campbell et al. (1986) and Green, Palmquist, and Schickler (2002). The same rationale is applicable to ideological identifications.

54. Ellis and Stimson (2012).

55. Ibid., 57.

56. Further, like ideological identifications, party identifications are derived from different sources, held for different reasons, and applied differently by those with different levels of political knowledge and education. These various causes and conditions of effects are just part of the complexity of the party identification origins and effects. For ideology, however, these complexities for some raise warnings about the measurement not being sufficiently nuanced (Ellis and Stimson 2012, 189–90).

57. Even if one were to accept the "conflicted conservative" findings using the flawed "operational ideology" measure, it would not explain the significant *increase* in declared ideologicals (conservatives plus liberals) since the 1970s. Presumably, the supposed bias detected in the self-reported ideology measure is a constant, rather than one that has itself increased in recent decades.

CHAPTER 4. ISSUES AND POLARIZATION

1. Lubell (1956).

2. DiMaggio et al. (1996); Evans (2003).

3. The DiMaggio team examined what they termed four principles of polarization: the dispersion principle, the bimodality principle, the constraint principle, and the consolidation principle. The second of these, the bimodality principle, might be considered to be an extreme level of dispersion. As already noted, there can be substantial polarization without bimodality of the opinion distribution. The consolidation principle involves the association of polarized opinions with individual characteristics. This concerns second-order rather than first-order polarization. Setting aside the DiMaggio team's second and fourth polarization principles leaves us with the dispersion of views on single issues and the association of views across issues.

4. DiMaggio et al. (1996, 708 and 738).

5. Ibid., 715.

6. See Abramowitz (2010, 38–40). Though mostly about the partisan polarization of ideological views (second-order polarization), Abramowitz (2010) and Abramowitz and Saunders (2008) found that American voters and particularly more politically engaged Americans had become more consistent in holding conservative or liberal views across a number of different issues (2010, 38–40). This finding was based on an examination of a seven-item policy scale from 1984 to 2004. The scale was composed of a count of liberal

(–1) or conservative (+1) responses to six issues plus the self-reported ideology measure (collapsed to –1, 0, +1, for a liberal, moderate, and conservative response). The reported standard deviations in table 3.1 and the displayed aggregate distributions of the index for 1984 and 2004 in figure 3.1 differ from the DiMaggio team's analysis. At least with respect to ANES data, the DiMaggio team was examining the dispersion of individual opinions and, therefore, tapping into the degree of deviation from the center. In Abramowitz's index an individual would be counted as an extreme conservative or an extreme liberal if he or she gave the barely right or left of center response consistently on each of the seven items used in the index. Seven responses of 1 are not distinguished from seven responses of 3, with 4 being the centrist response on an individual item. Abramowitz's measure taps consistency, not extremism. An increased association between partisanship, ideology, and issue positions had been observed beginning in the mid-1960s (Pomper 1971, 1972).

7. Fiorina (2006, 8).

8. Fiorina and Abrams (2008, 569).

9. Hetherington (2009, 431).

10. Key (1966).

11. Fiorina and Abrams (2008, 567).

12. As noted in chapter 2, Hetherington (2009, 433) attempted to establish a benchmark, but it was problematic and addressed only second-order polarization. Fiorina and Abrams (2008, 567) acknowledge the difference between the change and level questions, but note only that determining the level of polarization is the more difficult task.

13. The portion of the public thinking that an issue is important and the level of concern to qualify as being "important" are matters of degree. However, reasonable observers might agree on an issue or set of issues being of primary or tertiary interest to a substantial portion of the public as opposed to a relatively narrow issue public.

14. Fiorina et al. (2008, 556).

15. Key (1955); Sundquist (1983); Campbell (2006).

16. Rae and Taylor (1970); Sundquist (1983).

17. DiMaggio et al. (1996, 696–98); Fiorina and Abrams (2008, 577); Abramowitz (2010, 35).

18. Many of these policies are so complex that it is not practically possible to present even a brief summary of their various tradeoffs, side effects, and plausible repercussions in a survey question. The Affordable Health Care Act, popularly known as Obamacare, was well over 900 pages long. You can get the gist of it in shorter form, but not survey question-length shorter.

19. Abramowitz and Saunders (2008); Abramowitz (2010); Fiorina et al. (2008); Fiorina and Abrams (2008).

20. The government jobs issue was included in all nine of the ANES studies from 1972 to 2008. The government healthcare issue was included in each of the surveys except 1980. The apparent bivariate relationship of these issue preferences on the vote was statistically significant in each election (p<.01, one tailed).

21. Schattschneider (1960); Rae and Taylor (1970); Abramowitz (2006, 112); Fiorina and Abrams (2008, 577).

22. Along the same lines, positions on both issues were likely to be consistent with opinions about government spending versus services issue (recall table 3.1). The government spending versus services question was only asked since the early 1980s. Correlations with the other two issues were moderately strong (r's of .3 to over .4). Also, though measurement changes caution against strict comparisons, among domestic issues in 1958, Converse (1964) found average correlations of .23.

23. Though complicated by changes in question wordings, earlier studies had also noted an increase in the correlation among issue positions (Nie et al. 1976; Nie and Anderson 1974).

24. It cannot be taken for granted that a positive correlation among issue positions is indicative of high levels of polarization. The issue measures may, for instance, be duplicate measures of the same underlying issue. It is also possible that very moderate positions are highly correlated. As Achen (1977) observed long ago, this is a hazard of a standardized correlation statistic.

25. Ibid.

26. A number of additional issue preference data complications are not discussed here. One of these is the assumption that seven-point issue scales are equal-interval (Mouw and Sobel 2001).

27. See Stimson (1999).

28. In somewhat more technical terms, polarization is context dependent, but the issue data are treated as context independent—a response of X means the same thing regardless of the context or time in which it was expressed.

29. Ellis and Stimson acknowledge that responses to spending questions depend "in part on what government is doing" (2012, 46), but they conclude that these changes are only reversible short-term effects and that the public is "still operationally liberal, on average" (ibid.).

30. For the unconvinced reader a more extreme example might be convincing. Suppose you were asked whether Mr. X should be incarcerated for life or even executed. Most might properly regard a positive response as being quite extreme and vicious. Now suppose Mr. X goes out and commits the most heinous crime you could imagine. A positive response to the question might not now appear so unreasonable. Context is crucial and neglecting to consider it can lead to grossly misleading conclusions.

31. This problem for polarization measurement is addressed in some cases by the dispersion measure when the change on the issue is reflected in a changed mean preference on the issue scale. In some cases, however, the issue scale itself does not reflect how the issue has evolved. An opinion as an indicator of an ideological perspective may be appropriate in one context and time and not in another. The measurement of operational ideology is a case in point. Support for increased domestic spending is considered an indication of a liberal perspective at all times, regardless of what the current administration had done, the growth in the economy, the severity of the problem addressed, news about how previous funds had been spent, likely sources for the funding, or any other context that might be considered relevant.

32. In both 1976 and 1980 there were nine seven-point issue scales. In 2012 there were six.

33. Though unjustified, it is often assumed that attitudes on the small set of issue scales used in ANES studies represent the voters' preferences on all important issues. Some have gone even further to assume that attitudes on these few issues accurately reflect the entire political climate of an election year (Mebane 2000; Mebane and Sekhon 2002).

34. Fiorina (2009, 29).

35. Another problem with issue preference data is that the politically neutral response is often naively asserted to be the middle point of the seven-point scale. Unlike the ideological designation of "moderate," the political meaning of the middle point of the scale depends on the extremeness of the polar alternatives. If these are not properly balanced, then the moderate response may not be the middle response.

36. Bishop, Oldendick, and Tuchfarber (1978); Bishop, Tuchfarber, and Oldendick (1978); Jacoby (2000); Achen (1975); Sullivan, Pierson, and Marcus (1978); Shuman and Presser (1996).

37. Converse (1964, 1970); Achen (1975); Converse and Marcus (1979); Krosnick (1991); Pierce and Rose (1974); Erikson (1979).

38. Erikson (1979, 113).

39. Ansolabehere, Rodden, and Snyder (2014).

40. Zaller (1992).

41. Erikson (1979, 108).

42. Complicating this even further is Erikson's (1979) observation that the reliability of issue scales should increase somewhat with greater real polarization of views. Greater true variation in issue positions would somewhat offset what is assumed to be a constant amount of measurement error. This would dampen both the push to the middle and the attenuation of issue correlations, though we do not know by how much.

43. The reliability of issue data should increase with greater real polarization, thereby reducing the bias against observing polarization change, and the extent of bias should be a good deal smaller at middling levels of polarization, as some true moderates are wrongly counted as being more extreme are offset by some extremists being wrongly counted as more moderate.

44. Abramowitz (2006b, 114).

45. Jacoby (1991) and Campbell et al. (1960); Converse (1964).

46. Abramowitz and Saunders (1998); Bafumi and Shapiro (2009, 11).

47. A more rigorous analysis confirms the results displayed in table 4.5. Ideological views were significantly associated with positions on the government guaranteed jobs issue in each of the 17 ANES studies from 1972 to 2008 and on the government's role in funding healthcare in each of the 11 ANES studies over that period. Regression analyses of these data indicate that every 1 point movement on the seven-point ideology scale was typically associated with nearly a half of a point movement in positions on both the government jobs and the government healthcare involvement issue scales.

CHAPTER 5. CIRCUMSTANTIAL EVIDENCE

1. Ellis and Stimson (2012).

2. Law Dictionary (2014).

3. Layman, Carsey, and Horowitz (2006, 89).

4. Keith et al. (1992); Smith et al. (1995); Petrocik (2009); Bartels (2000); Campbell (2000).

5. For research documenting the strength of partisanship in the 1950s to mid-1960s, see Campbell et al. (1960) and Converse (1976). The decline of partisanship in the late 1960s and early 1970s is documented in Burnham (1970), Wattenberg (1981, 1994), Keith et al. (1992), Norpoth and Rusk (1982), Bartels (2000), and Campbell (2000). The resurgence of partisanship in the mid-1980s is documented in Norpoth (1987), Bartels (2000), Miller (1991), Campbell (2000, 2006) and Lewis-Beck et al. (2008).

6. Poole and Rosenthal (2007, 2014).

7. Poole and Rosenthal (2014).

8. McDonald and Popkin (2001); McDonald (2015).

9. McDonald (2015). The increase in turnout in recent presidential elections is not evident in recent midterm congressional elections. Turnout in the 2014 midterm elections was actually the lowest of post–World War II midterms. However, aside from 2014, there is no evidence of a downward trend in midterm turnout. The lack of turnout change in midterms is neutral evidence between the two party polarization hypotheses.

10. Trends in split-result districts (plurality votes for one party's presidential candidate and for the other party's House candidate) are consistent with the survey-based measure of ticket-splitting. About 28% of congressional districts had split results in presidential elections from 1952 to 1968. This rose to 37% in the 1972 to 1988 period and then declined to 18% in elections from 1992 to 2012. See Ornstein et al. (2013).

11. This is essentially an Analysis of Variance (ANOVA) situation. The variation in views in the public can be apportioned into the variation within the parties (more

heterogeneous and similar parties) or variation between the parties (more homogenous and distinct parties). In no case can the variation of views in the public be less than the sum of the between-party and within-party variation. This means the variation of views in the public must be greater than or equal to the variation of views between the parties. If the variation of views between the parties is sufficient to warrant a conclusion that they are highly polarized, the equal or greater polarization of views in the broader public should be regarded so as well.

12. While there appears to be a consensus about this, I suspect the question wording used by ANES undercounts true independents. This suspicion is based on the fact that independents are asked whether they are closer to one of the parties and are not explicitly offered the option of saying they are not closer to either one of the parties. Being what has been designated a "pure independent" must be volunteered. There is probably some number of respondents who accept one of the offered "leaning independent" alternatives rather than asserting their non-partisan neutrality. This possibility, however, is first only a possibility and second, even if true, is unlikely to be much of a threat to the argument since some percentage of pure independents declare a non-moderate ideological orientation. Although a large majority of the small number of pure independents routinely report not knowing their ideology in ANES surveys, of those who report an ideology, about as many say they are liberals or conservatives as say they are moderates. Finally, setting aside the consensus about counting "independent" leaners as partisans, the conclusions would not change much if leaners were (erroneously) counted as independents. Gallup data in 2011 indicate 55% of independents, broadly defined to include leaners, identified themselves as liberals or conservatives (Saad 2011).

13. The one possible loophole in this argument (assuming the parties in the electorate are accurately characterized as highly polarized) is the fact that the public is not 100% partisan. There is a small percentage of independents. If independents were numerous enough and moderate enough, the public could not be highly polarized despite a high level of polarization between the parties. Imagine a public in which better than half were moderate independents and less than half were divided between largely ideological parties that might also contain a smattering of moderates: party polarization with public polarization. The question is whether there are enough independents who are also centrist enough to make a difference. It appears not. First, the proportion of the electorate who are independents (not including "leaners") is typically only about 11% or 12% (less among reported voters). This represents about one column in any of the figure 5.1 panels. Second, independents are not wholly moderates. About a quarter to a third express a liberal or a conservative ideological orientation (compared to just over half of Democratic or Republican identifiers). This probably understates the number of independents with ideological views since a large percentage of pure independents do not or cannot identify their ideological perspective. Some percentage of these undoubtedly have an unarticulated non-centrist perspective but are counted among the non-ideological. In short, the public's non-centrist composition is not appreciably changed because of independents.

14. The arithmetic argument addresses the question of whether the public is now highly polarized, the level question. It does not address the question of whether there has been an increase in the polarization of the public, the change question.

15. Poole and Rosenthal (2014).

16. This distinction is similar to that between evaluations of Congress and of one's own representative, or between evaluations of political parties in general and an identification with a particular party. Americans dislike conflict and favor compromise in principle, but also want the outcome to go their way. Frequent calls for bipartisanship in Congress, usually by a side that wants the other side to cooperate with it, is another example of the "have your cake and eat it, too" or Americans' ambivalent perspective on politics (Ranney 1975).

17. A third premise can be added. This would be a conversion rule based on prior research about how people respond to the proximity of the policy positions of the parties and candidates: people prefer more proximate to more distant parties and candidates. Prior research and the rationale for linking the two main premises to the suspected effects are discussed for each of the three suspected effects (turnout, partisanship, and ticket-splitting).

18. There is a great deal of research attempting to explain changes in turnout, partisanship, and ticket-splitting. Most of this is from attempts to explain the earlier changes—declines in turnout and partisanship and a rise in ticket-splitting. While some of these factors are quite plausible, some are applicable to the earlier changes, but not the more recent (e.g., the drop in the minimum voting age to 18 years old before the 1972 election). Moreover, the polarization explanation offered here has Occam's Razor on its side. It offers a single simple explanation for all three changes both in the 2000s and in the 1970s (e.g., the partisan dealignment of the 1970s and the partisan restoration of the 1990s).

19. Zipp (1985, 58).

20. Adams, Dow, and Merrill (2006, 74); Leighley and Nagler (2013).

21. Fiorina with Abrams (2009).

22. Fiorina (1981).

23. Fiorina (1996); Erikson (1988).

24. The two tested premises concerning the public's polarization are static—that the public was and is moderate or that the public was and is highly polarized. The direct evidence, however, indicates that the public has become more polarized over the years. To the extent that the change in public polarization matched or was in sync with the change in the polarization of the parties in government we would have expected no change in the public reactions (turnout, partisanship, ticket-splitting). If public polarization, however, exceeded party polarization in government and then the parties caught up with the public's polarization, the expectations would be the same as those assuming a consistently highly polarized public. In this respect, the direct findings and those of this circumstantial evidence are in accord.

25. I reported the results of these three tests previously in Campbell (2006a).

26. Additional circumstantial evidence of polarization may be drawn from the evidence of directional issue voting (without a 'zone of acceptability' appended to the theory) (Rabinowitz and Macdonald 1989). According to directional issue voting theory as opposed to conventional proximity issue voting, those who appear even slightly left or right of center often prefer candidates or parties that are more extreme on the voter's side of the scale—more definitely and extremely in the voter's preferred direction. Though there are the many problems of issue scales (noted in chapter 4) and problems associated with comparing them and testing the two theories (Lewis and King 1999), to the extent that voters are voting in a directional way suggests that their preferences may be effectively more extreme than their stated issue positions would indicate. If a voter initially indicates that he or she is just slightly liberal, but then consistently prefers extremely liberal candidates over slightly liberal candidates, it seems reasonable to conclude that they might be underestimating the extent of their own liberalism. That said, as noted in chapter 3, great caution should be used in overriding a person's self-identification.

27. V.O. Key (1961, 56).

28. Ellis and Stimson's analysis of ideological self-identification (not including moderates) provides additional evidence of public opinion change. They observe a substantial decline in liberal identifications in the mid-1960s (2012, 70 and 87). Since their measure is of liberal identifications as a percentage of liberals plus conservatives, this suggests that the increased polarization of the public was produced by growth in the ranks of conservatives (p. 71).

29. Renowned campaign chronicler Theodore White sensed the contrast between the continuity of political leaders and the disruption experienced by everyday Americans. In the Foreword to *The Making of the President 1968*, White wrote how leadership seemed remarkably "stuck," but "If one studied the people, all was different. What was different was the entire nature of American life" (White 1969).

30. Campbell et al. (1960); Converse (1964).

31. Nie et al. (1976).

32. Lewis-Beck et al. (2008).

33. Carmines and Stimson (1989); Fiorina (2006, 59); Levendusky (2009).

34. Abramowitz and Saunders (2008).

35. Allen (2013).

CHAPTER 6. WHY ARE THE PARTIES MORE POLARIZED?

1. Dylan (1964).

2. Poole and Rosenthal (2014). An earlier and methodologically quite different analysis of roll-call votes by Richard Fleisher and Jon Bond (2000b, 166) found that the percentage of House members and senators who were ideologically closer to the opposite party (cross-pressured) had declined by the mid-1990s to only 15 members in the House and two in the Senate. This was a great decline from the post–1953 high water marks of 148 in the House (1955–56) and 33 in the Senate (1961–62). The number of cross-pressured representatives commonly exceeded 70 in the House and 25 in the Senate prior to the 1980s. Also see Binder (1996; 2003, 23–25).

3. Some criticize roll-call measures of party polarization as exaggerating polarization since many issues that might elicit bipartisan support are not brought to a vote since party leaders do not want to divide their caucuses. While the avoidance of issues internally divisive to a party is an explanation for why *party* polarization may be high, it is not a measurement problem. The issue agenda is never complete in real-world politics. Control of the agenda is part of politics whether at the mass or elite levels.

4. Committee on Political Parties (1950).

5. I offered early outlines of the staggered realignment in *Cheap Seats* (Campbell 1996, 162–68), the second edition of *The Presidential Pulse of Congressional Elections* (Campbell 1997, 226–33), and later in *The American Campaign* (Campbell 2000, 215–17).

6. Mann (2006); Theriault (2008); McCarty et al. (2009); Abramowitz (2010). If gerrymandering were a major force behind party polarization, we might also expect polarization to be more severe in states that were more severely gerrymandered and in states shortly after being gerrymandered (since redistricting effects should dissipate with later population shifts). These patterns are not evident.

7. Bartels (2008); Campbell (2012a).

8. McCarty et al. (2006).

9. Dettrey and Campbell (2013, 1078).

10. Ibid., 1069.

11. Lippmann (1922, 118–21).

12. Aldrich (2011); Owens (2013); Theriault (2008, 109–28).

13. Fiorina and Abrams (2006, 2009).

14. Wilson (1962); Constantini (1963); Wright (1971).

15. The establishment-moderate nominee and activist-ideological losers (only the major contenders) in the Democratic Party were: Carter over Kennedy (1980), Mondale over Hart (1984), Dukakis over Jackson (1988), Clinton over Brown and Tsongas (1992), Gore over Bradley (2000), and Kerry over Dean and Edwards (2004). In the Republican Party, the establishment-moderate winners were: Ford over Reagan (1976), Bush over Kemp and Robertson (1988), Dole over Buchanan and Forbes (1996), G. W. Bush over

McCain (2000), McCain over Huckabee and Paul (2008), and Romney over Santorum and Gingrich (2012). The three cases of activist-insurgent nomination winners were: McGovern over Muskie and Humphrey (1972), Reagan over Bush, Baker, and Dole (1980), and Obama over Hillary Clinton (2008). The one unclear case was Carter versus Udall, Church, and Brown in 1976. Carter was more moderate, but definitely not the establishment's candidate. It might also be noted that ideological activists are not the only reason that a party may veer too far toward an ideological extreme. The nomination of very conservative Republican Barry Goldwater who lost in a landslide to Lyndon Johnson in 1964 was made in the pre-reform period before activists exerted as much influence on the party's nomination.

16. Epstein, Epstein, and Koch (1942, 157).

17. Levendusky (2013a) emphasizes the media's contribution to party polarization.

18. Stroud (2008); Arceneaux and Johnson (2013).

19. Levendusky (2013b).

20. Jacobson (2008, 2011); Abramowitz (2010, 27); Edwards (2007, 26); Fiorina (2008, 93).

21. Jacobson (2008, 62).

22. Jones (2013).

23. The party approval gap over President G.H.W. Bush undoubtedly was narrowed by the post–Gulf War rally effect. A post–9/11 rally effect undoubtedly also narrowed the party approval gap for President G. W. Bush, but probably would not account for the full difference between his mean polarization gap (61%) and that of President Obama (70% as of January 2016).

24. See Obenshain (2012).

25. Another possibility is that presidents and their administrations may have governed in polarizing ways anticipating that ideologically pleasing policy decisions would be well received by their increasingly ideological base. These anticipated reactions are consistent with a bottom-up development of party polarization.

26. An extensive literature explaining this staggered ideological realignment has developed over a good deal of time. This includes Abramowitz and Saunders (1998); Stonecash et al. (2003); Taylor (1996); Campbell (1997, 2000, 2006b); Paulson (2006).

27. Key (1955, 1959); Sundquist (1983); Rosenof (2003).

28. Converse (1966); Campbell (2006).

29. Carmines and Stimson (1980); Poole and Rosenthal (2014).

30. Bain and Parris (1973). The 1912 convention also took 46 ballots to nominate Woodrow Wilson. The two-thirds rule, requiring the votes of two-thirds of convention delegates to secure a nomination, may have extended balloting in these conventions, though no candidate received a simple majority until the 10th ballot in 1912, the 43rd ballot in 1920, and the 103rd ballot in 1924, according to Bain and Parris (1972). One might also interpret the very existence of the two-thirds rule as evidence of the fragile nature of the Democrats' coalition, that minority elements of the coalition so distrusted other parts of the party that they required what amounted to a veto over nominations.

31. A rich and extensive literature developed that charted the rise and fall of different groups within the parties' coalitions. Axelrod (1972, 1986) identified and tracked six overlapping groups of voters that made up most of the Democratic coalition—the poor, African Americans, southerners, union members, Catholics, and residents of large cities. Among other notable studies of the dynamics of the parties' coalitions are Petrocik (1981); Erikson, Lancaster, and Romero (1989); Mayer (1996); Lawrence (1997); and Stanley and Niemi (2006).

32. The elimination of the two-thirds rule at the Democratic National Convention in 1936 was an earlier skirmish in the party's internal battles. The elimination of the rule effectively stripped southern conservatives of a good deal of their influence over nominations (CQ Press 2005).

33. Rusk (2001).

34. Rossiter (1960, 171).

35. Carmines and Stimson (1980).

36. National Bureau of Economic Research (2015).

37. Bureau of Economic Analysis (2015).

38. Carmines and Stimson (1980).

39. Gallup (2015).

40. American National Election Studies (2015). It is interesting to note that this initial 12-percentage-point surge in African American turnout predated the enactment of the Voting Rights Act of 1965.

41. Murphy and Gulliver (1971); Aistrup (1996).

42. Some suspected that an inclination of many southern whites to vote Republican at the presidential level and for Democrats for other offices reflected a "dual partisanship" (Hadley 1985).

43. Aistrup (1996).

44. Rusk (2001, 386).

45. Ibid., 260.

46. Campbell (1997, 202–3).

47. The percentages of Republican state legislators in southern states were calculated by the author from data gathered in volumes of *The Book of The States* (Council of State Governments, 2015).

48. Burnham (1970); Ladd (1978); Wattenberg (1994); Silbey (1990); Crotty and Jacobson (1980).

49. Broder (1971).

50. Wattenberg (1994, 156).

51. Keith et al. (1992); Smith et al. (1995); Petrocik (2009).

52. Campbell (2010a).

53. Green et al. (2002).

54. Black and Black (2002).

55. Erikson (1971); Mayhew (1974); Campbell (2003).

56. Craig (1988).

57. Ibid.

58. Carmines, McIver, and Stimson (1987, 376).

59. Norpoth (1987); Campbell (2010a).

60. Some speculated that the Republicans had achieved "a lock" on presidential elections, that they were now the majority party or were dominant in electoral votes. The Democrats' lead in party identification and subsequent election results proved otherwise.

61. Ladd (1985b, 23); Nelson (1989, 195); Wilson (1985).

62. Rosenof (2003); Ladd (1991); Mayhew (2002); Wattenberg (1987).

63. Campbell (2006b).

64. This corresponds closely to a multiple regression analysis of the three realignments (1896, 1932, and 1968–94) since the Civil War (Campbell 2006b). The original estimate of the presidential vote shift through 2004 was 5.7 percentage points. Including the 2008 and 2012 elections reduces the shift to 4.8 percentage points, approximately the difference in the medians in table 6.1. The pre-realignment median vote of 53.8% corresponds precisely with Converse's estimate of the normal vote (1966; Asher 1988, 48; Miller 1979).

65. The pre-realignment series begins in 1952 rather than 1932 because party identification data are not available prior to the 1952 election. This drop in the median of macropartisanhip is about two percentage points smaller than that estimated in a regression analysis of turnout and vote choice corrected ANES data. That analysis of macropartisanhip from 1952 to 2008 found a decline of about seven percentage points for the Democrats in 1984 among reported voters (Campbell 2010a, 630).

66. Bullock (1988); Bullock, Hoffman, and Gaddie (2006).

67. Reiter and Stonecash (2011).

68. Abramowitz and Saunders (1998).

69. Carmines and Stimson (1989); Fiorina (2006, 59); Fiorina and Abrams (2008, 581); Hetherington (2009, 441).

70. Levendusky (2009, 35).

71. Mayhew (1974); Jacobson (2001, 21–40).

72. Poole and Rosenthal (2007).

CHAPTER 7. ONE-SIDED PARTY POLARIZATION?

1. This quotation is from an exit interview in 2012 of four retiring House members and Senators (Tyrangiel 2012, 74).

2. Poole and Rosenthal (2014).

3. Mann and Ornstein (2012).

4. Mann (2014).

5. Mann and Ornstein are not alone in their belief that Republicans have moved much more to the right than Democrats have moved to the left. See Kabaservice (2012), Owens (2013), and Perlstein (2012), among others.

6. Mann and Ornstein (2012, 51–52).

7. Ibid., 52.

8. Poole and Rosenthal (2014).

9. Ibid.

10. La Raja and Schaffner (2015).

11. One option is that the Republican Party has become radicalized on the right, but the public failed to see it or had other reasons to overlook it. Given the intensity of campaigns and media scrutiny, this seems implausible. Moreover, even if accepted, this might explain why Republicans did not lose more ground to the Democrats, but does not explain why they actually improved their electoral standing.

12. As we will later determine, party polarization in the earlier period may have been asymmetrical, with Democrats overall being closer to the median voter than Republicans.

13. An even bigger problem may be in comparisons of the parties in terms of their differences from the political center (in figure 7.1). In a two-party center-right nation, the parties can only be competitive with each other if the more conservative party is further to the right than the more liberal party is to the left. If the Republican Party and the Democratic Party were equally removed from the center, the Republicans would dominate the Democrats because of the larger number of conservatives that they would draw on and their equal appeal to centrists.

14. Roper Center (2013).

15. I have elaborated elsewhere on this election-governing constituency connection in relation to the governing politics and the ideological inclinations of both the George W. Bush and the Barack Obama presidencies (Campbell 2008a, 2012b).

16. Taylor (1996, 279); Groseclose, Levitt, and Snyder (1999, 41).

17. The mean DW-NOMINATE scores for each party show the same staggered polarization. Democrats began their move to the left, before Republicans moved even further to the right (Poole and Rosenthal 2014). House Republicans had hardly changed at all ideologically from the early 1960s to the late 1970s; if anything they were a bit more moderate than they had been. House Democrats, on the other hand, had become somewhat more liberal through the 1960s and 1970s.

18. Taylor (1996).

19. These are unadjusted ADA scores. Groseclose et al. (1999) offer an adjustment to ADA scores that they indicate facilitates comparisons across time. Though we will

discuss reasons why these adjustments should *not* be made, like the unadjusted data, the adjusted ADA scores also indicate that House Democrats moved more to the left than Republicans moved to the right. According to the adjusted ADA scores, the Democrats' average support for liberal positions increased by 25 percentage points (50% to 75%) from the early 1960s to the 2000s. Liberal voting by House Republicans, in contrast, dropped on average by only seven percentage points (14% to 7%).

20. Senate ADA ratings for Democrats rose from 55% in the 1960s to 89% in the 2000s, a 34-point shift. ADA ratings for Senate Republicans dropped only from 24% in the 1960s to 16% in the 2000s, an 8-point drop.

21. Using the Groseclose et al. (1999) time and chamber adjusted ACU scores indicates that Republicans moved slightly further right (20 points, from 64% to 84% conservative) than Democrats moved left (13 points, from 31% to 18%). This may be a consequence of ACU beginning its ratings in the 1970s rather than the 1960s. As will be discussed shortly, though the adjustments are made in these data for the sake of comparability across years, there may also be reason not to make these adjustments.

22. The smaller difference in ACU numbers compared to ADA numbers may be the result of the later start of the ACU series. The ACU data for the Senate in these same years indicates a smaller difference but still a greater change for Democrats. Support for conservative positions among Senate Democrats dropped from 26% to 6%. Support for conservative positions among Senate Republicans increased from 62% to 77%.

23. The instability of the ADA and ACU ratings related to the small number of roll-call votes that change from year to year has been interpreted by some as evidence of the "invalidity of the nominal scores" (Groseclose et al. 1999, 38).

24. Based on Evans's (2001) research on partisan agenda-setting in Congress, Krehbiel (2008, 97) argues that roll-call measures of party polarization exaggerate its extent because party leaders set agendas that emphasize party differences and avoid intraparty divisions that would presumably be more moderate. He also argues that consensus votes have little or no effect on these scales and that also exaggerates the degree of party polarization. In defense of these scales, it can be observed that partisan agenda control is a fact of political life (and some extreme issues are also excluded from the mix). Agenda control is also better considered as an explanation of the degree of partisan polarization, rather than presenting a measurement problem. We are trying to gauge actual polarization, not what it might be like in a different political world. With respect to consensus issues, many of these votes are on trivial matters and would be excluded on those grounds if roll-call scales focused on the most important issues (Campbell 2006a). Recall our earlier discussions in chapter 1 about our tiny genetic differences from bonobos.

25. Brunell et al. (1999); Burden, Caldeira, and Groseclose (2000).

26. DW-NOMINATE scores are oriented so that higher values indicate greater conservative voting. It is expected to have a positive correlation with the ACU ratings and a negative correlation with the ADA ratings. The combination of the ADA and ACU ratings averaged the two after converting the ADA index to a conservatism scale by subtracting the ADA score from 100. The correlations are especially impressive given the lumpiness of the ACU and ADA ratings related to the small set of votes and to the ADA's practice of counting absences as a vote against the liberal position.

27. Hare, McCarty, Poole, and Rothenthal (2012).

28. The adjusted ADA and ACU scores also attempt to standardize scores to a common metric and meaning across years (Groseclose et al. 1999).

29. See Hare et al. (2012); Groseclose et al. (1999). There is also a question of whether the DW-NOMINATE scores have accurately adjusted for shifts in the expression or meaning of liberal and conservative perspectives (Ensley, Tofias, and de Marchi 2014). The application of DW-NOMINATE scores to *presidential* ideological orientations also raises question about the adjustments. Two pairs of comparisons, on both the left and the right,

illustrate the concern. According to the DW-NOMINATE application to Democratic presidents Bill Clinton and Barack Obama, President Clinton was more liberal than President Obama. On the Republican side, President George W. Bush is measured as having been more conservative than President Ronald Reagan. Both comparisons would seem to be at odds with common historical and contemporary evaluations of these presidents. This, of course, does not mean that the ratings are incorrect, only that there may be problems. More specifically, they may have overcorrected for the movement to the right. This might explain why Obama is seen as more moderate than Clinton and why Bush is seen as more conservative than Reagan.

30. From another perspective, the question of whether ideologies should be defined in context-sensitive or context-independent ways may be the wrong question. The important question is not which perspective is right, but *who* should be answering this question? Should the determination of who is a liberal or a conservative (whether voters or representatives) be imposed by analysts after the fact or by those actually involved in the politics of their time?

31. Or, at least, it requires a convincing explanation of exactly how an out-of-step party moving further away from the political center than its opposition not only fails to lose political ground to the opposing party but actually improves its political standing to the point of parity with its opposition.

32. Edwards (2012).

33. Smith (2015).

34. Pew Research Center (2015, 10). Pew asked respondents, "On issues that matter to you in politics today, has your side been winning or losing more often?" Liberal Democrats were about equally divided, with 46% seeing themselves more often on the winning side and 44% more often on the losing side. In sharp contrast, 81% of conservative Republicans saw themselves more often on the losing side and only 12% more often on the winning side.

CHAPTER 8. WHY ARE THE PARTIES POLARIZED AT ALL?

1. Scammon and Wattenberg (1970).

2. Strictly speaking, it is the party's candidates who are competing. For economy of exposition, a party and its candidates are combined here as the party.

3. Hotelling (1929); Smithies (1941); Downs (1957).

4. Downs (1957, 117).

5. Aldrich (2011, 176).

6. Scammon and Wattenberg (1970).

7. Ibid., 80.

8. Lippmann (1950).

9. Cohen (2012). For readers unfamiliar with the Etch A Sketch, it is a toy in which pictures can be drawn on a screen and then easily erased by shaking the device from side to side so that a new picture can be drawn on the screen.

10. Wood (2009); Druckman and Jacobs (2015).

11. Page (1978).

12. Ansolabehere et al. (2001).

13. Edwards (2007); Gutman and Thomson (2012).

14. The studies highlighted here are just two of the many studies that find that the parties fail to converge on the median position of the public. Among the many others supporting this conclusion are a study of party platforms (Monroe 1983) and my study of swing voters (Campbell 2008c).

15. Pomper (1972); Abramowitz and Saunders (1998).

16. The existential argument also may be made in different terms. If the major parties converged, they would leave the door open for a third party to outflank and replace them as the party of the left (or the right) (Palfrey 1989; Aldrich 2011). It seems unlikely, however, that the possible threats of hypothetical, potentially interloping third parties would make any significant difference in how the major parties positioned themselves against each other. Third parties in American politics face virtually insurmountable obstacles. These include difficulties obtaining ballot access, perceptions of nonviability, inadequate financing, inattention from the media, and the single-member district plurality rule electoral system. In short, even if the major parties were simple rational actors, rather than the unruly amalgams of different factions and participants that they are, there is normally little reason for them to pay much attention to what third parties, real or imagined, might do or say.

17. Mutz (2006); Huckfeldt, Johnson, and Sprague (2004).

18. Constantini (1963); Polsby (1983); Theriault (2008); Fiorina (1999, 16; 2009, 98); Fiorina and Levendusky (2006, 87); King (2003). Fiorina (1999, 16–18) offers an excellent review of the literature regarding activists as the impetus for the parties being pulled away from moderate positions.

19. The conventional wisdom drawn from early research (Wilson 1962; Constantini 1963) is that nomination participants are disproportionately ideological activists. Hershey, Birkhead, and Easter (2013), however, find that they are fairly representative of all those identifying with a party, and Hirano et al. (2010) find little evidence linking primaries to polarization in Congress.

20. Scammon and Wattenberg (1970, 318).

21. Fiorina (1974, 1999); Ardoin and Garand (2003).

22. Hadley (1976).

23. Key (1966); Fiorina (1981); Kiewiet and Rivers (1984); Miller and Wattenberg (1985).

24. The performance and values dimensions are empirically related. Liberals tend to see the performance of the more liberal party and officeholders in a more favorable light and are inclined to be more critical of the records of the more conservative party and its officeholders. Conservatives are similarly biased. However, these ideological and partisan predispositions do not entirely shield voters from the reality of the parties' records. See, for instance, Gary Jacobson's review of the partisan views of President George W. Bush's job performance (2011). It is also the case that performance affects ideologies. Like partisanship, a party that has had a successful record may attract more voters to its ideological perspective. Conversely, if a party is seen as being responsible for bad times or inept at turning things around, some voters may be repelled by its ideological perspective. In the 1980s, for instance, liberalism was in such bad repute that it was simply denoted as "the L-word" and liberals began referring to themselves instead as "progressives."

25. Something along these lines is routinely evident in partisan divisions on presidential approval ratings. As developments in a term run for or against a president, presidential approval numbers are most likely to resist negative changes among the president's partisans and most likely to resist positive changes among partisans of the opposition party (Jacobson 2011).

26. Wolfinger and Rosenstone (1980).

27. Grafstein (1995).

28. To withhold action because it may make only a tiny difference is to succumb to a "counsel of despair" (Collingwood 1956). Just because one's actions are not determinative or do not make a substantial difference does not mean that they are inconsequential.

29. Lewis-Beck et al. (2008, 90–92).

30. A third consideration influencing the strength of a potential voter's preference is the extent to which the potential voter disagrees with the disfavored party. A mildly disliked opposition party would not generate the same motivation that would be produced by a detested opposition party. Negative voting may be strongly motivating (Kernell 1977). However, any explanatory power of negative voting or a disliked second party is already taken into account by considering the distance to the preferred party and the difference between the two parties. Each of the three distances (in figure 8.2: V to C, C to L, and V to L) is a function of the other two.

31. Thinking of the spatial model in geographic terms, a distant first choice of a store might cause a potential customer to think, "if I were going to the store, the closer one is the one that I would go to, but it is so far away I don't think I want to bother making that long trip."

32. As Brody and Page (1973) found in examining the 1968 election, both candidate differences and how positively the preferred candidate is rated by the potential voter matter to the turnout decision. In the 2004 ANES, at the low end of the thermometer differences (less than 20 degrees difference), reported turnout was only 58%. At the high end (40 degree or greater differences), reported turnout was 86%.

33. Brody and Page (1973).

34. Smithies (1941).

35. Downs (1957, 117).

36. Converse (1966, 24) and Weisberg and Grofman (1981) concluded the effects were minimal. Brody and Page (1973) found them to be significant, but not large.

37. Zipp (1985, 55).

38. Adams et al. (2006, 79).

39. Leighley and Nagler (2013).

40. See Campbell (1987, 1997) on the theory of surge and decline on congressional election outcomes, and Campbell (2008b, 2008c) on the effects of presidential campaigns and swing voters on presidential election outcomes.

41. McClosky et al. (1960); Page (1978).

42. Axelrod (1972, 1986).

43. The reweighting process here involves first a cross-tabulation of the ideological-party identifications (liberal Democrat, non-liberal Democrat, independent, non-conservative Republican, or conservative Republican) by their reported presidential vote (voted for the Democrat, voted for the Republican, voted for a third-party candidate or non-voter). Weights are then determined based on the actual presidential vote distribution (e.g., actual Democratic vote % divided by the reported Democratic vote %). These weights are then applied to the cross-tabulation (e.g., reported Democratic vote of liberal Democrats multiplied by the associated weight for Democratic votes to obtain the actual Democratic vote of liberal Democrats). This is basically the process I used in my study of macropartisanship (Campbell 2010), though I do not attempt here to disentangle the misreported turnout issue (those who said that they voted, but did not).

44. There is some evidence, though slight, that the turnout of the ideological bases is also responsive to the ideological positions of the parties. Turnout in the ideological bases has increased a bit in recent years as the parties have become more polarized. Among liberal Democrats the median turnout in elections from 1972 to 1988 was 69.2%. This increased to 73.6% (+4.6 points) in the period from 2000 to 2012. Among non-liberal Democrats, even though there was greater room for growth, turnout increased by only 1.2 points (51.5% to 52.7%). Among conservative Republicans, turnout grew from by 2.3 points (76.0% to 78.3%). Turnout among non-conservative Republicans grew by 1.1 point (54.5% to 55.6%).

45. No statistical controls have been introduced for why those in the base may or may not see their parties as sharing their ideological views. What is important is that those

who feel that their party does not hold their ideological perspective, for whatever reason, are significantly less likely to vote. The withholding of votes by disillusioned non-centrists could potentially open the door to a less centrist third party (Palfrey 1989; Aldrich 2011), but whether these non-centrists cast their lot with a minor party or simply sit out the election is really beside the point. What is important to the party is that they are being deprived of votes from their base and there is good reason to be more responsive to these disgruntled non-centrists.

46. In both cases, calculations of the vote from the base are of a two-party popular vote majority and are based on exit poll data. Democrats received about 11% to 22% of the two-party vote from liberals. This is 22% to 44% of a bare majority. Republicans received about 22% to 29% of the vote from conservatives. This is 44% to 58% of a bare majority.

CHAPTER 9. POLARIZATION AND DEMOCRACY

1. Schattschneider (1960).

2. The causes of *party* polarization were addressed in chapters 6, 7, and 8. The short answer is that the parties are polarized and have grown more polarized because the public is polarized and had grown more polarized.

3. Hetherington and Weiler (2009) link ideological differences to authoritarianism. The measurement of authoritarianism is suspect, but the more basic problem is that the claim itself is perplexing. If authoritarianism is the basis for the left-right divide and conservatives are more authoritarian (more deferential to authority and respectful of order), then how does one explain why conservatives generally favor greater restraints on the powers of government authorities and how are insurgent conservatives like Barry Goldwater and Newt Gingrich possible? Even if measured well, authoritarianism seems an unlikely lynchpin for ideological perspectives.

4. Hibbing, Smith, and Alford (2014); Mondak and Hibbing (2012).

5. Some might contend that age and vocal development are the principal differences between crying infants and bickering adults.

6. Ideological perspectives may differ in the level of sophistication with which they are held as well as in their content (Campbell et al. 1960; Converse 1962; Lewis-Beck et al. 2008). Ideology here means the existence of a political orientation, not the sophistication with which that orientation is held or expressed. Someone may have a liberal or conservative orientation for any reason, from high-minded philosophical reasons to the crassest of gut-level self-interest reasons.

7. Jacoby (2014).

8. I say that there is roughly one dimension because the diversity within each general ideological label should not translate neatly on to a single orderly spectrum. Individual differences should create something of a cloud of ideological variants rather than a perfect lineup of views differing only by their degree of adherence to the most extreme view on the spectrum.

9. Allen (2013); Brewer and Stonecash (2015); Muirhead (2014, 256); Woodard (2016).

10. Clinton (1996).

11. Government action is not always so clearly intrusive. The case of the abortion issue is a classic example. Liberals favor government action is extending the right to "free choice," while conservatives see government action as protecting an individual's right to life. In all cases, we should remember that neither mainstream ideology, even in its extreme form, advocates either totalitarian unlimited government or the anarchy of no government. They are each within what Hartz (1955) referred to as the liberal tradition.

12. Evidence of the lack of trust in government among "pro-government" liberals is the long history of governmental reform movements that have come from the left, from civil service reforms in the late nineteenth century to campaign finance reforms and governmental ethics reforms in recent times.

13. Stimson (1999) in examining public opinion and Poole and Rosenthal (2007) in examining congressional roll-call voting have separately observed political decision-making to be made in a low dimensional space, roughly along the liberal-conservative ideological spectrum.

14. Duverger (1954).

15. Truman (1951); Dahl (1956, 1961); Polsby (1963). Pennock (1979) provides an excellent overview of pluralism. The pluralist perspective on mid-century American politics was not universally accepted. Among others, see Mills (1959) and Bachrach (1967). Ironically, the views that American politics was controlled by or heavily biased in favor of economic elites, like pluralism, differ from polarization in finding lower levels of expressed conflict in American politics.

16. Berelson (1952); Berelson, Lazarsfeld, and McPhee (1954).

17. Although Berelson's analysis is interesting, persuasive, and might be regarded as a precursor of David Easton's systems perspective of the political process (1957), it is also easy to see how some might see it as going easy on apathetic and slothful citizens in interpreting their deficiencies as assets for the political system.

18. Berelson et al. (1954, 318).

19. Rossiter (1960).

20. The change from pluralist and polarized government occurred over several decades and neither was cleanly at its extreme. Elements of polarization were present in the pluralist era and aspects of pluralism are present in the more polarized government of recent decades.

21. This is not to suggest that moderates do not care about their government or that some of them do not think of moderation as a principled direction. For some moderates, however, moderation is the absence of a preferred direction for the nation. It is essentially "muddling through" or splitting the difference between those who have preferences.

22. Huckfeldt et al. (2004); Mutz (2006); Arceneaux and Johnson (2013).

23. Motel (2013).

24. Tyrangiel (2012, 74).

25. Lippmann (1950, 4).

26. Campbell (2010b).

27. Fenno (1973).

28. Schattschneider (1960).

29. For the former, see Burns (1963). For the latter, see Bond and Fleisher (1990) and Fleisher and Bond (2000b, 2004).

30. See Lindblom (1968) and Wildavsky (1964). The one clear exception to incremental change was following realignments. See Brady (1991). This comports with large shifts in the gridlock space in models of congressional decision-making (Krehbiel 1998; Brady and Volden 2006).

31. Piven and Cloward (1988).

32. Bachrach (1967); Schattschneider (1960).

33. Schattschneider (1942); Committee on Political Parties (1950); Ranney (1962).

34. Binder (2003, 2014).

35. Ornstein and Mann (2013).

36. Summers (2013).

37. Stanley and Niemi (2013, 204); Ornstein et al. (2013, table 6-4).

38. Some number of these public laws do not deal with national public policy or do so in a very minor way. For example, the 383 laws enacted by the 111th Congress

(2009–10) included more than 80 laws naming different post offices, courthouses, and other federal buildings. A small number of other laws were appointments (e.g., to the Smithsonian board), awarding of honorific medals, ordering the minting of commemorative coins, and the designation of commemorative days (e.g., "Native American Heritage Day Act of 2009").

39. Mayhew (2005).

40. Binder (2014).

41. The enactment of major laws directed at valence issues may still involve a good deal of controversy as well as having a great deal of support. Examples of valence issue laws from Mayhew's list of 39 historic laws might include the enactment of the Housing Act of 1949, the creation of Medicare in 1965, the Elementary and Secondary Education Act of 1965, and Medicare Reform's prescription drug benefit in 2003. The four civil rights bills of 1957, 1964, 1965, and 1968 could also be added to this list.

42. Examples of historically important laws from Mayhew's list arising from crises might include the Marshall Plan in 1948, the Economic Recovery Tax Act of 1981, and the Persian Gulf Resolution of 1991. The enactment of four historically important laws was related to the terrorist attacks of 9/11. These were the Use of Force Resolution regarding terrorists in Afghanistan in 2001, the Patriot Act regarding intelligence gathering in 2001, the Iraq Resolution in 2002, and the creation of a new Homeland Security Department in 2002. Another four historically important laws related to the September 2008 meltdown of the financial institutions. These were the Housing Relief Program of 2008, the $700 Billion Bailout of the Financial Sector in 2008, the $787 billion stimulus of 2009, and the Financial Services Regulation Act of 2010.

43. Binder (2014).

44. Bachrach and Baratz (1963).

45. Elected party leaders and unelected party activists are and appear to be more polarized than their less politically obsessed counterparts in the public, but this reflects the routine McClosky Difference discussed in chapter 1.

46. Hibbing and Theiss-Morse (1995).

47. Issues can often be framed to either encourage or discourage division. For example, the problems of the poor can be seen as a problem of poverty or a problem of inequality. More Americans are likely to be rallied to reducing poverty than to redistributing incomes. Similarly, more Americans are likely to favor reducing pollution than fighting climate change. On healthcare issues, more could be enlisted to redouble efforts to cure cancer or heart disease than to cover more uninsured individuals with government mandated insurance plans.

48. See Connelly (2014).

49. Wilson (1962). Those with professional views about politics may also fail to work as hard as they might for compromise if they expect political gains can be made by holding on to the issue rather than reaching a deal. These prospective political gains, however, ultimately depend on the success of appeals to those having purist orientations toward compromise.

50. Mutz (2006).

51. Nivola and Galston (2008); Mann and Ornstein (2012).

52. Krehbiel (1998); Brady and Volden (2006).

53. An example of the escalation in conflict was the increase in what became widely known as "the politics of personal destruction" in a series of congressional set-tos that began with the opposition to the Supreme Court nomination of Robert Bork in 1987.

54. Allen (2013).

55. Mutz (2015).

56. Patterson (2013).

57. Hibbing and Theiss-Morse (1995); Ranney (1975).

58. Open, frank, and frequent discussions of political differences, even if conducted in a civil manner, require a good deal of effort. Most Americans need a positive reason to expend that effort. In short, Americans are unlikely to practice politics in a more civil and productive way until they learn how to enjoy politics more. See Mutz (2006, 2015).

59. Cantril (1965, 34–38).

60. Berelson et al. (1954).

AFTERWORD

1. Jones (2016), Pew Research Center (2017a).

2. Pew Research Center (2016).

3. Fox News Poll (2016).

4. The six new poll readings of self-reported ideology measure conservatives at 33% to 37% of the public, moderates plus "don't knows" at 39% to 43%, and liberals at 24% to 28%. The ANES measure uses only face-to-face interviews for comparability to earlier studies and uses the mean of the aggregate pre-election and post-election responses. The CBS/NYT measure takes the median of six surveys asking the self-reported ideology question. For comparison to Figure 3.4, the more precise distribution of ideological orientations in 2016 were 42.1% moderates, 35.6% conservatives, and 22.3% liberals. As the earlier discussions of the McClosky Difference and latent opinions suggest, these self-reported opinion numbers most likely undercount ideologicals in the public.

5. To determine whether liberal and conservative numbers increased at different times, I examined the percentage of each from 1972 to 2000 and then from 1994 to 2016. The overlapping subsets of years included 76 or 77 poll readings and each included dummy variables for the polling source (as in Appendix B). In the early series (ending in 2000), conservatives increased annually by .13 (p<.01) and liberals showed no trend (b= −.02, p>.10). In contrast, liberals since 1994 increased annually by .24 (p<.01) and conservatives showed no trend (b=.02, p>.10). Though an explanations awaits further research, we might speculate that liberal numbers grew with the passage of time and generations from when it was held in disrepute (avoiding "the L word" and using "progressive" instead), with the contrast of what some saw as the failures of the G.W. Bush years contrasted to the inspirational Obama years, or as a backlash to the overreach of hard-line conservatives.

6. Kinder and Kalmoe (2017) reaffirmed Converse's (1964) conclusion that most Americans are incapable of ideological thinking (recall my rebuttal in chapter 3, p.80) and concurred with Fiorina (2006) that Americans are neither highly nor increasingly polarized (2017, 54–57). Three points about this study deserve note. First, though nearly all of their analysis rests on ANES data, they do not examine *trends* in ANES self-reported ideology. As reported in Appendix B, Table B.1, there has been a statistically significant decline in non-ideologicals in each of the series, including the ANES series. The percentage of non-ideologicals has declined by an average of three-tenths of a point per year since 1972. This is certainly not a glacial change and began from a level of a good deal of polarization. Second, because ANES's self-reported ideology question (unlike all others) explicitly invites respondents to opt out with a "haven't thought much about it" response as Kinder and Kalmoe observe (2017, 171), the data overstate non-ideologicals. When ANES combined face-to-face interviews with Internet interviews not inviting the opt out, non-ideologicals dropped abruptly by 7 points from their 2008 level (47% to 40%). Had face-to-face interviews in 2012 eliminated the easy opt out option as the Internet questionnaire had, non-ideological numbers would have dropped even lower. Despite their tests of alternative measures of ideological identifications (2017, 139–155), based on comparisons to data collected by other prominent sources (GSS, Gallup, CBS/NYT and

the Exit Polls), their finding of a less ideologically polarized public appears to be an artifact of the unique opt out response option in ANES's ideology question. In reviewing the updated 126 poll observations from the five data sources of self-reported ideology examined in chapter 3, the ANES offered readings in 20 of the 44 years (1972 to 2016). Excluding the one year in which there were no competing ideological readings, ANES reported the highest percentage of non-ideologicals in 16 of the 19 years in which other survey measures were available. In the three years in which ANES did not report the most centrists, it reported the second most. Contrary to Kinder and Kalmoe's assertion, it is quite clearly *not* true that "liberals and conservatives are outnumbered by moderates and those who reject ideological terminology altogether" (2017, 87). Even in the ANES face-to-face surveys with their inflated number of non-ideologicals, liberals and conservatives (57.6% post-election) in 2016 outnumbered moderates and "haven't thought much about it" respondents (42.4%) by 15 percentage points. Finally, Kinder and Kalmoe (2017, 88) report lower percentages of overlapping ideological and party identifications than I report in table 1.3 because they include the entire ANES sample while my report includes only reported voters. More reported voters were ideologically aligned partisans in 2016 than in 2012 or in any previous election in the series.

7. There is also no mistaking the fact that incivility in politics has grown with greater polarization. As noted in chapter 9, incivility need not accompany polarization. In battling over political differences, one can take the high road or the low road. In the last several years, traffic on the low road has been heavy. President Trump has done much of this driving, but others have as well—often less crudely and certainly with more subtlety, but on the low road nevertheless. While not necessarily stimulating incivility, polarization may be more hospitable to low-road politics. A polarized public is likely to be more accepting of "low blows" struck in behalf of the views they hold and dismissive of complaints coming from the other side.

8. According to ANES data for reported voters in the 2016 election, 61% of Democrats were liberals and 78% of Republicans were conservatives.

9. Gallup (2017a).

10. Gallup (2017b).

11. Gallup (2017c); Pew Research Center (2017b).

12. One measure suggested public opinion about national conditions were not so bleak: President Obama's approval ratings. From July to Election Day, Obama's average approval rating was a mildly positive 52% (Gallup 2017d). Its contrast with more negative indicators suggests that Obama's approval ratings were substantially personal, rather that indicating satisfaction with how the nation had fared during his tenure.

13. The liberal vote split for Clinton was 89% in the exit poll and 94% in ANES. Put differently, based on the exit polls, 46% of Clinton's vote came from liberals.

14. Gallup (2017a); CNN (2016).

15. CNN (2016).

16. Data showing the Republican decline in Trump's unfavorables in the weeks before the election are from Gallup (2017a). The percentage of Trump's vote having an unfavorable view of him was calculated from the 2016 exit polls (CNN 2016). The conservative vote for Trump was 84% in the exit poll and 87% in ANES. Put differently, based on the exit polls, 61% of Trump's vote came from conservatives. Despite all the rancor and talk about sitting out the election, the exit polls found conservatives made up the same percentage of voters in 2016 as they had in 2012 (35%) and Trump ended up doing as well among them as Romney had four years earlier.

17. Too much has been made of the discrepancy between Trump's electoral vote majority and Clinton's popular vote plurality. Since the national popular vote has no official standing and has no direct impact on winning offices, campaigns are not run to win a popular vote plurality and voters may not feel pressure to vote or to vote for their

preferred viable candidate if they reside in safe states. In short, the national popular vote that is cast is not what it might have been had it mattered to candidates and to voters.

18. In a widely reported interview in May of 2017, Clinton asserted that she "was on the way to winning until the combination of Jim Comey's letter on October 28 and Russian Wikileaks raised doubts in the minds of people who were inclined to vote for me but got scared off–and the evidence for that intervening event is, I think, compelling [and] persuasive" (Rucker 2017). Although a bit more circumspect, Nate Silver (2017) basically agrees with Clinton, at least with respect to the Comey letter's impact. The AAPOR's Ad Hoc Committee on 2016 Election Polling, however, concluded that "evidence for a meaningful effect on the election from the FBI letter is mixed at best. . . . [It] appears that Clinton's support started to drop on October 24th or 25th." The Comey letter was released on three or four days later on October 28th (Ad Hoc Committee on 2016 Election Polling 2017).

19. Gallup (2017b), CNN (2016). It is difficult to determine what late breaking "bad news" from Wikileaks would have plausibly hurt Clinton. As to Comey's late October letter, the very fact that the mishandling of national security e-mails was in question was Clinton's chief political problem, not whether the FBI's investigation was active. Moreover, her detractors would already have figured the scandal into their unfavorable views and her supporters would have dismissed its relevance or importance. Finally, it should be observed that Clinton's lead over Trump did *not* increase when Comey announced earlier in July (when opinions were more fluid) that the investigation would be closed without recommending an indictment. This was widely regarded as good news for Clinton, but made no discernible difference in the polls, much less a lasting difference.

20. Gallup (2017a). It is typical in elections for disgruntled partisans to move back to supporting their party's candidate during the campaign and for the lead of the frontrunning candidate to decline during the campaign (Campbell 2008b). What was unusual in 2016 was the return of many disgruntled partisans did not occur until the last few weeks of the campaign. The obvious reason for this unusual delay is the unusual animosity within the Republican Party to its unusual presidential candidate.

21. If ideological orientations are often derived from impressions about the extent to which the use of government powers effectively promotes the public interest, Converse's claim that Americans are incapable of ideological thinking is even more dubious (Converse 1964). Basic impressions of the effectiveness of government do not require sophisticated or abstract thinking.

REFERENCES

Abramowitz, Alan I. 2006a. "Disconnected, or Joined at the Hip?"
In *Red and Blue Nation? Characteristics and Causes of America's
Polarized Politics*, edited by Pietro S. Nivola and David W. Brady,
72–84. Washington, DC: Brookings.

Abramowitz, Alan I. 2006b. "Rejoinder." In *Red and Blue Nation?
Characteristics and Causes of America's Polarized Politics*, edited by
Pietro S. Nivola and David W. Brady, 111–17. Washington, DC:
Brookings.

Abramowitz, Alan I. 2010. *The Disappearing Center: Engaged Citizens,
Polarization, and American Democracy.* New Haven, CT: Yale
University Press.

Abramowitz, Alan I. 2013. *The Polarized Public: Why American
Government Is So Dysfunctional*. New York: Pearson.

Abramowitz, Alan I. and Kyle L. Saunders. 1998. "Ideological
Realignment in the American Electorate." *Journal of Politics*,
60: 634–52.

Abramowitz, Alan I. and Kyle L. Saunders. 2006. "Exploring the
Bases of Partisanship in the American Electorate: Social Identity
vs. Ideology," *Political Research Quarterly*, 59 (2): 175–87.

Abramowitz, Alan I. and Kyle L. Saunders. 2008. "Is Polarization a
Myth?" *Journal of Politics*, 70 (2): 542–55.

Achen, Christopher H. 1975. "Mass Political Attitudes and the
Survey Response," *American Political Science Review*, 69: 1218–31.

Achen, Christopher H. 1977. "Measuring Representation: Perils of the Correlation Coefficient," *American Journal of Political Science*, 21 (4): 805–15.

Ad Hoc Committee on 2016 Election Polling. 2017. "An Evaluation of 2016 Election Polls in the U.S.," American Association for Public Opinion Research. http://www.aapor.org/Education -Resources/Reports/An-Evaluation-of-2016-Election-Polls-in -the-U-S.aspx. Accessed June 18, 2017.

Adams, James, Jay Dow, and Samuel Merrill III. 2006. "The Political Consequences of Alienation-Based and Indifference-Based Voter Abstention: Applications to Presidential Elections," *Political Behavior*, 28 (1): 65–86.

Aistrup, Joseph A. 1996. *The Southern Strategy Revisited: Republican Top-Down Advancement in the South*. Lexington: University Press of Kentucky.

Aldrich, John H. 2011. *Why Parties? A Second Look.* Chicago: University of Chicago Press.

Allen, Tom. 2013. *Dangerous Convictions: What's Really Wrong with the U.S. Congress.* New York: Oxford University Press.

American National Election Studies (ANES). 2015. *The ANES Guide to Public Opinion and Electoral Behavior*. http://www .electionstudies.org/utilities/utilities.htm. Accessed November 1, 2015.

Amos, Jonathan. 2012. "Bonobo's genetic code laid bare," *BBC: News Science and Environment*, http://www.bbc.co.uk/news/science -environment-18430420. Accessed June 12, 2013.

Ansolabehere, Stephen, Jonathan Rodden, and James M. Snyder, Jr. 2014. "The Strength of Issues: Using Multiple Measures to Gauge Preference Stability, Ideological Constraint, and Issue Voting," *American Political Science Review*, 102 (2): 215–32.

Ansolabehere, Stephen, James M. Snyder, Jr., and Charles Stewart III. 2001. "Candidate Positioning in U.S. House Elections," *American Journal of Political Science*, 45 (1): 136–59.

Arceneaux, Kevin and Martin Johnson. 2013. *Changing Minds or Changing Channels?: Partisan News in an Age of Choice*. Chicago: University of Chicago Press.

Ardoin, Philip J. and James C. Garand. 2003. "Measuring Constituency Ideology in U.S. House Districts: A Top-down Simulation Approach," *Journal of Politics*, 65 (4): 1165–89.

Asher, Herbert B. 1988. *Presidential Elections and American Politics: Voters, Candidates, and Campaigns since 1952*, 4th edition. Chicago: Dorsey Press.

Axelrod, Robert. 1972. "Where the Votes Come From: An Analysis of Electoral Coalitions, 1952–1968," *American Political Science Review*, 66 (1): 11–20.

Axelrod, Robert. 1986. "Presidential Electoral Coalitions in 1984," *American Political Science Review*, 80 (1): 281–84.

Bachrach, Peter. 1967. *The Theory of Democratic Elitism: A Critique.* Boston: Little, Brown.

Bachrach, Peter and Morton S. Baratz. 1963. "Decisions and Non-decisions: An Analytical Framework," *American Political Science Review*, 57 (3): 632–42.

Bafumi, Joseph and Robert Y. Shapiro. 2009. "A New Partisan Voter," *Journal of Politics*, 71 (1): 1–24.

Bain, Richard C. and Judith H. Parris. 1973. *Convention Decisions and Voting Records*, 2nd edition. Washington, DC: Brookings.

Bartels, Larry M. 2000. "Partisanship and Voting Behavior, 1952–1996," *American Journal of Political Science*, 44 (1): 35–50.

Bartels, Larry M. 2008. *Unequal Democracy: The Political Economy of the New Gilded Age.* Princeton, NJ: Princeton University Press.

Baumer, Donald C. and Howard J. Gold. 2010. *Parties, Polarization, and Democracy in the United States.* Boulder, CO: Paradigm Press.

Bell, Daniel. 1962. *The End of Ideology: On the Exhaustion of Political Ideas in the Fifties.* Cambridge, MA: Harvard University Press.

Berelson, Bernard. 1952. "Democratic Theory and Public Opinion," *Public Opinion Quarterly*, 16 (3): 313–30.

Berelson, Bernard R., Paul F. Lazarsfeld, and William N. McPhee. 1954. *Voting: A Study of Public Opinion Formation in a Presidential Campaign.* Chicago: University of Chicago Press.

Binder, Sarah A. 1996. "The Disappearing Political Center: Congress and the Incredible Shrinking Middle," *The Brookings Review*, 14 (4): 36–39.

Binder, Sarah A. 2003. *Stalemate: Causes and Consequences of Legislative Gridlock.* Washington, DC: Brookings.

Binder, Sarah A. 2005. "Elections and Congress's Governing Capacity." *Extensions: A Journal of the Carl Albert Congressional Research and Studies Center* (Fall): 10–14.

Binder, Sarah A. 2014. "Polarized We Govern?" *Center for Effective Public Management at Brookings* (May); http://www.brookings .edu/~/media/research/files/papers/2014/05/27%20 polarized%20 we%20govern%20binder/brookingscepm_polarized_figreplaced textrevtablerev.pdf. Accessed January 10, 2015.

Bishop, George F., Robert W. Oldendick, and Alfred J. Tuchfarber.1978. "Effects of Question Wording and Format on Political Attitude Consistency," *Public Opinion Quarterly*, 42 (1): 81–92.

Bishop, George F., Alfred J. Tuchfarber, and Robert W. Oldendick. 1978. "Change in the Structure of American Political Attitudes: The Nagging Question of Question Wording," *American Journal of Political Science*, 22 (2): 250–69.

Black, Earl and Merle Black. 2002. *The Rise of Southern Republicans.* Cambridge, MA: Harvard University Press.

Boller, Paul F., Jr. 1984. *Presidential Campaigns.* New York: Oxford University Press.

Bond, Jon R. and Richard Fleisher. 1990. *The President in the Legislative Arena.* Chicago: University of Chicago Press.

Bond, Jon R. and Richard Fleisher. 2000. *Polarized Politics: Congress and the President in a Partisan Era.* Washington, DC: CQ Press.

Boorstin, Daniel J. 1953. *The Genius of American Politics.* Chicago: University of Chicago Press.

Brady, David W. 1991. *Critical Elections and Congressional Policy Making.* Stanford, CA: Stanford University Press.

Brady, David W. and Charles S. Bullock, III. 1980. "Is There a Conservative Coalition in the House?" *Journal of Politics*, 42 (2): 549–59.

Brady, David W. and Craig Volden. 2006. *Revolving Gridlock: Politics and Policy from Jimmy Carter to George W. Bush*, 2nd edition. Boulder, CO: Westview.

Brewer, Mark D. and Jeffrey M. Stonecash. 2015. *Polarization and the Politics of Personal Responsibility.* New York: Oxford University Press.

Broder, David. 1971. *The Party's Over*. New York: Harper & Row.

Brody, Richard A. and Benjamin I. Page. 1973. "Indifference, Alienation, and Rational Decisions: The Effects of Candidate Evaluations on Turnout and the Vote," *Public Choice*, 15 (Summer): 1–17.

Brunell, Thomas L., William Koetzle, John DiNardo, and Scott L. Feld. 1999. "The R2 = .93: Where Do They Differ? Comparing Liberal and Conservative Interest Group Ratings," *Legislative Studies Quarterly*, 24 (1): 87–101.

Bullock, Charles S., III. 1988. "Regional Realignment from an Officeholding Perspective," *Journal of Politics*, 50 (3): 553–76.

Bullock, Charles S., III, Donna R. Hoffman, and Ronald Keith Gaddie. 2006. "Regional Variations in the Realignment of American Politics, 1944–2004," *Social Science Quarterly*, 87 (3): 494–518.

Burden, Barry C., Gregory A. Caldeira, and Tim Groseclose. 2000. "Measuring the Ideologies of U.S. Senators: The Song Remains the Same," *Legislative Studies Quarterly*, 25 (2): 237–58.

Bureau of Economic Analysis. 2015. "Gross Domestic Product: Percent Change from Preceding Period." http://www.bea.gov/national/index.htm#gdp. Accessed November 1, 2015.

Burnham, Walter Dean. 1970. *Critical Elections and the Mainsprings of American Politics*. New York: Norton.

Burns, James MacGregor. 1963. *The Deadlock of Democracy: Four-Party Politics in America*. Englewood Cliffs, NJ: Prentice-Hall.

Campbell, Angus, Philip E. Converse, Warren E. Miller, and Donald E. Stokes. 1960. *The American Voter*. New York: Wiley.

Campbell, Bruce A. and Richard J. Trilling. 1980. *Realignment in American Politics: Toward a Theory*. Austin: University of Texas Press.

Campbell, James E. 1983. "Ambiguity in the Issue Positions of Presidential Candidates: A Causal Analysis," *American Journal of Political Science*, 27 (2): 284–93.

Campbell, James E. 1985. "Sources of the New Deal Realignment: The Contributions of Conversion and Mobilization to Partisan Change." *Western Political Quarterly* 38 (3): 357–76.

Campbell, James E. 1987. "The Revised Theory of Surge and Decline," *American Journal of Political Science*, 31 (4): 965–79.

Campbell, James E. 1996. *Cheap Seats: The Democratic Party's Advantage in U.S. House Elections*. Columbus: Ohio State University Press.

Campbell, James E. 1997. *The Presidential Pulse of Congressional Elections*, 2nd edition. Lexington: University Press of Kentucky.

Campbell, James E. 2000. *The American Campaign: U.S. Presidential Campaigns and the National Vote.* College Station: Texas A&M University Press.

Campbell, James E. 2003. "The Stagnation of Congressional Elections." In *Life After Reform*, edited by Michael J. Malbin, 141–58. Lanham, MD: Rowman & Littlefield.

Campbell, James E. 2006a. "Polarization Runs Deep, Even by Yesterday's Standards." In *Red and Blue Nation? Characteristics and Causes of America's Polarized Politics*, edited by Pietro S. Nivola and David W. Brady, 106–16. Washington, DC: Brookings.

Campbell, James E. 2006b. "Party Systems and Realignments in the United States, 1868–2004," *Social Science History*, 30 (3): 359–86.

Campbell, James E. 2008a. "Presidential Politics in a Polarized Nation: The Re-election of George W. Bush." In *The George W. Bush Legacy*, edited by Colin Campbell, Bert A. Rockman, and Andrew Rudalevige, 21–44. Washington, DC: CQ Press.

Campbell, James E. 2008b. *The American Campaign: U.S. Presidential Campaigns and the National Vote*, 2nd edition. College Station: Texas A&M University Press.

Campbell, James E. 2008c. "Do Swing Voters Swing Elections?" In *The Swing Voter in American Politics*, edited by William G. Mayer, 118–32. Washington, DC: Brookings.

Campbell, James E. 2010a. "Explaining Politics, Not Polls: Examining Macropartisanship with Recalibrated NES Data," *Public Opinion Quarterly*, 74 (4): 616–42.

Campbell, James E. 2010b. "The Exceptional Election of 2008: Performance, Values, and Crisis," *Presidential Studies Quarterly*, 40 (2): 225–46.

Campbell, James E. 2012a. "The President's Economy: Parity in Presidential Party Performance," *Presidential Studies Quarterly*, 42 (4): 811–18.

Campbell, James E. 2012b. "Political Forces on the Obama Presidency: From Elections to Governing." In *The Obama Presidency:*

Appraisals and Prospects, edited by Bert A. Rockman, Andrew Rudalevige, and Colin Campbell, 67–93. Washington, DC. CQ Press.

Campbell, James E., Mary Munro, John R. Alford, and Bruce A. Campbell. 1986. "Partisanship and Voting." In *Research in Micropolitics, volume 1*, edited by Samuel Long, 99–126. Greenwich, CT: JAI Press.

Cantril, Hadley. 1965. *The Patterns of Human Concerns*. New Brunswick, NJ: Rutgers University Press.

Cantril, Hadley (with Mildred Strunk). 1951. *Public Opinion: 1935–1946*. Princeton, NJ: Princeton University Press.

Carlson, Keith, Michael A. Livermore, and Daniel Rockmore. 2016. "A Quantitative Analysis of Writing Style on the U.S. Supreme Court," *Washington University Law Review* 93 (6): 1461–1510.

Carmines, Edward G., Michael J. Ensley, and Michael W. Wagner. 2014. "Why American Parties Can't Get Beyond the Left-Right Divide." In *The State of the Parties*, 7th edition, edited by John C. Green, Daniel J. Coffey, and David B. Cohen, 55–71. Lanham, MD: Rowman & Littlefield.

Carmines, Edward, John P. McIver, and James A. Stimson. 1987. "Unrealized Partisanship: A Theory of Dealignment." *Journal of Politics*, 49 (2): 376–400.

Carmines, Edward G. and James A. Stimson. 1980. "The Two Faces of Issue Voting," *American Political Science Review*, 74 (1): 78–91.

Carmines, Edward G. and James A. Stimson. 1989. *Issue Evolution: Race and the Transformation of American Politics*. Princeton, NJ: Princeton University Press.

Cassel, Carol A. 2004. "Voting Records and Validated Voting Studies," *Public Opinion Quarterly*, 68 (1): 102–8.

Cavanagh, Thomas E. and James L. Sundquist. 1985. "The New Two-Party System." In *The New Directions in American Politics*, edited by John E. Chubb and Paul E. Peterson, 33–67. Washington, DC: Brookings.

Clausen, Aage R. 1968–69. "Response Validity: Vote Report," *Public Opinion Quarterly*, 32 (4): 588–606.

Clinton, Hillary Rodham. 1996. *It Takes a Village: And Other Lessons Children Teach Us*. New York: Simon & Schuster.

Clinton, Joshua D., Simon Jackman, and Doug Rivers. 2004. "'The Most Liberal Senator'? Analyzing and Interpreting Congressional Roll Calls," *PS: Political Science and Politics*, 37 (4): 805–11.

CNN. 2016. Exit Polls. http://edition.cnn.com/election/results/exit-polls. Accessed March 30, 2017.

Cohen, Tom. 2012. "Romney's big day marred by Etch A Sketch remark," (March 22, 2012). www.cnn.com/2012/03/21/politics/campaign-wrap/ Accessed December 15, 2014.

Collingwood, R. G. 1956. *The Idea of History*. New York: Oxford University Press.

Committee on Political Parties. 1950. *Toward a More Responsible Two-Party System: A Report.* New York: Rinehart and Company. Originally published as a Supplement to *American Political Science Review*, 64 (3), part 2.

Connelly, William F. Jr. 2014. "Partisan, Polarized, Yet Not Dysfunctional," In *The State of the Parties*, 7th edition, edited by John C. Green, Daniel J. Coffey, and David B. Cohen, 89–106. Lanham, MD: Rowman & Littlefield.

Conover, Pamela Johnston and Stanley Feldman. 1981. "The Origins and Meaning of Liberal/Conservative Self-Identifications," *American Journal of Political Science*, 25 (4): 617–45.

Constantini, Edmond. 1963. "Intraparty Attitude Conflict: Democratic Party Leadership in California," *Western Political Quarterly*, 25 (4): 956–72.

Converse, Philip E. 1964. "The Nature of Mass Belief Systems in Mass Publics." In *Ideology and Discontent*, edited by David E. Apter, 212–42. New York: Free Press.

Converse, Philip E. 1966. "The Concept of a Normal Vote." In *Elections and the Political Order*, edited by Angus Campbell, Philip E. Converse, Warren E. Miller, and Donald E. Stokes, 9–39. New York: Wiley.

Converse, Philip E. 1970. "Attitudes and Non-Attitudes: Continuation of a Dialogue." In *The Quantitative Analysis of Social Problems*, edited by Edward R. Tufte, 168–89. Reading, MA: Addison-Wesley.

Converse, Philip E. 1976. *The Dynamics of Party Support: Cohort Analyzing Party Identification*, Beverly Hills, CA: Sage.

Converse, Philip E. and Gregory B. Marcus. 1979. "Plus ca change …: The New CPS Election Study Panel," *American Political Science Review*, 73 (1): 32–49.

Council of State Governments. 2015. *The Book of the States* (various volumes). http://knowledgecenter.csg.org/kc/category/content-type/bos-archive. Accessed November 1, 2015.

CQ Press. 2005. *Guide to U.S. Elections, Fifth Edition, Volume I*. Washington, DC: CQ Press.

Craig, Stephen C. 1988. "The Decay of Mass Partisanship," *Polity*, 20 (4): 705–13.

Crotty, William J. and Gary C. Jacobson. 1980. *American Parties in Decline*. Boston: Little, Brown.

Dahl, Robert A. 1956. *A Preface to Democratic Theory*. Chicago: University of Chicago Press.

Dahl, Robert A. 1961. *Who Governs?* New Haven, CT: Yale University Press.

Dettrey, Bryan J. and James E. Campbell. 2013. "Has Growing Income Inequality Polarized the American Electorate? Class, Party, and Ideological Polarization," *Social Science Quarterly*, 94 (4): 1062–83.

DiMaggio, Paul, John Evans, and Bethany Bryson. 1996. "Have Americans' Social Attitudes Become More Polarized?" *American Journal of Sociology*, 102 (3): 690–755.

Downs, Anthony. 1957. *An Economic Theory of Democracy*. New York: Harper & Row.

Druckman, James N. and Lawrence R. Jacobs. 2015. *Who Governs?: Presidents, Public Opinion, and Manipulation.* Chicago: University of Chicago Press.

Dunn, Susan. 2010. *Roosevelt's Purge: How FDR Fought to Change the Democratic Party*. Cambridge, MA: Harvard University Press.

Duverger, Maurice. 1954. *Political Parties*. New York: Wiley.

Dylan, Bob. 1964. *The Times They Are a-Changin'*, album. New York: Columbia Records. http://www.bobdylan.com/us/music/the-times-they-are-a-changin. Accessed November 13, 2015.

Easton, David. 1957. "An Approach to the Analysis of Political Systems," *World Politics*, 9 (3): 383–400.

Edwards, George C., III. 2007. *Governing By Campaigning: The Politics of the Bush Presidency*. New York: Pearson Longman.

Edwards, George C., III. 2012. *Overreach: Leadership in the Obama Presidency*. Princeton, NJ: Princeton University Press.

Ellis, Christopher and James A. Stimson. 2012. *Ideology in America*. Cambridge: Cambridge University Press.

Ensley, Michael J., Michael W. Tofias, and Scott de Marchi. 2014. "Are These Boots Made for Walking? Polarization and Ideological Change among U.S. House Members." In *The State of the Parties*, 7th edition, edited by John C. Green, Daniel J. Coffey, and David B. Cohen, 107–20. Lanham, MD: Rowman & Littlefield.

Epstein, Julius J., Philip G. Epstein, and Howard Koch. 1942. "Casablanca." http://mckeestory.com/wp-content/uploads/Digital-CASABLANCA.pdf. Accessed November 1, 2015.

Erikson, Robert S. 1971. "The Advantage of Incumbency in Congressional Elections," *Polity*, 3 (3): 395–405.

Erikson, Robert S. 1979. "The SRC Panel Data and Mass Political Attitudes," *British Journal of Political Science*, 9 (1): 89–114.

Erikson, Robert S. 1988. "The Puzzle of the Midterm Loss," *Journal of Politics*, 50 (4): 1011–29.

Erikson, Robert S., Thomas D. Lancaster, and David W. Romero. 1989. "Group Components of the Presidential Vote, 1952–1984," *Journal of Politics*, 51 (2): 337–46.

Evans, C. Lawrence. 2001. "Committees, Leaders, and Message Politics," In *Congress Reconsidered*, 5th edition, edited by Lawrence C. Dodd and Bruce I. Oppenheimer, 217–43. Washington, DC: CQ Press.

Evans, John H. 2003. "Have Americans' Attitudes Become More Polarized?—An Update," *Social Science Quarterly*, 84 (1): 71–90.

Evans, John H., Bethany Bryson, and Paul DiMaggio. 2001. "Opinion Polarization: Important Contributions, Necessary Limitations," *American Journal of Sociology*, 106 (4): 944–59.

Feldman, Stanley and Jeanne Zaino. 2012. "Election Confirms Deep Ideological Divide," CBS News website. http://www.cbsnews.com/8301-250_162-57546153/election-confirm-deep-ideological-divide/. Accessed November 7, 2012.

Fenno, Richard F., Jr. 1973. *Congressmen in Committees*. Boston: Little, Brown.

Field, John Osgood and Ronald E. Anderson. 1969. "Ideology in the Public's Conceptualization of the 1964 Election," *Public Opinion Quarterly*, 33 (3): 380–98.

Fiorina, Morris P. 1974. *Representatives, Roll Calls, and Constituencies.* Lexington, MA: D.C. Heath.

Fiorina, Morris P. 1981. *Retrospective Voting in American National Elections*, New Haven, CT: Yale University Press.

Fiorina, Morris P. 1996. *Divided Government, Second Edition.* New York: Allyn and Bacon.

Fiorina, Morris P. 2017. *Unstable Majorities: Polarization, Party Sorting, and Political Stalemate.* Stanford, CA: Hoover Institution Press.

Fiorina, Morris P. 1999. "Whatever Happened to the Median Voter?" Presented at the MIT Conference on Parties and Congress (October 2), Cambridge, MA.

Fiorina, Morris P. 2002. "Parties, Participation, and Representation in America: Old Theories Face New Realities." In *Political Science: State of the Discipline*, edited by Ira Katznelson and Helen V. Milner, 511–41. Washington, DC: American Political Science Association and New York: Norton.

Fiorina, Morris P. 2008. "A Divider, Not a Uniter—Did It Have to Be?" In *The George W. Bush Legacy*, edited by Colin Campbell, Bert A. Rockman, and Andrew Rudalevige, 92–111. Washington, DC: CQ Press.

Fiorina, Morris P. with Samuel J. Abrams. 2009. *Disconnect: The Breakdown in Representation in American Politics.* Norman: University of Oklahoma Press.

Fiorina, Morris P. and Samuel J. Abrams. 2008. "Political Polarization in the American Public," *Annual Review of Political Science*, 11: 563–88.

Fiorina, Morris P. with Samuel J. Abrams and Jeremy C. Pope. 2006. *Culture War? The Myth of a Polarized America*, 2nd edition. New York: Pearson.

Fiorina, Morris P., Samuel A. Abrams, and Jeremy C. Pope. 2008. "Polarization in the American Public: Misconceptions and Misreadings," *Journal of Politics*, 70 (2): 556–60.

Fiorina, Morris P. and Matthew S. Levendusky. 2006. "Rejoinder to 'Disconnected, or Joined at the Hip?'" In *Red and Blue Nation? Volume One, Characteristics and Causes of America's Polarized Politics*, edited by Pietro S. Nivola and David W. Brady, 95–110. Washington, DC: Brookings.

Fleisher, Richard and John R. Bond. 2000a. "Congress and the President in a Partisan Era." In *Polarized Politics: Congress and the President in a Partisan Era*, edited by Jon R. Bond and Richard Fleisher, 1–8. Washington, DC: CQ Press.

Fleisher, Richard and John R. Bond. 2000b. "Partisanship and the President's Quest for Votes on the Floor of Congress." In *Polarized Politics: Congress and the President in a Partisan Era*, edited by Jon R. Bond and Richard Fleisher, 154–85. Washington, DC: CQ Press.

Fleisher, Richard and John R. Bond. 2001. "Evidence of Increasing Polarization among Ordinary Citizens." In *American Political Parties: Resurgence and Decline*, edited by Jeffrey E. Cohen, Richard Fleisher, and Paul Kantor, 55–77. Washington, DC: CQ Press.

Fleisher, Richard and John R. Bond. 2004. "The Shrinking Middle in the U.S. Congress," *British Journal of Political Science*, 34 (3): 429–51.

Fox News Poll. 2016. http://www.foxnews.com/politics/interative/2016/12/20/fox-news-poll-december-20–2016.html. Accessed December 24, 2016.

Free, Lloyd A. and Hadley Cantril. 1967. *The Political Beliefs of Americans: A Study of Public Opinion.* New Brunswick, NJ: Rutgers University Press.

Gallup. 2015. "Election Polls: Vote by Groups, 1960–1964," http://www.gallup.com/poll/9454/Election-Polls-Vote-Groups-19601964.aspx. Accessed November 1, 2015.

Gallup. 2017a. "Presidential Election 2016: Key Indicators," http://www.gallup.com/poll/189299/presidential-election-2016-key-indicators.aspx#pcf-image. Accessed January 12, 2017.

Gallup. 2017b. "Favorability: People in the News," http://www.gallup.com/poll/1618/Favorability-People-News.aspx Accessed July 10, 2017.

Gallup. 2017c. "Satisfaction with the United States," http://www.gallup.com/poll/1669/General-Mood-Country.aspx. Accessed August 3, 2017.

Gallup. 2017d. "Presidential Approval Ratings—Barack Obama" http://www.gallup.com/poll/116479/Barack-Obama-Presidential-Job-Approval.aspx. Accessed August 3, 2017.

Galston, William A. and Thomas E. Mann. "The GOP's Grass-Roots Obstructionists," *Washington Post*, May 16, 2010.

Garner, Andrew D. and Harvey D. Palmer. 2011. Polarization and Issue Consistency Over Time. *Political Behavior* 33 (2): 225–46.

Gibbons, Ann. 2012. "Bonobos Join Chimps as Closest Human Relatives," *Science (Now)* http://news.sciencemag.org/science now/2012/06/bonobo-genome-sequenced.html.

Grafstein, Robert. 1995. "Rationality as Conditional Expected Utility Maximization," *Political Psychology*, 16 (1): 63–80.

Green, Donald, Bradley Palmquist, and Eric Schickler. 2002. *Partisan Hearts and Minds: Political Parties and the Social Identities of Voters.* New Haven, CT: Yale University Press.

Greenberg, Stanley B. 2004. *The Two Americas: Our Current Political Deadlock and How to Break It.* New York: Thomas Dunne Books.

Groseclose, Tim, Steven D. Levitt, and James M. Snyder, Jr. 1999. "Comparing Interest Group Scores across Time and Chambers: Adjusted ADA Scores for the U.S. Congress," *American Political Science Review*, 93 (1): 33–50.

Gutman, Amy and Denis Thomson. 2012. *The Spirit of Compromise: Why Governing Demands It and Campaigning Undermines It.* Princeton, NJ: Princeton University Press.

Hadley, Arthur T. 1976. *The Invisible Primary: The Inside Story of the Other Presidential Race.* Englewood Cliffs, NJ: Prentice-Hall.

Hadley, Charles D. 1985. "Dual Partisan Identification in the South," *Journal of Politics* 47 (1): 254–68.

Hamilton, Alexander, James Madison, and John Jay. 1787 (republished 1961). *The Federalist Papers.* Edited by Clinton Rossiter. New York: New American Library.

Hare, Christopher, Nolan McCarty, Keith T. Poole, and Howard Rosenthal. 2012. "Polarization Is Real (and Asymmetric)," Voteview Blog (May 16, 2012), Accessed June 11, 2013.

Hartz, Louis. 1955. *The Liberal Tradition in America*. New York: Harcourt, Brace, and Jovanovich.

Hershey, Marjorie Randon, Nathaniel Birkhead, and Beth C. Easter. 2013. "Party Activists, Ideological Extremism, and Party Polarization." In *The Parties Respond: Changes in American Parties and Campaigns*, 5th edition, edited by Mark D. Brewer and L. Sandy Maisel, 75–102. Boulder, CO: Westview.

Hetherington, Marc J. 2008. "Turned Off or Turned On? How Polarization Affects Political Engagement." In *Red and Blue Nation? Volume Two: Consequences and Correction of America's Polarized Politics*, edited by Pietro S. Nivola and David W. Brady, 1–33. Washington, DC: Brookings.

Hetherington, Marc J. 2009. "Review Article: Putting Polarization in Perspective," *British Journal of Political Science*, 39 (2): 413–48.

Hetherington, Marc J. and Jonathan D. Weiler. 2009. *Authoritarianism and Polarization in American Politics*. New York: Cambridge University Press.

Hibbing, John R., Kevin B. Smith, and John R. Alford. 2014. *Predisposed: Liberals, Conservatives, and the Biology of Political Differences*. New York: Routledge.

Hibbing, John R. and Elizabeth Theiss-Morse. 1995. *Congress As Public Enemy: Public Attitudes Toward American Political Institutions*. New York: Cambridge University Press.

Hinich, Melvin J. and Michael C. Munger. 1996. *Ideology and the Theory of Political Choice*. Ann Arbor: University of Michigan Press.

Hirano, Shigeo, James M. Snyder, Jr., Stephen Ansolabehere and John Mark Hansen. 2010. "Primary Elections and Partisan Polarization in Congress," *Quarterly Journal of Political Science*, 5 (2): 169–91.

Holm, John D. and John P. Robinson. 1978. "Ideological Identification and the American Voter," *Public Opinion Quarterly*, 42 (2): 235–46.

Hotelling, Harold. 1929. "Stability in Competition," *Economic Journal*, 39: 41–57.

Huckfeldt, Robert, Paul Johnson, and John Sprague. 2004. *Political Disagreement*. New York: Cambridge University Press.

Hunter, James Davison. 1991. *Culture Wars: The Struggle to Define America*. New York: Basic Books.

Iyengar, Shanto, Gaurav Sood, and Yphtach Lelkes. 2012. "Affect, Not Ideology: A Social Identity Perspective on Polarization," *Public Opinion Quarterly*, 76 (3): 405–31.

Jacobson, Gary C. 2000. "Party Polarization in National Politics: The Electoral Connection." In *Polarized Politics: Congress and the President in a Partisan Era,* edited by Jon R. Bond and Richard Fleisher, 9–30. Washington, DC: CQ Press.

Jacobson, Gary C. 2001. *The Politics of Congressional Elections*, 5th edition. New York: Longman.

Jacobson, Gary C. 2006. "Why Other Sources of Polarization Matter More." In *Red and Blue Nation? Characteristics and Causes of America's Polarized Politics*, edited by Pietro S. Nivola and David W. Brady, 284–90. Washington, DC: Brookings.

Jacobson, Gary C. 2008. "George W. Bush, Polarization, and the War in Iraq." In *The George W. Bush Legacy*, edited by Colin Campbell, Bert A. Rockman, and Andrew Rudalevige, 62–91. Washington, DC: CQ Press.

Jacobson, Gary C. 2011. *A Divider, Not a Uniter: George W. Bush and the American People*, 2nd edition. New York: Pearson Longman.

Jacobson, Gary C. 2013. "Partisan Polarization in American Politics: A Background Paper," *Presidential Studies Quarterly*, 43 (4): 688–708.

Jacoby, William G. 1991. "Ideological Identification and Issue Attitudes," *American Journal of Political Science*, 35 (1): 178–205.

Jacoby, William G. 2000. "Issue Framing and Public Opinion Toward Government Spending," *American Journal of Political Science*, 44 (4): 750–67.

Jacoby, William G. 2005. "Is It Really Ambivalence? Public Opinion Toward Government Spending." In *Ambivalence and the Structure of Political Opinion*, edited by Stephen C. Craig and Michael D. Martinez, 149–72. New York: Palgrave MacMillan.

Jacoby, William G. 2009. "Ideology and Vote Choice in the 2004 Election," *Electoral Studies*, 28 (4): 584–94.

Jacoby, William G. 2014. "Is There a Culture War? Conflicting Value Structures in American Public Opinion," *American Political Science Review*, 108 (4): 754–71.

Jones, Jeffrey M. 2013. "Obama's Fourth Year in Office Ties as Most Polarized Ever"; http://www.gallup.com/poll/160097/obama-fourth-year-office-ties-polarized-ever.aspx. Accessed April 15, 2014.

Jones, Jeffrey M. 2016. "Record-High 77% of Americans Perceive Nation as Divided," Gallup (November 21); http://www.gallup.com/poll/197828/record-high-americans-perceive- nation-divided.aspx. Accessed August 3, 2017.

Kabaservice, Geoffrey M. 2012. *Rule and Ruin: The Downfall of Moderation and the Destruction of the Republican Party*. New York: Oxford University Press.

Keith, Bruce E., David B. Magleby, Candice J. Nelson, Elizabeth Orr, Mark C. Westlye, and Raymond E. Wolfinger. 1992. *The Myth of the Independent Voter*. Berkeley and Los Angeles: University of California Press.

Kelley Stanley, Jr. and Thad W. Mirer. 1974. "The Simple Act of Voting," *American Political Science Review*, 68 (2): 572–91.

Kernell, Samuel. 1977. "Presidential Popularity and Negative Voting: An Alternative Explanation of the Midterm Congressional Decline of the President's Party," *American Political Science Review*, 71 (1): 44–66.

Kessel, John H. 1972. "Comment: The Issues in Issue Voting," *American Political Science Review*, 66 (2): 459–76.

Key, V. O., Jr. 1955. "A Theory of Critical Elections," *Journal of Politics*, 17 (1): 3–18.

Key, V. O., Jr. 1959. "Secular Realignment and the Party System." *Journal of Politics*, 21 (2): 198–210.

Key, V. O., Jr. 1961. *Public Opinion and American Democracy*. New York: Alfred A. Knopf.

Key, V. O., Jr. with Milton C. Cummings, Jr. 1966. *The Responsible Electorate: Rationality in Presidential Voting, 1936–1960.* New York: Vintage Books.

Kiewiet, Roderick and Douglas Rivers. 1984. "Retrospective on Retrospective Voting," *Political Behavior*, 6 (4): 369–93.

Kinder, Donald R. and Nathan P. Kalmoe. 2017. *Neither Liberal nor Conservative: Ideological Innocence in the American Public*. Chicago: University of Chicago Press.

King, David C. 2003. "Congress, Polarization, and Fidelity to the Median Voter," manuscript.

Knight, Kathleen. 1984. "The Dimensionality of Partisan and Ideological Affect: The Influence of Positivity," *American Politics Quarterly*, 12 (3): 305–34.

Krehbiel, Keith. 1998. *Pivotal Politics: A Theory of U.S. Lawmaking*. Chicago: University of Chicago Press.

Krehbiel, Keith. 2008. "Comment on Sinclair's 'Spoiling the Sausages: How a Polarized Congress Deliberates and Legislates.'" In *Red and Blue Nation? Consequences and Correction of America's Polarized Politics*, edited by Pietro Nivola and David W. Brady, 93–105. Washington, DC: Brookings.

Krosnick, Jon A. 1991. "The Stability of Political Preferences: Comparisons of Symbolic and Nonsymbolic Attitudes," *American Journal of Political Science*, 35 (3): 547–76.

Ladd, Everett Carll, Jr. 1969. *Ideology in America: Change and Response in a City, a Suburb, and a Small Town*. Ithaca, NY: Cornell University Press.

Ladd, Everett Carll, Jr. 1978. *Where Have All the Voters Gone? The Fracturing of American Political Parties*. New York: Norton.

Ladd, Everett Carll, Jr. 1981. "The Brittle Mandate: Electoral Dealignment and the 1980 Presidential Election," *Political Science Quarterly*, 96 (1): 1–25.

Ladd, Everett Carll, Jr. 1985a. "As the Realignment Turns: A Drama in Many Acts," *Public Opinion*, 7 (6): 2–7.

Ladd, Everett Carll, Jr. 1985b. "On Mandates, Realignments, and the 1984 Presidential Election," *Political Science Quarterly*, 100 (1): 1–25.

Ladd, Everett Carll, Jr. 1991. "Like Waiting for Godot: The Uselessness of 'Realignment' for Understanding Change in Contemporary American Politics." In *The End of Realignment? Interpreting American Electoral Eras*, edited by Byron E. Shafer, 24–34. Madison: University of Wisconsin Press.

Ladd, Everett Carll, Jr. 1994. *The American Ideology: An Exploration of the Origins, Meaning, and Role of American Political Ideas*. Storrs, CT: Roper Center for Public Opinion Research.

Ladd, Everett Carll, Jr. with Charles D. Hadley. 1975. *Transformations of the American Party System: Political Coalitions from the New Deal to the 1970s*. New York: Norton.

Lane, Robert E. 1962. *Political Ideology: Why the American Common Man Believes What He Does*. New York: Free Press.

Lane, Robert E. 1965. "The Politics of Consensus in an Age of Affluence," *American Political Science Review*, 59 (4): 874–95.

Lane, Robert E. 1969. *Political Thinking and Consciousness: The Private Life of the Political Mind.* Chicago: Markham Publishing.

LaPalombara, Joseph. 1966. "Decline of Ideology: A Dissent and an Interpretation," *American Political Science Review*, 60 (1): 5–16.

La Raja, Raymond J. and Brian F. Schaffner. 2015. *Campaign Finance and Political Polarization: When Purists Prevail.* Ann Arbor: University of Michigan Press.

Law Dictionary. 2014. "What Is Circumstantial Evidence?" http://thelawdictionary.org/circumstantial-evidence/. Accessed February 26, 2014.

Lawrence, David G. 1997. *The Collapse of the Democratic Presidential Majority: Realignment, Dealignment, and Electoral Change from Franklin Roosevelt to Bill Clinton.* Boulder, CO: Westview.

Layman, Geoffrey C. and Thomas M. Carsey. 2002. "Party Polarization and 'Conflict Extension' in the American Electorate," *American Journal of Political Science*, 46 (4): 786–802.

Layman, Geoffrey C., Thomas M. Carsey, and Juliana Menasce Horowitz. 2006. "Party Polarization in American Politics: Characteristics, Causes, and Consequences," *Annual Review of Political Science*, 9: 83–110.

Lazarsfeld, Paul F., Bernard Berelson, and Hazel Gaudet. 1948. *The People's Choice.* New York: Columbia University Press.

Leighley, Jan E. and Jonathan Nagler. 2013. *Who Votes Now? Demographics, Issues, Inequality, and Turnout.* Princeton, NJ: Princeton University Press.

Levendusky, Matthew. 2009. *The Partisan Sort: How Liberals Became Democrats and Conservatives Became Republicans.* Chicago: University of Chicago Press.

Levendusky, Matthew. 2013a. *How Partisan Media Polarize America.* Chicago: University of Chicago Press.

Levendusky, Matthew S. 2013b. "Why Do Partisan Media Polarize Viewers?" *American Journal of Political Science*, 57 (3): 611–23.

Lewis, Jeffrey B. and Gary King. 1999. "No Evidence on Directional vs. Proximity Voting," *Political Analysis*, 8 (1): 21–33.

Lewis-Beck, Michael S., William G. Jacoby, Helmut Norpoth, and Herbert F. Weisberg. 2008. *The American Voter Revisited*. Ann Arbor: University of Michigan Press.

Lindblom, Charles E. 1968. *The Policy-Making Process*. Englewood Cliffs, NJ: Prentice-Hall.

Lindqvist, Erik and Robert Östling. 2010. "Political Polarization and the Size of Government," *American Political Science Review*, 104 (3): 543–65.

Lippmann, Walter. 1922 (reprinted 1997). *Public Opinion*. New York: Free Press.

Lippmann, Walter. 1950. "Today and Tomorrow," *Wilmington Morning Star*, Wilmington, NC (January 30, 1950), p. 4; http://news.google.com/newspapers?nid=1454&dat=19500130&id=zl9g AAAAIBAJ&sjid=B3INAAAAIBAJ&pg=2232,7452656. Accessed January 4, 2015.

Lipset, Seymour Martin. 1960. *Political Man*. New York: Doubleday.

Lipset, Seymour Martin. 1966. "Some Further Comments on 'The End of Ideology'," *American Political Science Review*, 60 (1): 17–18.

Liptak, Adam. 2014. "The Polarized Court," *The Buffalo News* (May 18), pp. H1–2.

Lubell, Samuel. 1956. *Revolt of the Moderates*. New York: Harper.

Lubell, Samuel. 1965 (originally published 1951). *The Future of American Politics*, 3rd edition, revised. New York: Harper.

Lubell, Samuel. 1970. *The Hidden Crisis in American Politics*. New York: Norton.

MacKuen, Michael B., Robert S. Erikson, and James A. Stimson. 1989. "Macropartisanship," *American Political Science Review*, 83 (4): 1125–42.

Maddox, William S. and Stuart A. Lilie. 1984. *Beyond Liberal and Conservative: Reassessing the Political Spectrum*. Washington, DC: Cato Institute.

Manley, John F. 1973. "The Conservative Coalition in Congress," *American Behavioral Scientist*, 17 (4): 223–47.

Mann, Thomas E. 2006. "Polarizing the House of Representatives: How Much Does Gerrymandering Matter." In *Red and Blue Nation? Characteristics and Causes of America's Polarized Politics*, edited by Pietro S. Nivola and David W. Brady, 263–83. Washington, DC: Brookings.

Mann, Thomas E. 2014. "Admit It, Political Scientists: Politics Really Is More Broken Than Ever," *The Atlantic* (May 26); http://www .theatlantic.com/politics/archive/2014/05/dysfunction/371544/. Accessed September 10, 2014.

Mann, Thomas E. and Norman J. Ornstein. 2012. *It's Even Worse Than It Looks: How the American Constitutional System Collided with the New Politics of Extremism.* New York: Basic Books.

Mann, Thomas E. and Raffaela Wakeman. 2013. "Growing Gridlock in Congress: An Interactive Graphic." Fixgov Blog. Washington, DC: Brookings. http://www.brookings.edu/blogs/fixgov/posts/ 2013/11/25-gridlock-congress-party-polarization-mann-wakeman. Accessed May 7, 2014.

Maraniss, David. 1999. *When Pride Still Mattered: A Life of Vince Lombardi.* New York: Simon & Schuster.

Mayer, William G. 1996. *The Divided Democrats: Ideological Unity, Party Reform, and Presidential Elections.* Boulder, CO: Westview.

Mayhew, David R. 1974. *Congress: The Electoral Connection.* New Haven, CT: Yale University Press.

Mayhew, David R. 2002. *Electoral Realignments: A Critique of an American Genre.* New Haven, CT: Yale University Press.

Mayhew, David R. 2005. *Divided We Govern*, 2nd edition: *Party Control, Lawmaking, and Investigations, 1946–2002.* New Haven, CT: Yale University Press.

Mayhew, David R. 2015. "Data and Materials: Divided We Govern." http://davidmayhew.commons.yale.edu/datasets-divided-we -govern/. Accessed January 8, 2015.

McCarty, Nolan, Keith T. Poole, and Howard Rosenthal. 2006. *Polarized America: The Dance of Ideology and Unequal Riches.* Cambridge, MA: MIT Press.

McCarty, Nolan, Keith T. Poole, and Howard Rosenthal. 2009. "Does Gerrymandering Cause Polarization?" *American Journal of Political Science*, 53 (3): 666–80.

McClosky, Herbert, Paul J. Hoffman, and Rosemary O'Hara. 1960. "Issue Conflict and Consensus Among Party Leaders and Followers," *American Political Science Review*, 54 (2): 406–27.

McDonald, Michael P. 2015. "United States Election Project." http:// www.electproject.org/home. Accessed October 12, 2015.

McDonald, Michael P. and Samuel L. Popkin. 2001. "The Myth of the Vanishing Voter," *American Political Science Review*, 95 (4): 963–74.

Mebane, Walter R., Jr. 2000. "Coordination, Moderation, and Institutional Balancing in American Presidential and House Elections," *American Political Science Review*, 94 (1): 37–57.

Mebane, Walter R., Jr. and Jasjeet S. Sekhon. 2002. "Coordination and Policy Moderation at Midterm." *American Political Science Review*, 96 (1): 141–57.

Meffert, Michael F., Helmut Norpoth, and Anirudh V. S. Ruhil. 2001. "Realignment and Macropartisanship," *American Political Science Review*, 95 (4): 953–62.

Miller, Arthur H. 1979. "Normal Vote Analysis: Sensitivity to Change Over Time," *American Journal of Political Science*, 23 (2): 406–25.

Miller, Arthur H., Warren E. Miller, Alden S. Raine, and Thad A. Brown. 1976. "A Majority Party in Disarray: Policy Polarization in the 1972 Election," *American Political Science Review*, 70 (3): 753–78.

Miller, Arthur H. and Warren E. Miller. 1976. "Ideology in the 1972 Election: Myth or Reality—A Rejoinder," *American Political Science Review*, 70 (3): 832–47.

Miller, Arthur H. and Martin P. Wattenberg. 1985. "Throwing the Rascals Out: Policy and Performance Evaluations of Presidential Candidates, 1952–1980," *American Political Science Review*, 79 (2): 359–72.

Miller, Warren E. 1991. "Party Identification, Realignment, and Party Voting: Back to the Basics," *American Political Science Review*, 85 (2): 557–68.

Miller, Warren E. and Teresa E. Levitan. 1976. *Leadership and Change: The New Politics and the American Electorate.* Cambridge, MA: Winthrop.

Mills, C. Wright. 1959. *The Power Elite.* New York: Oxford University Press.

Mondak, Jeffrey J. and Matthew V. Hibbing. 2012. "Personality and Public Opinion." In *New Directions in Public Opinion*, edited by Adam J. Berinsky, 217–38. New York: Routledge.

Monroe, Alan D. 1983. "American Party Platforms and Public Opinion," *American Journal of Political Science*, 27 (1): 27–42.

Montjoy, Robert S., William R. Shaffer, and Ronald E. Weber. 981. "Policy Preferences of Party Elites and Masses: Conflict or Consensus?" In *Public Opinion and Public Policy: Models of Political Linkage*, edited by Norman R. Luttbeg, 280–96. Itasca, IL: F.E. Peacock.

Motel, Seth. 2013. "Public wants compromise, but not on issues they care about." Pew Research Center (October 10). http://www.pewresearch.org/fact-tank/2013/10/10/public-wants-compromise-but-not-on-issues-they-care-about/. Accessed January 4, 2015.

Mouw, Ted and Michael E. Sobel. 2001. "Culture Wars and Opinion Polarization: The Case of Abortion," *American Journal of Sociology*, 106 (4): 913–43.

Muirhead, Russell. 2014. *The Promise of Party in a Polarized Age*. Cambridge, MA: Harvard University Press.

Murphy, R. and H. Gulliver. 1971. *The Southern Strategy*. New York: Scribner's.

Mutz, Diana. 2006. *Hearing the Other Side: Deliberative versus Participatory Democracy*. New York: Cambridge University Press.

Mutz, Diana. 2015. *In-Your-Face Politics: The Consequences of Uncivil Media.* Princeton, NJ: Princeton University Press.

National Bureau of Economic Research. 2015. "US Business Cycle Expansions and Contractions." http://www.nber.org/cycles/cyclesmain.html. Accessed November 1, 2015.

Nelson, Michael. 1989. "Constitutional Aspects of the Elections." In *The Elections of 1988*, edited by Michael Nelson, 181–209. Washington, DC: CQ Press.

Neuman, W. Russell. 1986. *The Paradox of Mass Politics: Knowledge and Opinion in the American Electorate*. Cambridge, MA: Harvard University Press.

Newhart, Bob. 1975. "My Business Is Shrinking," Episode of *The Bob Newhart Show*. Originally aired February 1.

Nice, David C. 1984. "Polarization in the American Party System," *Presidential Studies Quarterly*, 14 (1): 109–16.

Nie, Norman and Kristi Anderson. 1974. "Mass Belief Systems Revisited: Political Change and Attitude Structure," *Journal of Politics*, 36 (3): 540–91.

Nie, Norman, Sidney Verba, and John Petrocik. 1976. *The Changing American Voter*. Cambridge, MA: Harvard University Press.

Nivola, Pietro S. and William A. Galston. 2008. "Toward Depolarization." In *Red and Blue Nation? Volume Two: Consequences and Correction of America's Polarized Politics*, edited by Pietro S. Nivola and David W. Brady, 235–84. Washington, DC: Brookings.

Noel, Hans. 2013. *Political Ideologies and Political Parties in America*. New York: Cambridge University Press.

Norpoth, Helmut. 1987. "Under Way and Here to Stay: Party Realignment in the 1980s?" *Public Opinion Quarterly*, 51 (3): 376–91.

Norpoth, Helmut and Jerrold D. Rusk. 1982. "Partisan Dealignment in the American Electorate: Itemizing the Deductions Since 1964," *American Political Science Review*, 76 (3): 522–37.

Obenshain, Kate. 2012. *Divider-in-Chief: The Fraud of Hope and Change*. New York: Regnery.

Office of the Clerk, U.S. House of Representatives. 2014. "Election Statistics, 1920 to Present"; http://history.house.gov/Institution/Election-Statistics/Election-Statistics// Accessed August 10, 2014.

Ornstein, Norman J. and Thomas E. Mann. 2013. "Gridlock Is No Way to Govern," *Washington Post* (August 18); http://www.washingtonpost.com/opinions/gridlock-is-no-way-to-govern/2013/04/18/5f884506-a6ce-11e2-8302-3c7e0ea97057_story.html. Accessed January 7, 2013.

Ornstein, Norman J., Thomas E. Mann, Michael J. Malbin, and Andrew Rugg. 2013. *Vital Statistics on Congress*; http://www.brookings.edu/research/reports/2013/07/vital-statistics-congress-mann-ornstein. Accessed: May 5, 2014.

Owens, John E. 2013. "The Onward March of (Asymmetric) Political Polarization in the Contemporary Congress." In *Issues in American Politics: Polarized Politics in the Age of Obama*, edited by John Dumbrell, 98–121. New York: Routledge.

Page, Benjamin I. 1978. *Choices and Echoes in Presidential Elections: Rational Man and Electoral Democracy*. Chicago: University of Chicago Press.

Palfrey, Thomas R. 1989. "A Mathematical Proof of Duverger's Law." In *Models of Strategic Choice in Politics*, edited by Peter C. Ordeshook, 69–91. Ann Arbor: University of Michigan Press.

Patterson, Thomas E. 2013. *Informing the News: The Need for Knowledge-Based Journalism*. New York: Vintage.

Paulson, Arthur S. 2006. *Electoral Realignment and the Outlook for American Democracy*. Boston: Northeastern University Press.

Pennock, J. Roland. 1979. *Democratic Political Theory.* Princeton, NJ: Princeton University Press.

Perlstein, Rick. 2012. "Why Conservatives Are Still Crazy After All These Years," *Rolling Stone* (March 16, 2012); http://www.rolling stone.com/politics/news/why-conservatives-are-still-crazy-after-all -these-years-20120316. Accessed October 4, 2014.

Petrocik, John R. 1981. *Party Coalitions: Realignments and the Decline of the New Deal Party System*. Chicago: University of Chicago Press.

Petrocik, John R. 1987. "Realignment: New Party Coalitions and the Nationalization of the South," *Journal of Politics*, 49 (2): 347–75.

Petrocik, John Richard. 2009. "Measuring Party Support: Leaners Are Not Independents," *Electoral Studies*, 28 (4): 562–72.

Pew Research Center. 2012. *Trends in American Values: 1987–2012*. Survey Report 6/4/12. www.people-press.org/2012/06/04/ partisan-polarization-surges-in-bush-obama-years/. Accessed July 1, 2013.

Pew Research Center. 2014. *Political Polarization in the American Public*. www.pewresearch.org.

Pew Research Center. 2015. *Beyond Distrust: How Americans View Their Government*. http://www.pewresearch.org/. Accessed December 1, 2015.

Pew Research Center. 2016. "Partisanship and Political Animosity in 2016." (June 22); http://assets.pewresearch.org/wp-content/ uploads/sites/5/2016/06/06–22–16-Partisanship-and-animosity -release.pdf Accessed August 3, 2017.

Pew Research Center. 2017a. "On Eve of Inauguration, Americans Expect Nation's Deep Political Divisions to Persist," (January 19); http://www.people-press.org/2017/01/19/on-eve-of-inaugura-tion-americans-expect-nations-deep-political-divisions-to-persist/ Accessed August 3, 2017.

Pew Research Center. 2017b. "Economic Conditions." http://www .pewresearch.org/data-trend/national-conditions/economic

-conditions/ Accessed August 3, 2017. Pierce, John C. 1970. "Party Identification and the Changing Role of Ideology in American Politics," *Midwest Journal of Political Science*, 14 (1): 25–42.

Pierce, John C. and Douglas D. Rose. 1974. "Nonattitudes and American Public Opinion," *American Political Science Review*, 68 (2): 626–49.

Piven, Francis Fox and Richard A. Cloward. 1988. *Why Americans Don't Vote*. New York: Pantheon Books.

Polsby, Nelson W. 1963. *Community Power and Political Theory.* New Haven, CT: Yale University Press.

Polsby, Nelson W. 1983. *Consequences of Party Reform*. New York, Oxford University Press.

Pomper, Gerald M. 1967. "'If Elected, I Promise': American Party Platforms," *Midwest Journal of Political Science*, 11 (3): 318–52.

Pomper, Gerald M. 1971. "Toward a More Responsible Two-Party System? What, Again?" *Journal of Politics*, 33 (4): 916–40.

Pomper, Gerald M. 1972. "From Confusion to Clarity: Issues and American Voters, 1956–1968," *American Political Science Review*, 66 (2): 415–28.

Poole, Keith T. 2005. "The Decline and Rise of Party Polarization in Congress During the Twentieth Century." *Extensions: A Journal of the Carl Albert Congressional Research and Studies Center* (Fall): 6–9.

Poole, Keith T. 2014. "The Polarization of the Congressional Parties"; http://voteview.com/political_polarization_2014.htm. Accessed: March 1, 2014.

Poole, Keith T. and R. Steven Daniels. 1985. "Ideology, Party, and Voting in the U.S. Congress, 1959–1980," *American Political Science Review*, 79 (2): 373–99.

Poole, Keith T. and Howard Rosenthal. 1984. "The Polarization of American Politics," *Journal of Politics*, 46 (4): 1061–79.

Poole, Keith T. and Howard Rosenthal. 1991. "Patterns of Congressional Voting," *American Journal of Political Science*, 35 (1): 228–78.

Poole, Keith T. and Howard Rosenthal. 1997. *Congress: A Political-Economic History of Roll Call Voting.* New York: Oxford University Press.

Poole, Keith T. and Howard Rosenthal. 2007. *Ideology and Congress.* New Brunswick, NJ: Transaction.

Rabinowitz, George and Stuart Elaine Macdonald. 1989. "A Directional Theory of Issue Voting," *American Political Science Review*, 83 (1): 93–121.

Rae, Douglas W. 1967. *The Political Consequences of Electoral Laws*, New Haven, CT: Yale University Press.

Rae, Douglas W. and Michael Taylor. 1970. *The Analysis of Political Cleavages*. New Haven, CT: Yale University Press.

Ranney, Austin. 1962. *The Doctrine of Responsible Party Government: Its Origins and Present State*. Urbana: University of Illinois Press.

Ranney, Austin. 1975. *Curing the Mischiefs of Faction: Party Reform in America*. Berkeley: University of California Press.

Ranney, Austin and Willmoore Kendall. 1956. *Democracy and the Party System*. New York: Harcourt, Brace, and Company.

Rasinski, Kenneth A. 1989. "The Effect of Question Wording on Public Support for Government Spending," *Public Opinion Quarterly*, 53 (3): 388–94.

Reiter, Howard L. and Jeffrey M. Stonecash. 2011. *Counter Realignment: Political Change in the Northeastern United States*. New York: Cambridge University Press.

RePass, David E. 1971. "Issue Salience and Party Choice," *American Political Science Review*, 65 (2): 389–400.

Riker, William H. and Peter C. Ordeshook. 1968. "A Theory of the Calculus of Voting," *American Political Science Review*, 62 (1): 25–42.

Roper Center. 2013. The Exit Polls, various years. http://www.roper center.uconn.edu/how_groups_voted/. Accessed May 6, 2013.

Rosenof, Theodore. 2003. *Realignment: The Theory That Changed the Way We Think About American Politics*. Lanham, MD: Rowman & Littlefield.

Rossiter, Clinton. 1960. *Parties and Politics in America*. Ithaca, NY: Cornell University Press.

Rucker, Philip. 2017. "'I would be your president': Clinton Blames Russia, FBI Chief for 2016 Election Loss." *The Washington Post* (May 3); https://www.washingtonpost.com/politics/hillary -clinton-blames-russian-hackers-and-comey-for-2016-election- loss/2017/05/02/e62fef72-2f60-11e7-8674-437ddb6e813e_story .html?utm_term=.b341b4ae981 Accessed June 10, 2017.

Rusk, Jerrold G. 2001. *A Statistical History of the American Electorate*. Washington, DC: CQ Press.

Saad, Lydia. 2011. "U.S. Political Ideology Stable with Conservatives Leading," Gallup; http://www.gallup.com/poll/148745/Political -Ideology-Stable-Conservatives-Leading.aspx. August 1, 2011. Accessed March 22, 2014.

Saad, Lydia. 2012. "Most in U.S. Say Americans Are Divided on Important Values," Gallup; http://www.gallup.com/poll/159257/ say-americans-divided-important-values.aspx. Accessed July 1, 2013.

Scammon, Richard M. and Ben J. Wattenberg. 1970. *The Real Majority: An Extraordinary Examination of the American Electorate.* New York: Coward, McCann, and Geohegan.

Schattschneider, E. E. 1942. *Party Government.* New York: Holt, Rinehart, and Winston.

Schattschneider, E. E. 1960. *The Semisovereign People.* New York: Holt, Rinehart and Winston.

Schlafly, Phyllis. 1964. *A Choice Not an Echo.* Alton, IL: Pere Marquette Press.

Schlesinger, Arthur M., Jr. 1949. *The Vital Center: The Politics of Freedom.* Boston, MA: Houghton Mifflin.

Schneider, Jerrold E. 1979. *Ideological Coalitions in Congress.* Westport, CT: Greenwood Press.

Schuman, Howard and Stanley Presser. 1996. *Questions and Answers in Attitude Surveys: Experiments on Question Wording, Form, and Context.* Thousand Oaks, CA: Sage Publications.

Shelley, Mack C., II. 1983. *The Permanent Majority: The Conservative Coalition in the United States Congress.* University: University of Alabama Press.

Silbey, Joel H. 1990. "The Rise and Fall of American Political Parties." In *The Parties Respond: Changes in the American Party System,* edited by L. Sandy Maisel, 3–18. Boulder, CO: Westview.

Silver, Nate. 2017. "The Comey Letter Probably Cost Clinton the Election," (May 3) https://fivethirtyeight.com/features/the-comey -letter-probably-cost-clinton-the-election. Accessed August 3, 2017.

Sinclair, Barbara. 1992. "Senate Democratic Leadership in the 101st Congress." In *The Atomistic Congress: An Interpretation of Congressional Change,* edited by Allen D. Hertzke and Ronald M. Peters, Jr., 259–92. Armonk, NY: M.E. Sharpe.

Smith, Andrew E., Alfred J. Tuchfarber, Eric W. Rademacher, and Stephen E. Bennett. 1995. "Partisan Leaners Are Not Independents," *The Public Perspective* (October/November), 9–12.

Smith, Eric R.A.N. 1989. *The Unchanging American Voter*. Berkeley: University of California Press.

Smith, Samantha. 2015. "24% of Americans Now View Both GOP and Democratic Party Unfavorably," Pew Research Center. http://www.pewresearch.org/fact-tank/2015/08/21/24-of-americans-now-view-both-gop-and-democratic-party-unfavorably/, August 21, 2015. Accessed October 1, 2015.

Smith, Tom W. 1990. "Liberal and Conservative Trends in the United States since World War II," *Public Opinion Quarterly*, 54 (4): 479–507.

Smithies, Arthur. 1941. "Optimum Location in Spatial Competition," *Journal of Political Economy*, 49: 423–39.

Stanley, Harold W. 1988. "Southern Partisan Changes: Dealignment, Realignment, or Both?" *Journal of Politics*, 50 (1): 64–88.

Stanley, Harold W. and Richard G. Niemi. 2006. "Partisanship, Party Coalitions, and Group Support, 1952–2004," *Presidential Studies Quarterly*, 36 (2): 172–88.

Stanley, Harold W. and Richard G. Niemi. 2013. *Vital Statistics on American Politics 2013–2014.* Washington, DC: CQ Press.

Stewart, Potter. 1964. "Concurrence: Jacobellis v. Ohio," 173 Ohio St. 22, 179 N.E.2d 777, reversed. Supreme Court Decision (June 22, 1964). https://www.law.cornell.edu/supremecourt/text/378/184#writing-USSC_CR_0378_0184_ZC1. Accessed October 26, 2015.

Stimson, James A. 1999. *Public Opinion in America: Moods, Cycles, and Swings*, 2nd edition. Boulder, CO: Westview.

Stimson, James A. 2004. *Tides of Consent: How Public Opinion Shapes American Politics.* New York: Cambridge University Press.

Stonecash, Jeffrey M. 2006. *Political Parties Matter: Realignment and Return of Partisan Voting*. Boulder, CO: Lynne-Rienner.

Stonecash, Jeffrey M., Mark D. Brewer, and Mack D. Mariani. 2003. *Diverging Parties: Social Change, Realignment, and Party Polarization*. Boulder, CO: Westview.

Stroud, Natalie Jomini. 2008. "Media Use and Political Predispositions: Revisiting the Concept of Selective Exposure," *Political Behavior*, 30 (3): 341–66.

Sullivan, John L., James E. Piereson, and George E. Marcus. 1978. "Ideological Constraint in the Mass Public: A Methodological Critique and Some New Findings," *American Journal of Political Science*, 22 (2): 233–49.

Summers, Larry. 2013. "When Gridlock Is Good," *Washington Post* (August 14); http://www.washingtonpost.com/opinions/lawrence -summers-when-gridlock-is-good/2013/04/14/8bfeab9c-a3c3-11e2 -9c03-6952ff305f35_story.html. Accessed January 7, 2015.

Sundquist, James L. 1983. *Dynamics of the Party System: Alignment and Realignment of Political Parties in the United States*, revised edition. Washington, DC: Brookings.

Sundquist, James L. and Richard M. Scammon. 1981. "The 1980 Election: Profile and Historical Perspective." In *A Tide of Discontent: The 1980 Elections and Their Meaning*, edited by Ellis Sandoz and Cecil V. Crabb, Jr., 19–44. Washington, DC: CQ Press.

Taagepera, Rein and Matthew Soberg Shugart. 1989. *Seats and Votes: The Effects and Determinants of Electoral Systems*. New Haven, CT: Yale University Press.

Taylor, Andrew W. 1996. "The Ideological Development of the Parties in Washington, 1947–1994," *Polity*, 29 (2): 273–92.

Theriault, Sean M. 2008. *Party Polarization in Congress*. New York: Cambridge University Press.

Traugott, Michael W. and John P. Katosh. 1979. "Response Validity in Surveys of Voting Behavior," *Public Opinion Quarterly*, 43 (3): 359–77.

Truman, David B. 1951. *The Governmental Process*. New York: Alfred A. Knopf.

Tyrangiel, Josh. 2012. "Farewell to the Swamp," *Bloomberg Businessweek*, June 25–July 1, 2012, pp. 72–76.

U.S. Bureau of the Census. 1985. "No. 540. National Defense Outlays and Veterans Benefits: 1955 to 1985," *Statistical Abstract of the United States: 1986* (106th edition). Washington, DC: U.S. Government Printing Office, p. 331.

Wattenberg, Martin. 1981. "The Decline of Partisanship in the United States: Negativity or Neutrality?" *American Political Science Review*, 75 (4): 941–50.

Wattenberg, Martin. 1987. "The Hollow Realignment: Partisan Change in a Candidate-Centered Era," *Public Opinion Quarterly*, 51 (1): 58–74.

Wattenberg, Martin. 1994. *The Decline of American Political Parties: 1952–1992.* Cambridge, MA: Harvard University Press.

Weisberg, Herbert and Bernard Grofman. 1981. "Candidate Evaluations and Turnout," *American Politics Quarterly,* 9 (2): 197–219.

White, John Kenneth. 2003. *The Values Divide: American Politics and Culture in Transition.* New York: Chatham House.

White, Theodore H. 1969. *The Making of the President 1968.* New York: Atheneum Publishers.

Wildavsky, Aaron. 1964. *The Politics of the Budgetary Process.* Boston, MA: Little, Brown.

Wilson, James Q. 1962. *The Amateur Democrat: Club Politics in Three Cities.* Chicago: University of Chicago Press.

Wilson, James Q. 1985. "Realignment at the Top, Dealignment at the Bottom." In *The American Elections of 1984,* edited by Austin Ranney, 297–310. Durham, NC: Duke University Press.

Wolfinger, Raymond E. and Steven J. Rosenstone. 1980. *Who Votes?* New Haven, CT: Yale University Press.

Woodard, Colin. 2016. American Character: *A History of the Epic Struggle Between Individual Liberty and the Common Good.* New York: Penguin.

Wood, B. Dan. 2009. *The Myth of Presidential Representation.* New York: Cambridge University Press.

Wood, Thomas and Eric Oliver. 2012. "Toward a More Reliable Implementation of Ideology in Measures of Public Opinion," *Public Opinion Quarterly,* 76 (4): 636–62.

Wright, William E. 1971. "Comparative Party Models: Rational-Efficient and Party Democracy." In *A Comparative Study of Party Organization,* edited by William E. Wright, 17–54. Columbus, OH: Charles E. Merrill Publishing.

Wroe, Andrew. 2013. "The Culture War: Is America Polarizing?" In *Issues in American Politics: Polarized Politics in the Age of Obama,* edited by John Dumbrell, 83–97. New York: Routledge.

Zaller, John R. 1992. *The Nature and Origins of Mass Opinion.* New York: Cambridge University Press.

Zipp, John F. 1985. "Perceived Representativeness and Voting: An Assessment of the Impact of 'Choices' vs. 'Echoes,'" *American Political Science Review,* 79 (1): 50–61.

INDEX